JOHN MARSHALL

JOHN MARSHALL

The Man Who Made the
Supreme Court

RICHARD
BROOKHISER

Author of *James Madison*

BASIC BOOKS
New York

Cover design by Ann Kirchner
Cover image: Portrait of John Marshall, 1832 (Oil on canvas), Lambdin, James Reid (1807–89) / Virginia Historical Society, Richmond, Virginia, USA / Bridgeman Images
Cover © 2018 Hachette Book Group, Inc.

Basic Books
Hachette Book Group
1290 Avenue of the Americas, New York, NY 10104
www.basicbooks.com

Printed in the United States of America

First Edition: November 2018

Published by Basic Books, an imprint of Perseus Books, LLC, a subsidiary of Hachette Book Group, Inc. The Basic Books name and logo is a trademark of the Hachette Book Group.

The Hachette Speakers Bureau provides a wide range of authors for speaking events. To find out more, go to www.hachettespeakersbureau.com or call (866) 376-6591.

The publisher is not responsible for websites (or their content) that are not owned by the publisher.

PRINT BOOK INTERIOR DESIGN BY JEFF WILLIAMS.

Library of Congress Cataloging-in-Publication Data
Names: Brookhiser, Richard, author.
Title: John Marshall : the man who made the Supreme Court / Richard Brookhiser.
Description: New York : Basic Books, 2018. | Includes bibliographical references and index.
Identifiers: LCCN 2018018016 (print) | LCCN 2018020347 (ebook) | ISBN 9780465096237 (ebook) | ISBN 9780465096220 (hardcover)
Subjects: LCSH: Marshall, John, 1755–1835. | United States. Supreme Court—Biography. | Judges—United States—Biography.
Classification: LCC KF8745.M3 (ebook) | LCC KF8745.M3 B76 2018 (print) | DDC 347.73/2634 [B]—dc23

LC record available at https://lccn.loc.gov/2018018016

ISBNs: 978-0-465-09622-0 (hardcover), 978-0-465-09623-7 (ebook)

LSC-C

10 9 8 7 6 5 4 3 2 1

To Lewis E. Lehrman

CONTENTS

SECTION III:
MAGISTERIAL CHIEF JUSTICE

SECTION IV:
CHIEF JUSTICE: THE WANING YEARS

A NOTE ON
SPELLING AND USAGE

J OHN MARSHALL SPELLED BADLY, AS DID REPORTERS FOR the Supreme Court, who had a penchant for mangling surnames (*Sturges* for *Sturgis*, *Sandford* for *Sanford*). The reporters' mistakes are enshrined in legal nomenclature. I have corrected Marshall's. Cornelius Vanderbilt's spelling is too good to lose.

Capitalization signals the federal government: *Bank* means *Bank of the United States*, *Constitution* means Constitution of the United States, and *Court* means *Supreme Court of the United States*. But *Federalism* always means the political party. (NB: The Republicans of Marshall's lifetime are the ancestors of today's Democrats; the GOP is a different, later organization.)

Justices of the Supreme Court were called *judges* in Marshall's day. I have used modern etiquette. Inconsistently, I write of Native Americans as *Indians*.

INTRODUCTION

John Marshall and George Washington

J OHN MARSHALL IS THE GREATEST JUDGE IN AMERICAN
history. As chief justice of the Supreme Court for thirty-four
years—a record that still stands—he impressed, charmed,
and defied colleagues, skeptics, and enemies, transforming an institution to which the Founding Fathers had given relatively little
thought into a pillar of the nation. In 1801 when Marshall became
chief justice, the job lacked "dignity," as one contemporary put it,
while the judiciary was, in the words of another, the "weakest"
branch of the federal government. When Marshall died in 1835,
he and the Court he led had rebuked two presidents, Congress,
and a dozen states and laid down principles of law and politics
that still apply. Now, when the Supreme Court makes the news
every day it sits, and every time a new justice must be appointed,
there is no question of its prominence—a prominence it owes, in
the first instance, to Marshall, the man who made it.

But the most formative experiences of Marshall's life came not
in court but in battle. That was where he met George Washington, the man he called simply "the greatest Man on earth," whose
example would inspire and guide him for the rest of his life.

In September 1777, the Continental Army, led by commander in chief George Washington, met a British army led by Lord Howe at Brandywine Creek in Pennsylvania, thirty miles southwest of Philadelphia, the new nation's capital. Washington lost the battle of Brandywine, and the British took the city. In October, he counterattacked at Germantown, a hamlet north of Philadelphia, but once again he was defeated.

Before the year ended, Washington faced a third fight. His troops were dug in behind a line of redoubts at White Marsh, northwest of the city; in early December, Howe and his men marched out of Philadelphia toward them.

Washington was threatened by more than the enemy. Congress, dismayed by the loss of the capital, demanded that he strike the enemy and recover it.

John Marshall was in Washington's army that winter, a lieutenant in a Virginia regiment. He was tall, strong, and slovenly, with black hair and bright black eyes. He had recently turned twenty-two and was already a two-year veteran who had fought in four engagements. Decades later, in a biography of George Washington—the only book he ever wrote—he recalled his commander's predicament at White Marsh.

Washington knew his troops were in no shape to launch another attack. They had fought two battles in two months and lacked shoes, uniforms, and weapons. Washington, wrote Marshall, had "too much discernment" and "too much firmness of temper" to be distracted by "the torrent of public opinion . . . the clamors of faction or the discontents of ignorance." Yet if the enemy attacked, he must be ready to meet them. So "the American chief rode through every brigade of his army, delivering, in person, his orders respecting the manner of receiving the enemy, exhorting his troops to rely principally on the bayonet, and encouraging them by the steady firmness of his countenance, as well as by his words, to a vigorous performance of their duty. . . . The author states this on his own observation," Marshall added (proudly: *I was there;* self-effacingly: he put it in a footnote). After two days of skirmishing, the British withdrew; Washington would not be lured from his prepared positions, and Howe decided it would be too risky to assault them. Marshall explained the enemy's retreat thus: Howe's return "to Philadelphia without bringing on an action, after marching out with the avowed intention of fighting, is the best testimony of the respect which he felt for the talents of his adversary, and the courage of the troops he was to encounter."

Washington's talents, soldiers' courage: Marshall would never forget them. The revolutionary army drew patriotic young men from every state who risked privation, injury, and death for their common country. The man who commanded them struck where he could and stood firm when he had to; he was judicious, brave, and a leader of men.

For the rest of his life, John Marshall saw Washington as his commander and himself as one of his troops. In 1787, Washington left his postwar retirement to preside over the Constitutional Convention in Philadelphia. Marshall, still in his early thirties, was not yet eminent enough to be sent as a delegate to that meeting, but in 1788, he served in the Virginia Ratifying Convention in Richmond, defending the Constitution that Washington had signed. In 1798, Washington summoned his former junior officer to Mount Vernon and told him to run for Congress; Marshall obeyed. In 1799, after the great man died, it was Marshall who eulogized him, on the floor of the House, as "first in war, first in peace, and first in the hearts of his countrymen."

But Washington was more than a hero to Marshall. He was a man with principles and an agenda, who had learned from the privations of his army the need for a capable national government, and who then worked as a Constitution-maker and president to design and lead one. How could Marshall support Washington while he lived and defend his handiwork after he was gone?

The most obvious way was politics, and Marshall had an abiding interest in it. In the first national two-party system that emerged in the 1790s, the party Marshall joined was the Federalists. Their policies were Washington's: a strong federal government that could pay its debts, foster commerce, and sustain a unified nation in a turbulent world. Marshall was friendly with every prominent Federalist—Washington, John Adams, Alexander Hamilton, Timothy Pickering—even when, as their party began to sink at the turn of the century, they turned on each other. The only man Marshall ever hated was Federalism's enemy and destroyer (and his own cousin)—Thomas Jefferson.

Federalism withered and died, new parties emerged; Marshall kept tabs on them all. He was touted as a presidential candidate himself in one election season, and in another he attended America's first national political convention, organized by America's first third party (the Marshall campaign went nowhere, as did the third party).

Yet although politics was a lifelong interest of Marshall's, it was not his main one. He had a vocation, which was the law. His father, Thomas, had decided that his eldest child should be a lawyer; William Blackstone's *Commentaries on the Laws of England,* then the most popular legal text in the English-speaking world, was part of John's homeschooling. In 1780, while on a furlough from the army, he attended a course of lectures in the law at William and Mary—the only formal legal instruction he would ever receive, but since the course was given by George Wythe, one of the top legal minds in the country, it was first-rate. After the war, Marshall established a practice in Richmond, Virginia's new capital, quickly joining the state's legal elite. His practice was so engrossing that he refused several offers of national public office. In 1801, however, after serving in Congress and as secretary of state, he agreed to become the nation's chief justice.

The Supreme Court that Marshall led was the federal government's fledgling, almost its orphan. In twelve years, it had traveled, with the nation's capital, through three cities—New York, Philadelphia, and the brand-new site on the Potomac; between terms, justices were required to ride circuit over hundreds of miles of woeful roads. Partly because of these hardships, three men had already cycled through the post of chief justice before Marshall took the job.

The law that the Court administered was in no better shape. Americans were already famously litigious, but the legal arena in which they struggled was poorly marked. Colonial precedents had been upset by the Revolution; many Americans, from pioneers on the margins of settlement to wealthy grandees, simply broke whatever laws there were, old or new. Americans went to court to scramble for land and to exploit new technology; to defend their religious and political beliefs and to attack the beliefs of their neighbors. Black men and red men went to court—mostly, though not always, unsuccessfully—for relief from injustices committed by white men; white men went to court to gouge each other.

At the helm of the Supreme Court, Marshall brought order to this chaos. He did it by expressing and implementing the principles he had imbibed from Washington and from other Federalists such as Alexander Hamilton. In a series of landmark decisions, he defended contracts and corporations from meddlesome state laws and struck down state-sponsored monopolies, unblocking what Hamilton called "the veins of commerce"; he affirmed the constitutionality of a national bank, one of the keystones of Washington's economic policy; he compelled state courts to acknowledge the supremacy of the federal judiciary (Hamilton had likened unchecked state courts to "a hydra in government"); and he tried, in vain, to sustain Washington's Indian policy, whereby native peoples who signed and honored treaties with the United

States could keep their tribal lands. In 1801, Jefferson, who had been inaugurated president only five weeks after Marshall was confirmed as chief justice, complained that Federalism had "retired into the judiciary as a stronghold." Marshall held his position as resolutely as Washington at White Marsh.

More important than the substance of Marshall's rulings was what they said about the power of the Supreme Court and the nature of the Constitution. He disclaimed any intention to judge matters that were strictly political, but he insisted that in defense of the Constitution's text or of constitutionally protected rights, the Supreme Court could overturn a law passed by Congress or compel a president to testify in a courtroom. In so ruling, he made the Supreme Court a definer of its own powers and a peer—sometimes, the superior—of Congress and the president.

Marshall was, at the deepest level of his thought, a populist; he believed that the people had expressed their incontrovertible will when they debated and ratified the Constitution. But until they willed something new, they and their representatives—citizens, legislators, and chief executives alike—were bound by their first foundational act. And the Supreme Court was a guardian—a protector and an expounder—of that act.

In his conduct as chief justice, Marshall imitated his former commander in chief as much as a judge can imitate a president or a general. Marshall's description of Washington in action outside Philadelphia described what he himself wished to be. Some of the phrases he used—"firmness of temper," "steady firmness"—applied equally to himself. If his courtroom exhortations were not always as stern as Washington's battlefield appeals—Marshall listened and persuaded as often as he commanded—they were as persistent and as successful.

In one respect, Marshall exceeded his idol. Washington's combined service as commander in chief during the Revolution (1775–83) and first president (1789–97) made him the nation's chief executive for sixteen and a half years. But Marshall's tenure as chief justice was more than twice as long.

When he died, he was eulogized as "a Federalist of the good old school of which Washington was the acknowledged head."

THERE HAVE BEEN several excellent biographies of Marshall over the years, though not as many as record the lives of his great peers. Marshall's career in the law keeps the number down: writers and readers fear that the subject is too technical. As someone who had even less legal training than Marshall had, I am forced in this biography to see and describe legalisms afresh. As a political journalist, I keep my eye, as Marshall always did, on the politics that surrounded him. As a storyteller, I try to show that the cases that generated his decisions were anything but technical. Blackstone wrote, early in his *Commentaries,* that society arose from "the wants and the fears of individuals." The parties that came before Marshall's Court wanted money, jobs, power; they feared chicanery, oppression, extinction, the noose. People do not go to court over nothing; every legal case is a short story.

Marshall's career is a long story. Over four decades, he dealt with a shifting cast of judges and lawyers, many brilliant and willful, others odd, a few alcoholic or insane. He established his preeminence among them by the force of his mind, which one attorney general compared to "an Atlantic Ocean," the minds of his peers being "mere ponds." He established it also by his never-failing courtesy, good humor, and high spirits, lubricated by frequent applications of Madeira; during his tenure, the wine merchants of Washington, DC, called their best stuff "the Supreme Court," in honor of his many purchases and his generous distribution of their wares.

There are gaps in the record of Marshall's life. He left less to work with than other founders; he kept no diary or journal and was careless with his papers. (The modern collected edition of

Marshall's papers is twelve volumes long; the comparable edition of the papers of Hamilton, who lived thirty-two fewer years than Marshall, fills twenty-seven volumes.) Because I am interested in Marshall's public career and its effects, I am less interested in some aspects of his life than others: less interested in his children than his colleagues, or in his wife than his enemies. Because they did affect his public career, however, I am interested in the games he played, the land deals he made, and what he learned from Alexander Pope.

There are also blots on Marshall's record. In some of his greatest decisions, he contradicts himself, or nearly so; one of his characteristic techniques is to advance a sweeping principle, then draw back to hang his decision on a lesser point. He boldly defended Cherokee Indians; he did nothing for blacks. There were moments when even he lost heart; toward the end of his life, he feared that the great constitutional holding operation and defense of Federalism that was his career had failed.

Considering the Supreme Court's role in American life today, we must also ask: Was John Marshall right? Is his vision of the Constitution as the supreme statement of popular will and the Supreme Court as its defender in fact workable? Do judicial guardians inevitably decay into unelected legislators? Are we too far away from the Constitution to think about it as intelligently, or care about it as passionately, as he did?

Marshall was a man of the founding who lived through the first third of the nineteenth century. His rulings touched on corporations and steam power, the Napoleonic Wars and the campaign against the slave trade. Washington's devotee saw the age of Jackson. Although he did not foresee the precise cause of the Civil War, he feared his country would split apart, and he tried to prevent it. He was a backward-looking man who lived and ruled forward. The implications of his career reach even further forward, into our century.

Section I

EARLY LIFE

Chapter 1

SOLDIER

J OHN MARSHALL, ELDEST CHILD OF THOMAS AND MARY Marshall, was born in September 1755, in a cabin near Germantown, twenty miles west of the Potomac River in northern Virginia, in what is now Fauquier County (pronounced faw-*keer*). Over the next twenty years, the family would move twice, to Leeds Manor in the Blue Ridge Mountains, then to North Cobbler Mountain, but never leaving John's home county.

The Marshalls were not pioneers—their second house was a frame house, and their third had glass in the windows, marks of prosperity and civilization. But they lived, as most Virginians did, in the country.

Two marks of Marshall's upbringing stayed with him all his life. Fauquier County lay within a 5.2 million–acre tract of land between the Rappahannock and the Potomac Rivers, larger than the entire colony of New Jersey, which had been granted in the seventeenth century by the Crown to a noble family, the Culpepers. This domain passed via a married daughter to another noble family, the Fairfaxes. To make money off their property by renting or selling parcels of it, the new owners had to know its exact dimensions. Over the years, the Fairfaxes hired surveyors, one of them a young in-law, George Washington. Another was

Thomas Marshall. Mapping and ultimately buying a portion of the Fairfax Grant would engage the attention of the Marshall family for decades. When a tenacious lawsuit concerning the property made its way to the Supreme Court in 1816, John Marshall would have to recuse himself (though he maintained a keen offstage interest in the case).

Marshall bore a second mark of rural Virginia on his personality. He would spend his adult life in cities—Richmond, Philadelphia, Washington, half a year in Paris—but he never lost his country tastes and habits. Old friends and new acquaintances alike noted his simplicity. The first time he served as a circuit court judge (an assignment that justices of the Supreme Court were required to perform until after the Civil War), he lodged in a rude inn in Raleigh, North Carolina, one of the seats of his circuit. Over the years, Raleigh grew while the inn went downhill. Marshall nevertheless continued to patronize it, even after the innkeeper was no longer able to afford servants; Marshall carried logs from the woodpile into his room himself.

When Marshall was seventy years old, a scholar researching a biography of George Washington called on him at what was then his country house (the house with the glass windows, which he had lived in growing up). The visitor described entering the yard "through a broken wooden gate, fastened by a leather strap and opened with some difficulty." He found Marshall in his "office"—a little brick building in a corner of the yard. The two men had a brief talk, Marshall passing on some advice. "All things about him," the scholar concluded, "his house, grounds, office, himself, bear marks of a primitive simplicity and plainness rarely to be seen."

His simple manners attracted stories as a magnet attracts filings. One story that became famous in Richmond, his primary residence, showed that he was not above using his manners to tease. A newcomer to town bought a turkey in the market and asked a countryman to carry it home for him. The rustic slung it over his shoulder and did as he was bid, refusing any tip. Only later did the newcomer learn that his deliveryman was the chief justice of the United States. No doubt Marshall enjoyed the joke at the newcomer's expense as much as the Richmonders who regaled themselves with it.

Virginia gentlemen loved, or pretended to love, the simple life. Marshall took it to an extreme, without a hint of pretense. He must have kept his earliest habits because he had enjoyed his youth and felt no reason—neither the pull of fashion, nor the sting of family conflicts—to repudiate it.

Mary Marshall's father was an Anglican clergyman, the Reverend James Keith. More important, in the class- and clan-conscious world of Virginia, her mother was a Randolph, one of the colony's first families, thus giving John Marshall a cousin's link to several men he would encounter in later life—Edmund Randolph, John Randolph of Roanoke, Thomas Jefferson.

Mary Marshall was eighteen when John was born; she had fourteen more children. We know little more about her than that. When he was an old man, Marshall was asked to write a recommendation for a book of lectures on the education of women. "Precepts from the lips of a beloved mother," he wrote, "inculcated in the amiable, graceful, and affectionate manner which belongs to the parent and the sex, sink deep in the heart." This was conventional language of the time for describing mothers and their importance in raising children, especially sons. Of Mary Marshall, perhaps it was true.

Thomas Marshall left a larger public record. A grandson of Welsh immigrants, he became a big man in a small world: a vestryman of his Anglican parish; the sheriff of Fauquier County; a member of the House of Burgesses, the elected house of the colonial legislature. Working for the Fairfaxes as a surveyor helped boost him into all these positions. It also enabled him, as it did a young George Washington, to cultivate an eye for land and to begin buying promising tracts with his earnings.

Thomas Marshall oversaw his children's education. There were no schools in their county, so when John was fourteen, Thomas sent him away from the Blue Ridge to board for a year in the Tidewater at a school run by an Anglican minister (one of his classmates was James Monroe). After John returned home, Thomas hired another clergyman to live with the Marshalls for a year, serving the parish and doubling as the family tutor. The rest of John's early education came at home, from his father. Thomas Marshall steered his sons toward the law. Thomas was a subscriber to the first American edition of William Blackstone's *Commentaries on the Laws of England*. "From my infancy," John later wrote, "I was destined to the bar." Four of John's six brothers also became lawyers.

Thomas gave him Alexander Pope's long, didactic poem, "An Essay on Man," which John memorized by copying it out. No one today would nominate "An Essay on Man" for Pope's best work. It is a string of platitudes; even in Pope's own day, Samuel Johnson complained that "he tells us much that every man knows." But the platitudes are exceedingly well put; everything Pope tells us, he tells so well that we believe every man has always known it. John Marshall never became a poet beyond a few simple verses for himself and friends. But the technique of authoritative pronouncement, which he encountered in Pope, would serve him well in later years.

John Marshall adored his father, calling him "a watchful parent and affectionate friend," and "my only intelligent companion" growing up. That last, rather stern comment (my *only* intelligent companion) sets a limit to his remarks on the guiding role of mothers.

When John was nineteen years old, he and his father became companions in revolution.

FOR ALL THAT intelligent Americans read English law books and English poets, the policies of the British Empire clamped hard on the thirteen colonies. Americans evaded commercial regulations and harassed imperial tax collectors; more important, they thought and wrote about their situation, analyzing and proclaiming their violated rights. Colonists hundreds of miles apart joined in angry idealism. When Britain closed the port of unruly Boston in the spring of 1774, the Virginia House of Burgesses, meeting in Williamsburg that June, called for a day of "Fasting, Humiliation and Prayer." Virginia's royal governor dismissed the burgesses and sent them home. Instead of leaving, they reconstituted themselves in August as a convention, an illegal independent institution, which called for an embargo of British goods and a continental congress.

Britain was unmoved by these protests. A second meeting of the Virginia Convention, in a Richmond church in March 1775, heard Patrick Henry: "Our chains are forged. Their clanking may be heard on the plains of Boston. . . . I know not what course others may take, but as for me, give me liberty, or give me death!" Thomas Marshall was in the church, a member of the convention, when the speech was delivered, and reported it to his family.

A month later came news of the battles of Lexington and Concord. The Marshalls plunged into the patriotic current, John showing, as he wrote years later, "all the zeal and enthusiasm which belonged to my age." He volunteered for the county militia and was elected by his comrades as their lieutenant. Thomas, equally zealous, became a major. The volunteers of Fauquier and two other counties mustered at the Culpeper County courthouse in September 1775. One of them described their dress: "brown linen hunting shirts . . . the words 'Liberty or Death' worked in large white letters on the breast, bucktails [deer tails] in each hat, and a leather belt about the shoulders with tomahawk and scalping knife."

In December, Marshall and his comrades put their bold words and bold gear to the test. British troops had occupied Norfolk, Virginia's largest port, and erected a small fort at the head of a causeway, known as the Great Bridge, that led away from the town. Patriots, including Marshall's unit, threw up a barricade at the causeway's far end. One morning, British grenadiers charged the patriot position, expecting to sweep all before them, but American musketry and rifle fire inflicted heavy losses—a hundred killed or wounded, the Americans claimed; sixty, the British admitted. The enemy retired to a warship that bombarded Norfolk, burning it to the ground on New Year's Day.

In 1776, Thomas and John Marshall enlisted in a more regular force: the newly formed Continental Army, made up of regiments raised in the individual states but directed by the Continental Congress and commanded by George Washington. After the burning of Norfolk, Virginia was clear of British troops. The main action of the war shifted to the south and to the north: Charleston, South Carolina; Long Island and White Plains, in New York; Trenton and Princeton, in New Jersey. John Marshall's regiment fought in none of these engagements but did what many units spend much of their time doing in war: marching to battles that never happened; hurrying up and waiting. In 1777, his regiment was sent to Philadelphia, then to New Jersey; in one two-and-a-half-week stretch, he and his comrades marched to the Hudson Highlands in New York and back, a round trip of three hundred miles.

As the summer of 1777 turned to fall, Marshall saw action again. A British armada sailed into Chesapeake Bay and landed an army at the mouth of the Elk River in northern Maryland. The British had occupied New York City, the second-largest city in the United States, the year before; Philadelphia, fifty miles away from their present landing, was the largest and the seat of Congress. Marshall was assigned to a thousand-man light infantry corps intended to slow the British advance. The light infantry was a truly national force, drawn from the regiments of North Carolina, Virginia, Maryland, Pennsylvania, and New Jersey. They engaged the enemy at Cooch's Bridge in northern Delaware on September 3, losing fifty killed, and fell back.

They fought again at Brandywine Creek in southern Pennsylvania on September 11, where George Washington decided to make a stand with his full army. Marshall was on the American left at a crossing called Chadd's Ford. (His father, now a colonel, shared the battle with him, upstream on the American right.) But the British managed to ford the creek even farther upstream and attacked the American right flank. The defenders gave way, losing three hundred killed. The enemy marched into Philadelphia on the twenty-sixth of September. Congress fled west to the small Pennsylvania town of York.

The members of the light infantry having been reassigned to their original regiments, Marshall fought in an American attack on Germantown, a northern suburb of Philadelphia, on October 4. The Americans struck at dawn, achieving surprise. But the enemy rallied in a large stone house that could not be reduced by musket fire or artillery. In darkness and fog, the Americans lost their cohesion, then retreated, leaving almost two hundred dead. Marshall was injured in the hand.

The British attempt to bring on yet another battle at White Marsh in December has been described. After the fighting was done for the year, Marshall and his comrades went into winter quarters at Valley Forge.

Valley Forge was not the coldest winter encampment during the Revolution. What made it a misery was the lack of clothing and food. Legend has it that the desperate conditions drove Washington, an Enlightenment Anglican not given to such behavior, to fall to his knees in prayer. The desperate conditions inspired

John Marshall to good humor. "Nothing discouraged, nothing disturbed him," one of his fellow officers remembered. "If he had only bread to eat, it was just as well; if only meat, it made no difference. If any of the officers murmured at their deprivations, he would shame them by good-natured raillery, or encourage them by his own exuberance of spirits. [The] gloomy hours were enlivened by his inexhaustible fund of anecdote." Young Marshall had a gift, which he never lost, for weaving an air of good fellowship around him. His enjoyment was infectious, and his company a blessing.

Under the instruction of the Prussian volunteer Baron von Steuben, the army at Valley Forge learned a modified European drill that imparted discipline and confidence. In 1778, the British pulled their forces in Philadelphia back to New York. The Americans followed and engaged them at Monmouth Court House in central New Jersey in June. Marshall was at that battle, though he saw no action. It was a confusing conflict, bedeviled on the American side by cross-purposes and miscommunication, but unlike at Brandywine or Germantown, the Americans held the field and fought to an honorable draw. The British felt, for the first time, that they had encountered professional peers, not armed rustics. In the summer of 1779, promoted to captain, Marshall served a supporting role in two small, sharp conflicts meant to test the enemy's control of the lower Hudson River—Stony Point and Paulus Hook. Both were American victories.

Marshall would recount all these actions in his biography of George Washington, published almost two decades later. There he tracked the movement of troops in detail, though his descriptions of terrain and atmosphere were laconic (of Valley Forge, he said only that "the sufferings of the army were extreme"). His reserve extended to himself; he recorded his presence as an eyewitness only in footnotes and did not mention his injury at Germantown (we know of it only from a reference in a pension request by a fellow soldier).

Two themes resounded, however, in Marshall's telling of the story. One was the incompetence of a weak government. The Congress that had declared independence and directed the war—a one-house legislature in which each state's delegation cast one vote—had no power to levy taxes or tariffs. It could only ask the states for money; if they refused or were unable to pay, there was no revenue. Loans from foreign allies and bankers closed some of the gap; so, disastrously, did inflation. The result was that soldiers suffered, unsupplied and unpaid—not just at Valley Forge but continuously as the war dragged on. Marshall made the point repeatedly. In Congress "opinions of the most pernicious tendency prevailed." "Measures essential to the safety of the nation were never taken in season." There were "radical defects in the system itself." A captain's pay (Captain Marshall's pay?) could not buy "the shoes in which he marched." "The purse of a nation alone can supply the expenditures of a nation . . . when all are interested in a contest all ought to contribute to its support." Instead, an empty-handed Congress gave a "philosophic lecture on the virtues of temperance to men who were often without food."

What held the army and the cause together, according to Marshall, despite the fecklessness of the politicians and the feebleness of the government, was the character and presence of George Washington. Most Americans admired Washington. Marshall's reverence was personal, powerful, and enduring.

Marshall may have met Washington at Valley Forge, for he served for a few months there as a judge advocate—his first judicial experience—presiding over one court-martial. This was a job that might have brought him into contact, however briefly, with the commander in chief. (If it did, Marshall's modesty as a historian prevented him from saying so.) His impression of Washington was formed by observing him in the middle distance, in action.

The praise that Marshall heaped on Washington for rallying the army at White Marsh in 1777 echoed throughout his account of the entire war. "In no situation could Washington despond." The "machinations" of critics made "no undue impression on his steady mind." When he was not in the thick of the fight, he "look[ed] anxiously towards the scene of action through a glass." When he appeared on the scene, he brought relief from disaster. "His fine appearance on horseback, his calm courage . . . gave him the air best calculated to excite enthusiasm" (quoted by Marshall from a letter written to him by the Marquis de Lafayette). Marshall inscribed his conclusive judgment of Washington in this paean: "To this unconquerable firmness, to this perfect self-possession under the most desperate circumstances, is America, in a great degree, indebted for her independence."

Marshall's Washington possessed another valuable trait beyond his physical and moral stature: he grasped the underlying political problem that weakened the war effort and lobbied for a remedy. Marshall quoted from one of Washington's many appeals to Congress: "A long and continual sacrifice of individual interest for the general good ought not to be expected or required. The nature of man must be changed before institutions built on the presumptive truth of such a principle can succeed." The nation would have to find some means of paying and supporting the men who defended it, Washington believed, or independence would be lost.

Marshall's conclusions in his Washington biography had been shaped by years of after-the-fact reflection. But his reflections had begun on the spot, as the Revolution, simultaneously glorious and mismanaged, unfolded.

There is one more noteworthy quality about Marshall's Washington. As Marshall revered his own father, so he revered the father of his country.

It is an almost universal human experience to seek surrogates to correct the errors or supply the lacks of one's parents. Marshall found nothing amiss in Thomas Marshall, and his devotion extended seamlessly to George Washington. Washington and the elder Marshall had had the same youthful job, and they were senior officers in the same war. John Marshall followed and admired them both.

Nor did their (literally) commanding presence stunt or diminish him. In their footsteps, but not in their shadows, he flourished as an officer and as a man.

Marshall put one final thought about his war experience in a letter he wrote in his old age to a fellow Supreme Court justice: it was in the army "where I was confirmed in the habit of considering America as my country." Not all Americans did so, during the war or later. When an American spoke of his country, he often meant his state. Thomas Jefferson, living in Philadelphia in 1776 while serving in the Continental Congress, complained that it was "a painful sensation to be 300 miles from one's country." He had just written the Declaration of Independence, but in his mind, his country was Virginia. Marshall fought in Delaware, Pennsylvania, New Jersey, and New York, alongside comrades from the length of America. They starved, bled, and won together; they were his countrymen.

THE BEGINNING OF 1780 marked a lull in the war. Marshall took a furlough and paid an extended visit to his father, who was commanding an artillery company in York, Virginia (later called Yorktown), a small port on Chesapeake Bay. It was a family reunion—Thomas had two other sons and a nephew serving under him. It was also an opportunity to socialize with the family that lived next door to Thomas Marshall, the Amblers.

Jacquelin Ambler—the French first name reflected Huguenot ancestry—had been collector of customs in York, once a lucrative job, though the disruption of the war had left him pinched. He had four daughters, who would be provided for only if they married well.

Two of them were young girls, but Elizabeth (or Betsy) and Mary (or Polly) were nearly fifteen and fourteen, respectively—old enough, in those days, for the joys, and the fevers, of courtship. A letter of Betsy's describing a ball in Williamsburg, the old colonial capital, might have been written by one of Jane Austen's young women: "Of the brilliancy of the company too much cannot be said; it consisted of more Beauty and Elegance than I had ever witnessed before, and I was transported with delight at being considered a distinguished personage . . . so much attention did your giddy friend receive as almost turned her poor distracted brain."

The prospect of Captain John Marshall's arrival in York added to the Ambler sisters' distractions. His siblings had sung his praises; his father had shared his letters home. When at last he appeared, Betsy was at first disappointed. "When I beheld his awkward figure, unpolished manners, and total negligence of person"—she specified a "slouched hat" and "slovenly garb"—"I . . . lost all desire of becoming agreeable in his eyes." Polly lost no desire; she had decided to catch him, sight unseen. "She," wrote Betsy, "had made up her mind to go to [a] ball, though she had not even been at dancing school, and was resolved to set her cap at him, and eclipse us all." The war hero captain soon showed qualities that justified Polly's determination. He "used to read to us from the best authors," Betsy went on, "particularly the Poets, with so much taste and feeling, and pathos too, as to give me an idea of their sublimity, which I should never have had an idea of." There are passages in "An Essay on Man" that, if read well, could produce such an effect. So could "The Rape of the Lock," also by Pope—an erotic tale, presented as wit and froth, of a beau clipping a curl of a young woman's hair.

MARSHALL DID NOT spend his furlough entirely with the Amblers. In the spring and early summer of 1780, he took a course of law lectures at William and Mary College in Williamsburg, given by George Wythe. Wythe, then in his mid-fifties, was a well-regarded politician and judge. As a member of Virginia's congressional delegation, he had signed the Declaration of Independence; on the bench, he could be as venturesome as Marshall would later become. Wythe was equally eminent as a teacher. Thomas Jefferson had learned law as an apprentice in Wythe's office; Wythe's professorship at William and Mary, to which Jefferson, now governor, had appointed him, was the first of its kind in the United States. Marshall was not the only bright young Virginian in the class: among his fellow students were two eighteen-year-olds, Bushrod Washington, a nephew of George, who would serve with Marshall on the Supreme Court, and Spencer Roane, who would become a justice of the Virginia Supreme Court of Appeals and a thorn in Marshall's side.

The core of Wythe's curriculum was Blackstone's *Commentaries,* which Marshall was already familiar with—an attempt to organize and explain the English legal system, which had grown up, like a coral reef of precedents and laws, over centuries. Wythe also held mock legislatures and courts, in which his students debated new laws and argued hypothetical cases. This was a heady load; one of Wythe's students wrote that you either learned a lot from him or nothing at all.

Marshall did not always concentrate. He kept, at Wythe's direction, a commonplace book of laws and cases, organized alphabetically by topic. Marshall got as far as *L* ("Limitation of Action"). Polly Ambler's name, sometimes coupled with his, is doodled throughout the pages. Williamsburg and York were thirteen miles apart, an easy walk for a soldier in war or love.

At the end of his course, Marshall applied for a law license in the new state capital at Richmond (his license was signed by Governor Jefferson).

IN JANUARY 1781, when the turncoat Benedict Arnold raided Virginia, Marshall saw his last action in an ambush of an enemy landing party along the James River. The British would not be driven from the state until Lord Cornwallis was surrounded and captured at Yorktown in October.

John Marshall had by then resigned his commission and resumed his peacetime life. He pressed his courtship of Miss Ambler. He was not well off; his father had many heirs, and he had only just begun in his profession. But he was a young man of energy and intelligence—a good match.

There was a near disaster in the home stretch: John proposed, Polly refused; he left the Ambler household disappointed, she was distressed that he had gone. But a quick-witted cousin of Polly's snipped a lock of her hair and sent it after Marshall as a pledge that his love was in fact returned. Pope had written about the potency of women's hair: "Love in these Labyrinths his Slaves detains / And Mighty Hearts are held in slender Chains." One of Marshall's modern biographers argues that Polly snipped and sent the lock herself, family tradition substituting the cousin to shield her from responsibility for such a bold and intimate act. She and John were married in January 1783. The groom was twenty-seven, the bride almost sixteen. For a wedding present, John's father gave him a slave named Robin and three horses.

Polly's life would shrink and darken, but in her teens, she was a lively and spirited woman who knew what she wanted and got it.

CORNWALLIS'S DEFEAT AT Yorktown had ended Britain's hope of victory in the Revolutionary War, although long negotiations delayed the evacuation of their last troops until the end of 1783. Two days before Christmas, George Washington returned his commission as commander in chief to Congress. In the new year, Marshall wrote about him in a letter to his old schoolmate James Monroe: "At length then the military career of the greatest Man on earth is closed. May happiness attend him wherever he goes. . . . When I speak or think of that superior Man my full heart overflows with gratitude."

Marshall showed the gift, essential to good citizenship, of admiring greatness without forfeiting his own manhood.

Chapter 2

LAWYER

JOHN MARSHALL MOVED TO RICHMOND IN 1784. THE RAW
town stood at the falls of the James River—not a single
plunge but a miles-long rocky descent, making a constant
roar. Benedict Arnold had burned Richmond during his raid in
1781, but it was quickly rebuilt. As the new state capital, it was
the site of Virginia's highest courts and, in time, of a United States
circuit court. It would be the focus of Marshall's professional life
for the next fifteen years.

The law in Virginia, and in the United States generally, was in
a fluid state. A remark of James Kent, a New York judge, about
his prerevolutionary legal education applied to the profession
throughout the thirteen colonies: "We had no law of our own, and
no one knew what it was." Blackstone had erected a great ratio-
nalistic monument of the English common law, useful as a study
guide and for organizing lawyers' thoughts, though how far it actually applied in America was unclear. Blackstone himself noted
that many of the common law's "refinements and distinctions"
were not relevant in "our American plantations": "The common
law of England, as such, has no allowance or authority there;
they being no part of the mother country." American lawyers
and judges who relied on Blackstone after independence could

find themselves at loggerheads with legislators who wanted to jettison the mother country's precedents and make a fresh start.

Day-to-day legal decisions in Virginia were issued by county courts, run by justices of the peace, and served by lawyers who were their cronies. These local figures often knew little of the law, nor did they care so long as the interests of their patrons and friends were safeguarded. In a letter to a fellow veteran-turned-lawyer, Marshall called them "the county court establishment." Its lawyers, he wrote, feared "that they do not possess abilities or knowledge sufficient to enable them to stand before [real] judges of law."

Beneath and beyond the reach of the law lay a powerful fact of Virginia life: the mighty did what they wanted. There was a legendary instance in Marshall's own family. His maternal grandmother, Mary Randolph, was said to have eloped as a teenager with the Randolph family's Irish overseer and had a child by him. Her brothers hunted them down, killed the overseer and the child, and took Mary back. She had a breakdown but recovered to marry a clergyman and raise a new family, including Marshall's mother-to-be. In her middle age, however, she got a letter from the overseer, who said he had survived the long-ago attack but would not now claim her. This letter, whether it was really from her old beloved or the work of a prankster, caused a second breakdown that afflicted her for the rest of her days. Marshall never mentioned this gruesome tale but surely knew of it: the old lady lived into his teens. In the old days, the first families of Virginia made their own law, and there was no power to rebuke them.

But efforts to order the chaos and to curb or at least soften the brutality were under way. The revolutionary elite wanted to lead a respectable nation, not a mob of rubes and barbarians. Learned Virginia jurists such as Wythe and his peer Edmund Pendleton raised the standard of the Virginia bench. There was an effort in the legislature to establish circuit courts, modeled on England's assizes, in which senior judges would rotate throughout the state, holding sessions as they went, making it easier to appeal decisions from the county level. The effort failed, but it showed a desire to make justice more accessible.

There was, finally, a hunger throughout America to learn more about the law. Marshall's father, paying for his prewar American edition of Blackstone and raising a family full of lawyers, typified the trend. Edmund Burke, the English statesman, had warned Parliament on the eve of the Revolution that America was full of "smatterers in law. . . . This study renders men acute, inquisitive, dexterous, prompt in attack, ready in defense, full of resources." Whichever came first, the smattering or the temperament, the two went hand in hand in postindependence America.

ONE OF MARSHALL'S cousins, Edmund Randolph, a former aide to George Washington, now a rising politician, let Marshall do business out of his Richmond law office, and the young man went to work.

Marshall's talents found their way, as did so many things about him, into anecdotes. A country gentleman, in Richmond to have a case argued, was advised by the landlord at his hotel to hire Marshall. But when he saw the young lawyer in the street, in a plain linen shirt, picking cherries out of his hat and eating them, he decided instead to hire an advocate who looked the part—older, with a wig and a black coat. The litigant arrived in court to find that the first case of the day pitted his new lawyer against Marshall. After watching the two in action, he went to Marshall, abashed, and told him that, although he had come to town with a hundred dollars to spend on his case, he had already given most of it to the lawyer with the wig and had only five dollars left. Would Marshall represent him for the remainder? Marshall agreed to take him on.

Like the story of Marshall carrying the turkey, this has the shape of a folk tale: the Simpleton Triumphant. Marshall was simple in his shirts and his snacks, not in his skills.

One of his important early cases concerned the Fairfax Grant. In the 1730s, Joist Hite, a German immigrant and land speculator, had bought 140,000 acres along the Rappahannock River, the title to be guaranteed by the royal governor of Virginia provided Hite find settlers for them. Lord Fairfax objected that the land lay within his grant and took his case to the Privy Council, the king's advisors, in London, which ruled for him. Hite then sued in a Virginia court to get the decision overturned. The litigation wound on until the Revolution, when it paused, to be resumed after the war.

By 1786, Hite and Lord Fairfax were dead, but their heirs and partners and those who had bought land from them carried on the struggle. Each group retained two lawyers to argue its case before the Virginia Court of Appeals. Edmund Randolph, opening for Hite, presented the case as David versus Goliath—simple settlers, fighting the old claim of an English lord. Marshall, closing for Fairfax, cited the family's "long and quiet possession." The Fairfax claim "could not have been unknown to any body."

The decision in *Hite v. Fairfax* was a loss for Marshall and his clients, wrapped in a victory. The Court of Appeals awarded ninety-four thousand acres to Hite's purchasers. But the decision acknowledged the legitimacy of the original Fairfax Grant—an important point at a time when Virginians, relishing their independence, were minded simply to void colonial arrangements. The fate of the Fairfax Grant would be in court for years to come.

Richmond had one church, St. John's, the same in which Patrick Henry had given his blazing oration. It was Anglican before the Revolution, Episcopal thereafter; Marshall, though his convictions were Unitarian, belonged to it, out of good-neighborliness (also out of deference to Polly, "a firm believer," as he put it, in "the church in which she was bred"). Richmond had many taverns, in which Marshall also was a regular. His favorite was run by Serafino Formicola, an Italian who had been the steward of Virginia's last royal governor. Formicola's second story had beds for travelers; when the courts and the legislature were in session, according to a guest who stayed there, visitors and locals "sat all together about the fire, drinking, smoking, singing, and talking ribaldry." Marshall led a sociable life, in and out of taverns; his account books show him spending on liquor, barbecues, plays, and gambling (whist and backgammon). Occasionally, there is a payment to a barber. He also bought slaves to serve him in town and to work on the farms he would soon acquire.

He and Polly had their first child, Thomas, in 1784. Then, two years later, disaster. A girl, born in June, died after five days; in September, Polly miscarried. Infant mortality was high in those days, but common fates can strike different people differently. Polly's losses were as crushing to her as the lurid events that had unseated the reason of Marshall's grandmother. The bright, willful girl he had married began to slide into a lifelong depression. The form it took with her was an extreme sensitivity to noise or contact with strangers. Her response would be to withdraw from the world; Marshall's was to cater to her.

Thomas, Marshall's father, moved in 1785 with his family to Kentucky, which was cut off from the rest of Virginia by the Appalachians and bound soon for statehood itself. Thomas had raised his sons to a profession, but he was a surveyor and a land speculator: Kentucky was the land of fresh opportunity. He left to John the family's third home at North Cobbler Mountain; John would be the clan's eastern patriarch.

MARSHALL HAD A second, parallel career suited to life in Richmond: politics. He had several reasons for taking it up. Most obviously, he had a knack for it. He liked people and people liked him, the irreducible basis of vote-getting. In his early days as a lawyer, when he was still being underestimated by wealthy clients, he needed the additional income that office-holding provided. Revolutions, especially those that accompany wars of independence, always create jobs for the winners as old elites are disrupted and foreigners sent home; a patriot of Marshall's energy and intelligence would be thrust into public service even if he did not seek it. Finally, Marshall had opinions about public affairs, about what was not being done and what had to be.

Marshall was first elected to the House of Delegates, the lower house of the Virginia legislature, in 1782, as a representative from Fauquier County before he even moved to Richmond. His fellow legislators elected him to sit on the governor's eight-man advisory council—quite an honor for a freshman (some of his elders grumbled at it). When he relocated to Richmond, he was elected to the city council. In 1787, he was returned to the House of Delegates from his new home.

Marshall had conceived a low opinion of Congress during his wartime service. He was not impressed by his state-level colleagues now. The Treaty of Paris, which ended the Revolution, had guaranteed that British creditors could recover the debts incurred by Americans before the war. Virginia planters in hock to their British factors, or agents, were loath to settle. Their reluctance mirrored an impulse among debtors nationwide to use the new powers of postindependence legislatures to delay payments to British and American creditors alike. Whether because his legal training made him tidy-minded or because as a family ally of the Fairfaxes and a potential land-buyer himself he wanted engagements enforced, Marshall complained of this spirit. "There are many members," he wrote of his fellow legislators, "who really appear to be determined against every measure which may expedite . . . recovering debts and compelling a strict compliance with contracts."

At the end of 1786, the politics of debt became violent in Massachusetts, as armed bands shut courts to prevent them from foreclosing on the properties of tax delinquents. Reports of Shays's Rebellion that came to Virginia were simultaneously exaggerated and unclear. Was the violence really a British plot directed from Canada? A cover for a local faction fight? Marshall likened disorder in Massachusetts to the "strong tendency" of his fellow Virginians "to promote private and public dishonesty. . . . I fear, and there is no opinion more degrading to the dignity of man, that those have truth on their side who say that man is incapable of governing himself. I fear we may live to see another revolution."

WHAT AMERICA SAW instead was a push to change America's government. A convention of delegates from every state (except Rhode Island, which boycotted the meeting) met in Philadelphia in the summer of 1787 to alter or replace America's first constitution, the Articles of Confederation. Virginia's delegation was the strongest, a sign of the seriousness with which the state's leaders took the country's problems. Marshall's patron, Edmund Randolph, newly elected governor, led it. It included famous men such as George Wythe; a man rapidly becoming famous, James Madison, at age thirty-six already a veteran of state and national politics; and the most famous man in the country, and Marshall's idol, George Washington. Washington had been lobbying behind the scenes for reform, corresponding with politicians and former comrades, canvassing new plans of government, assessing the popular mood. As soon as the convention had a quorum, the delegates unanimously picked him to preside over their deliberations. Washington wanted radical change. If the current system were merely amended, he wrote, "it will be like the propping of a house which is ready to fall."

Not everyone in Virginia shared Washington's urgency. The legislature had picked Patrick Henry to go to Philadelphia, but he declined. "I smelt a rat," he explained, fearing that a new system would curtail state power and liberty itself. Henry's enemies thought him vain, lazy, and demagogic, but everyone admitted that when roused he was a force of nature.

What Virginia decided would resonate nationwide, for, besides the eminence of its patriots, Virginia was the most populous state. One fifth of all Americans were Virginians.

Marshall did not belong to the top tier of Virginia's leaders, and no one thought of sending the thirty-one-year-old to Philadelphia. But after the new Constitution was finished in September 1787, he played a supporting role in the struggle for ratification.

Marshall's new term in the House of Delegates began in October. The Constitution specified that it should be submitted to conventions called in each state; it would go into effect once nine of them ratified. When the Constitution's supporters in the Virginia legislature offered a motion calling for a convention in Richmond, Henry was ready with a ploy: an amendment allowing the convention to ratify on condition that the Constitution itself be amended first, if necessary.

Henry's proposal was the equivalent of a vote of no confidence. How good could the Constitution be if it needed amending at birth? If Henry's proposal ever went into effect, it would create havoc; what would happen if other states rejected Virginia's amendments or made amendments of their own? Adopting Henry's proposal would send a bad signal nationwide, which is exactly why Henry offered it. Marshall muffled it with an emollient compromise: the Constitution should be submitted to a convention for "free and ample discussion." Who, pro or con, could be against that? Marshall's motion passed unanimously.

Marshall showed a gift for careful, neutral-seeming language that served a larger goal—in this case, defending the Constitution from preemptive criticism.

Virginia decided on a late date for the Richmond convention: May 1788, later pushed back to June. This was a risk for both opponents and supporters of the Constitution. It might win nine quick ratifications, leaving Virginia voiceless. Or it might be so buffeted in multiple state contests that Virginia could deliver the final fatal blow.

THE ARTICLES OF Confederation, which the Constitution proposed to replace, had been hammered out by the Continental Congress over sixteen months, from July 1776 to November 1777. It was a true committee document, verbose and picayune. (Sample: "Whenever the legislative or executive authority or lawful agent of any state in controversy with another shall present a petition to congress, stating the matter in question and praying for a hearing, notice thereof shall be given by order of congress to the legislative or executive authority of the other state in controversy, and a day assigned for the appearance of the parties by their lawful agents . . . " (This particular sentence, from Article IX, went on for several hundred more words.) The Articles created a "firm league of friendship" among the states. Its governing body was a one-house Congress, in which each state cast one vote. Congress appointed secretaries to conduct diplomatic, military, and financial business, subject to its supervision, and a court of appeals to decide the fate of enemy ships captured at sea, but there were no equivalents of the governors or court systems that almost every state had.

Congress itself was governed by the states, which held the power of the purse and passed all the laws that Americans actually obeyed. Congress could make requisitions on the states for money, but the states contributed as much as they could or as they liked.

Congress could raise armies but had no power (as Marshall knew) to pay them. It could sign treaties but could not (as Virginia's debtors knew) enforce them. Any change to this system required the approval of every state—virtually an impossible hurdle.

The Constitution that came out of Philadelphia was better written, even though it was more complex; Gouverneur Morris, a peg-legged aristocrat from New York, was the draftsman responsible for its sheen and smoothness. The new system envisaged a Congress with two houses—a Senate in which the states were represented equally, and a House of Representatives in which representation was based on population. The executive power was assigned to a president; there was also a judiciary, consisting of a supreme and inferior courts. These three branches were given an expansive list of powers: Congress could levy its own taxes and pass laws concerning a variety of subjects, from borrowing money to issuing patents; the president could pick his own secretaries, command the military, and negotiate treaties; the courts could pass judgment on cases arising under the Constitution and a dozen other specified situations.

The different branches controlled each other in several ways: only the House of Representatives could propose a budget; the president could veto Congress's laws, which Congress could pass again only with supermajorities; the president, with the approval of the Senate, picked judges of the Supreme Court; the House could impeach and the Senate remove from office the president or judges. The process for amendments, Patrick Henry should have been pleased to learn if he were interested in improving the document instead of killing it, was complicated but less onerous than that of the Articles of Confederation.

In March 1788, Marshall was elected as one of two delegates from Henrico County, in which Richmond lay, to the Ratifying Convention (Governor Randolph was the other). Marshall later admitted that his constituents probably opposed the Constitution but chose him because they liked him. He prepared for the meeting in characteristic style, buying bottles, corks, glasses, and food for entertaining out-of-town delegates. For himself, he bought volume 1 of the *Federalist,* thirty-six pro-Constitution essays by Madison, Alexander Hamilton, and John Jay, which had been appearing since the fall of 1787 in New York newspapers. He even, uncharacteristically, bought new clothes.

The convention opened on June 2 and—after one cramped day in the statehouse, which could not accommodate 170 delegates plus spectators—it adjourned to the Academy, a new building that was a combination dancing school and theater. The delegates met six days a week, six or seven hours a day, for three and a half weeks.

The hopes and fears of both sides of the ratification struggle had been borne out over the last eight months. Eight states had ratified—the most recent, South Carolina, at the end of May—but four, besides Virginia, had yet to decide: North Carolina, New York, New Hampshire (whose convention had adjourned when panicked supporters of the Constitution feared defeat), and incorrigible Rhode Island. Most of the country wanted the Constitution, but Virginia held its fate in its hands.

Patrick Henry was the star of the convention, giving one-quarter of the speeches himself. He used sarcasm, mocking the notion that amendments could wait until after ratification: "You agree to bind yourselves hands and foot—For the sake of what? Of being unbound. You go into a dungeon—For what? To get out." He used melodrama, invoking "beings which inhabit the aetherial mansions . . . anxious concerning our decision." The pro-Constitution side was led by Madison, who, despite his slight frame and weak voice, wrangled learnedly over every detail that critics raised.

Marshall gave three substantial speeches. His skills as a performer were limited to moving his right arm up and down stiffly as he spoke. His power came from the force of his arguments.

In an early speech making a general argument for the new Constitution, he defended giving the government expanded powers. Even "if a system of government were devised by more than human intelligence, it would not be effectual if the means were not adequate to the power." Could such power be abused? Of course. "All delegated powers are liable to be abused. Arguments drawn from this source go in direct opposition to every government, and in recommendation of anarchy." The Constitution's supporters wished only "to give the government powers to secure and protect it." The veteran cited the Revolutionary War as an instance of the government's feebleness under the Articles of Confederation. "It would have been much sooner terminated had [the] government been possessed of due energy." The lawyer and budding land speculator cited postwar anti-debt laws as another instance. "The present government . . . takes away the incitements to industry by rendering property insecure and unprotected."

In a speech on militias—opponents of the Constitution feared that Congress's power to summon state militias would supersede a state's power to call up its own—Marshall made a passing reference to the foundation on which the new Constitution would rest. "When the government is drawn from the people . . . and depending on the people for its continuance, oppressive measures will not be attempted, as they will certainly draw on their authors the resentment of those on whom they depend. On this government, thus depending on ourselves for its existence, I will rest my safety." The Preamble to the Constitution derived its authority from "We the People of the United States of America." Gouverneur Morris opened the Preamble this way to avoid listing the signatory states, since Rhode Island had sent no delegates to the Philadelphia convention, and most of New York's had gone home in disgust halfway through. But Morris's rhetorical maneuver also expressed a thought and a hope: the Constitution, if ratified, would be an act of the people. So Marshall understood it.

His third speech concerned the judiciary. The Constitution's opponents feared that the new government would exceed its powers. Marshall argued that the judiciary was the safeguard that would hold the government in check. "If [it] were to make a law not warranted by any of the powers enumerated, it would be considered by the Judges as an infringement of the Constitution which they are to guard. They would not consider such a law as coming under their jurisdiction. They would declare it void. . . . To what quarter will you look for protection from an infringement of the Constitution if you will not give power to the Judiciary? There is no other body that can afford such a protection."

One of the Constitution's opponents had slyly raised the question of the Fairfax Grant, which Marshall and his family were well known to defend. Could Fairfax's heirs take their case out of state to the new supreme and inferior courts, as to the Privy Council in colonial times? Marshall defended himself and the new judiciary by defending the independence and impartiality of judges. "If a law be executed tyrannically in Virginia, to what can you trust? To your judiciary. What security have you for justice? Their independence. Will it not be so in the Federal Court?"

More eloquent than the arguments of Henry, Madison, Marshall, and everyone else who spoke in Richmond was the silent presence of George Washington. Since returning from Philadelphia in 1787, Washington had stayed at Mount Vernon, making no appearances, issuing no statements. But everyone knew that he supported the new Constitution. His was the first of the thirty-nine signatures: G. Washington, Presidt. and Deputy from Virginia. Many had received his letters, anxious or hortatory by turns, but always engaged, following the progress of ratification, complimenting Hamilton on the *Federalist,* plotting strategy with Madison. Madison alluded to Washington during the Richmond debates: "Could we not adduce a [great] character . . . on our side?" William Grayson, an opponent of the Constitution, tried to argue around him: "I think that were it not for one great character in America, so many men would not be for this government." Marshall had followed Washington during the war; now he followed him in peace.

On June 24, the Virginians voted. They approved the Constitution, 89–79. Days later, they learned that they had been preceded by New Hampshire, whose convention, returning from adjournment, had become the ninth to ratify, on June 21. New York followed in July, North Carolina in 1789, and Rhode Island in 1790.

The United States had a new government. In it, Marshall would find new avenues of law and politics.

Chapter 3

LOCAL POLITICIAN

I N THE CLOSING YEARS OF THE 1780S, A RICHMOND INSTITU-
tion was formed that would play a considerable role in Marshall's life, variously called the Barbecue Club, Buchanan's
Spring Quoits Club, or simply the Quoits Club. Quoits was an
old British game, like horseshoes, except that it was played with
metal rings. Medieval kings banned it on the grounds that it distracted their subjects from archery, England's military specialty.
Two teams of players pitched their quoits at iron pins, or megs,
the goal being to see who could come closest to, or at the best
encircle, the meg.

The club met every Saturday, from May to October, at the
farm of the Reverend John Buchanan, a Presbyterian minister.
Membership was limited to thirty, carefully chosen; two black-
balls could block a candidate. The governor was allowed to attend
ex officio as an honorary member. Eating, drinking, and talking
were as important as quoits. Members sang, recited poems, and
gave mock heroic speeches on fine points of the game. Religion
and politics were forbidden topics; an infraction cost the offender
a case of champagne, to be consumed at the next meeting. No
other wine was served; julep, toddy, porter, ale, and punch were
the drinks of choice.

Marshall was devoted to games and exertion. All his life, he walked several miles before breakfast. His nickname in the army had been Silverheels, partly because his mother sewed him socks with white heels, partly because he was so agile he could jump over a bar resting on the heads of two men. He took to quoits with equal relish. Marshall's technique at the game has been recorded: "Mr. Marshall, with his long arms hanging loosely by his side . . . leaning slightly to the right, carried his right hand and right foot to the rear; then, as he gave the quoit the impetus of his full strength, brought his leg up, throwing the force of the body" into his toss.

On the particular day that this account described, Marshall ringed the meg, but another player then pitched his quoit on top of Marshall's. Who won the point? Marshall delivered a speech in defense of his throw. "He was the first occupant, and his right extended up from the ground to the vault of heaven. . . . If his opponent had adversary claim, he must obtain a writ of ejectment."

Why remember such things—the elaborate japes of unbuttoned lawyers, the boys' games played by men? Because Marshall loved the japes and the games. His partying and his playing eased his mind of its labors; they aided his labors, encouraging friendships across partisan and intellectual lines. All players of the game were equal, and sometimes Marshall's bonhomie induced other players—in law and politics, if not quoits—to switch sides.

As MARSHALL ADVANCED in his profession, the days when he would be mistaken for a tyro faded. When Edmund Randolph became governor at the end of 1786, he had ceded his law office and his practice to Marshall. Marshall did legal business for the elite—George Washington, James Madison, George Mason, author of the state's bill of rights. (Mason thought him indolent.) He tried cases alongside his rival at the Virginia Ratifying

Convention, Patrick Henry. This is a quality of lawyers, especially in small communities: your opponent today may be your cocounsel tomorrow. Even political differences outside the courtroom do not stand in the way of business. The community of lawyers is like the Quoits Club: professional competence is the price of admission, the esteem of peers seals it; once you are in, every other member is a potential partner.

The year 1793 saw Marshall appearing with Henry in two major cases. *Commonwealth v. Randolph,* a criminal matter, involved a branch of the Randolph family and was quite as gothic as what had happened to Marshall's grandmother.

In 1789, Richard Randolph married his cousin Judith, also surnamed Randolph, and took her to Bizarre, his plantation in Cumberland County. Two years later, Judith's younger unmarried sister Nancy came to live with them. In October 1792, the three Randolphs visited yet another cousin, Randolph Harrison, at his plantation. In the night, the Harrisons were wakened by Nancy's screams. She appeared to have had a hysterical fit; she recovered after a few days, and the guests left. The Harrisons' slaves, however, whispered that a white newborn had been found dead on a woodpile. As the rumor spread and mutated, the father and murderer was identified as Nancy's cousin and brother-in-law, Richard.

To stop the gossip, Richard Randolph announced that he would appear at Cumberland County Court in April 1793 to answer "any charge or crime" that anyone might bring against him. He hired Patrick Henry for the handsome sum of 140 pounds. Henry cross-examined the witnesses, an assortment of Harrisons, Randolphs, and their neighbors (slaves could not testify in a felony matter involving white people). Henry tricked one old lady into making a fool of herself: when she testified that she had seen an undressed and pregnant-looking Nancy through a crack in the door of her room, Henry asked, "Which eye did you peep with?"

Richard Randolph also retained Marshall to defend Nancy. Marshall's case notes summarized the depositions, some of them damaging—Nancy appeared (to more than the spying lady) to have gained weight; she had asked about procuring gum guaiacum, a medicine that induced abortions; she and Richard had been noticed exchanging "imprudent familiarities." Marshall then listed, with equal care, all the reasons that might explain such damning testimony away. Some of Nancy's acquaintances had not noticed any weight gain. Gum guaiacum had other uses besides abortions. As for "imprudent familiarities," Marshall wrote gallantly, "there is no man in whose house a young lady lives who does [not] occasionally pay her attentions . . . which a person prone to suspicion may consider as denoting guilt." Look to your own dirty minds, gossips. "But had [Richard and Nancy] been conscious of guilt they would have suppressed any public fondness." Their guilty behavior proved their innocence.

Marshall's summation was splendid. "The friends of Miss Randolph cannot deny, that there is some foundation on which suspicion may build: nor can it be denied by her enemies but that every circumstance may be accounted for, without imputing guilt to her." By seeming to split the difference, Marshall stacked the deck for acquittal.

In the event, the court dismissed all charges. The case would come back into Marshall's life years later.

W ARE v. HYLTON, Marshall's second partnership with Henry, involved the most inflamed political issue of the 1780s, debt to British creditors.

In 1777, two years into the Revolution, Virginia had passed a law making all debts owed to British creditors payable instead to a state loan office. Yet the Treaty of Paris that ended the war stipulated that creditors on either side should face no legal bar to securing what was owed them.

The most industrious lawyer in Virginia defending the state's debtors was John Marshall—this, despite his complaints about "private and public dishonesty" and his belief in "strict compliance with contracts." Marshall's willingness to argue for debtors reflects another quality of the law: just as any practitioner can be your partner, so anyone can be your client. A good lawyer goes where the business is and makes the best case he can.

One client that Marshall and Henry represented was Daniel Hylton, a Richmond merchant who in 1780 made a payment to the state loan office in lieu of paying 933 pounds to a firm of Bristol factors. After the war, John Ware, the executor for one of the firm's partners, sued to recover. Hylton hired Marshall in April 1793, and the case went to trial the following month.

The venue was Richmond's new federal Circuit Court, envisioned by the Constitution, Article III, Section 1 ("Congress may from time to time . . . establish" inferior courts). In 1789, Congress had established district courts in each state and grouped these into three circuits, with Virginia belonging to the middle circuit. Twice a year, the local district judge—Cyrus Griffin, a veteran of the Continental Congress—and two itinerant justices of the Supreme Court heard cases in Richmond. *Ware v. Hylton* was a matter for a federal court because (as per Article III, Section 2) it pitted "Citizens" against "foreign . . . Citizens."

Henry displayed his usual eloquence—"Gracious God," exclaimed James Iredell, one of the visiting Supreme Court justices, "he is an orator indeed!"—bolstered on this occasion with diligent reading in dusty tomes on international law (Henry was not in fact as lazy as his enemies maintained).

The only record of what Marshall argued in this case is in notes jotted by Justice Iredell. Marshall's most persuasive argument was that Hylton's payment to the loan office had abolished his debt and transferred it to the State of Virginia. Ware sought a "recovery—from whom? From him who owes nothing. From him who does not owe *the Debt*. . . . If [Ware] has a debtor it is" the government of Virginia, "not he whom the law has declared is discharged." Chief Justice John Jay, who was riding circuit with Iredell, did not buy this argument, but Iredell and Griffin did, which made a victory for Marshall. Ware would appeal his case to the Supreme Court.

M ARSHALL COULD ARGUE before juries and before judges; he could handle criminal investigations and complex lawsuits. The longest-lasting suit in which he was personally involved took a turn in 1793, not in a courtroom but in London, where Marshall, long an advocate for the Fairfax interest, became a potential purchaser as well.

Thomas, Lord Fairfax, had died in 1781, age eighty-eight, at his hunting lodge in the Shenandoah Valley (he was the only English nobleman ever to move to his property in the thirteen colonies). A childless bachelor, he named a nephew, the Reverend Denny Martin, an English clergyman, his heir, provided Martin took Fairfax as his surname. Though Lord Fairfax had opposed the Revolution, he had retained the esteem of his longtime neighbors in Virginia. Denny Martin Fairfax, who had never set foot in America, inherited the claim and the surname, but not the respect. Despite Marshall's 1786 victory in *Hite v. Fairfax*, which had wrung acknowledgment of the Fairfax Grant from the Court of Appeals, the new proprietor foresaw only endless difficulties in maintaining his windfall.

The Marshall family, seeing an opportunity, sent one of their own to London to negotiate with the new landowner. James Markham Marshall was eight and a half years younger than his brother John. He too had served in the Revolution (volunteering in 1779, age only fifteen); he too had become a lawyer, after moving with their father, Thomas, to Kentucky. In February 1793, James made a deal with Denny Martin Fairfax: he, John, and Rawleigh Colston (the husband of their eldest sister, Elizabeth) would buy 215,000 acres of prime Fairfax land for 20,000 pounds.

This was a huge purchase for a huge sum (the pounds the Marshall syndicate promised to come up with were the pounds sterling of Great Britain, the strongest currency in the world, not the depreciated paper of old Virginia, which Daniel Hylton had used to pay the state loan office). It also exposed the purchasers to huge risks. They might become wealthy by reselling. They might go bust if they defaulted after making their down payment. Win or lose, they were sure to be entangled in the counterclaims and litigation that had beset the Fairfax Grant for sixty years. John Marshall had confidence in his legal and political savvy. He would need all of it, over many years, to defend his family's Fairfax purchase.

MARSHALL'S SUCCESS AS a lawyer had augmented his income stream. He no longer needed the salary of an officeholder, and he found the work increasingly distracting. In 1789, George Washington himself, newly elected the nation's first president, asked him to become the United States attorney for the Virginia district; Marshall passed. ("It is with real regret," he wrote, "I decline accepting an office which has to me been rendered highly valuable by the hand which bestowed it.") In 1791, he declined to run again for the House of Delegates; years later, he remembered that he meant his refusal to be his "final adieu to political life."

Neither politics nor George Washington had said good-bye to Marshall, however. In the summer of 1793, national politics reached into Richmond to claim his attention.

Once the Constitution went into effect, it seemed at first as if there might be no more politics. In January 1789, Washington had been elected president unanimously, receiving every electoral vote. His trip from Mount Vernon to New York City, the nation's capital, for his inauguration in April had been a rolling festival of cheering crowds and ceremonial welcomes, all the large pride and little pomposities of a new country. Congress fussed with trivialities; one representative foresaw long debates about "whether a man shall be called doorkeeper or sergeant-at-arms." Once Congress got down to substance, one of its first accomplishments, during the summer of 1789, was to approve a set of amendments to the Constitution that should function as a bill of rights—an olive branch to critics like Henry, who had deplored the absence of one in the original.

But politics never ends, because ambition never rests. Honest differences of opinion gave ample material for contention.

One lightning rod was the first treasury secretary, Alexander Hamilton. Born and raised in the Caribbean, Hamilton had immigrated to New York. Like Marshall, he was a veteran—a captain of artillery, promoted to Washington's staff. He and Marshall had served in three battles together (Brandywine, Germantown, Monmouth) and shared the winter at Valley Forge. Conceivably, Marshall met Hamilton there, as a judge advocate reporting up the chain of command. Marshall certainly knew Hamilton's contributions to the *Federalist*.

Hamilton's plans for putting the nation's finances in order passed Congress in the summer of 1790. Hamilton wanted the federal government to take on the debts of all the states, as well as its own; tariffs and excise taxes would pay them off. His plans were deeply unpopular in Virginia, where the General Assembly professed to see in them a "striking resemblance" to the operations of the Bank of England. Hamilton's Virginia critics were right: England had entered a modern fiscal world, in which a national debt, prudently managed, boosted a country's credit. Hamilton wanted the United States to enjoy the same benefits.

Marshall, once the unpaid captain, approved; so did Washington, once the unsupplied commander in chief. Most Virginians, however, hated the English model, because it was English and because it seemed to promise an overbearing federal government. Hamilton's "whole funding system," wrote Marshall, "was censured."

The great flashpoint in Marshall's life, however, was the French Revolution and its aftershocks in America.

France's Revolution coincided with America's new form of government: the Bastille fell in July 1789, just three months after Washington's inauguration. The French Revolution initially struck most Americans as a godsend. Our revolutionary ally would now enjoy the blessings of liberty. Lafayette, a hero of our struggle, led a people's army, the National Guard, and designed a red, white, and blue cockade (still the national colors). Thomas Jefferson, who was America's minister to France, advised him on a Declaration of the Rights of Man. Louis XVI would become a constitutional monarch. Only Gouverneur Morris, who was in Paris on business, had doubts. The French "want an American constitution," he wrote in his diary, "without reflecting that they have not American citizens to support" it. His doubts, however, were lost in the enthusiasm of the moment.

In only a few years, the French Revolution changed its character, both in France and in American politics. Plagued by divisions at home and declarations of war by Britain and other European powers, the revolution radicalized, murdering its enemies wholesale. Louis was deposed in 1792, and Lafayette fled the country; the ex-king went to the guillotine in January 1793.

Meanwhile, in America, those who opposed Hamilton's measures realized that sympathy for France could be a useful counterweight. If the treasury secretary wanted to foist English policies

on America, then Americans could show their resistance by praising and emulating France. Republicanism abroad would bolster
republican sentiment at home.

American Francophiles had another target besides Hamilton—Vice President John Adams, the Massachusetts patriot and
diplomat. Adams was deeply learned, disputatious, and inclined
to gloom, at least when he theorized. He was also the first vice
president to discover that he had hardly anything to do. To fill
up his time, he wrote a series of essays on political philosophy
for the nation's premier newspaper, in which he speculated that
hereditary succession might prove less disruptive than contested
elections. If Hamilton emulated England's financial system, Adams seemed to be calling for monarchy.

America's leading Francophile was Jefferson, who, after returning home in 1790, had become secretary of state. Jefferson's
mother, like Marshall's, was a Randolph; the two men were second cousins, once removed. Jefferson was twelve years older and
had started faster and higher in public life, serving in the House
of Burgesses and the Continental Congress. His singing prose
and his clear, simple thoughts made him an obvious choice to
write the Declaration of Independence. Jefferson was governor of Virginia when Marshall was a captain skirmishing with
Benedict Arnold's invaders. Jefferson left the governorship just
before Marshall began his career in Virginia politics, and spent
the last half of the 1780s in Paris, so the two men had scarcely
crossed paths.

In public, Jefferson branded Adams's articles "political heresies." Privately, he wrote that Hamilton intended to "undermine
and demolish the Republic," and that "the liberty of the whole
earth" depended on the success of the French Revolution.

James Madison, once Hamilton's *Federalist* coauthor, now followed Jefferson. Washington, who was used to working with all
these men—Jefferson and Hamilton were in his cabinet, Adams

was his vice president, and Madison had ghosted his first inaugural address—tried to keep them in harness.

Washington was reelected president in March 1793, once again winning every electoral vote, but the quarrels of his first term carried on into his second. In April, he tried to calm them by issuing a proclamation declaring America's neutrality in the struggle between France and its counterrevolutionary enemies.

The president was challenged from an unlikely source. Edmond Charles Genet, France's newly appointed minister to the United States, arrived that same month in Charleston. He meant to present his credentials in Philadelphia, the country's capital since 1790, but his ship had been blown off course. His trip north became a triumphal tour. Genet was young, ardent, and a passionate believer in worldwide revolution. Americans eager to show their fondness for France cheered him on, and Genet took their cheers to heart. "I live here in the midst of perpetual fetes," he wrote home happily.

Genet sought a specific benefit from the United States: permission to arm French privateers in American ports to prey on the shipping of France's enemies. Secretary of State Jefferson, for all his Francophilia, explained to Genet the policy of the Washington administration: France could not arm privateers here since that would amount to an American act of war on France's side. Genet then threatened to appeal over Washington's head directly to the American people.

Hamilton leaked word of the Frenchman's threat to the press at the end of July. So began Genet's undoing. Americans might have loved France and been charmed by Genet, but they loved Washington more. Pro-administration rallies were organized in American cities; the rally in Richmond, in mid-August, was the work of John Marshall.

Marshall enlisted Virginia jurist George Wythe to preside, but he wrote the resolutions that the meeting approved. These praised "our illustrious fellow citizen, George Washington," declared that "the constitution of our country" outlined the proper means of communication between diplomats and the government (e.g., not by fetes and threats), and condemned "the intervention of foreign ministers" in American politics as "a high indignity."

Genet's misbehavior struck at Marshall's deepest beliefs. The man who had learned patriotism in wartime could not abide being lectured by a foreigner. The man who had labored to ratify the Constitution did not want it circumvented by mass meetings and bluster. The man who venerated George Washington would not see him snubbed.

Genet crystallized Marshall's stand in domestic politics. Fights over finance had inclined him to support Alexander Hamilton, but France's arrogance made him deplore its supporters, including his cousin.

Two YEARS LATER came another foreign policy storm brewed by the wars of the French Revolution, this one involving Britain. Britain had been stopping American ships on the high seas and seizing cargos bound for France that it considered contraband (chiefly grain). There were also unresolved issues hanging over from the Treaty of Paris: American debtors had still not paid off their British creditors, and Britain still occupied forts on the American frontier. Washington sent John Jay to London to smooth these problems out. Jay had been serving as chief justice of the Supreme Court since 1789, but he had once been a diplomat. He willingly put his judicial duties on hold to take up his former ones.

In the spring of 1795, the treaty Jay negotiated arrived in Philadelphia. The pro-French party read it with outrage. Jay had gotten the British out of their frontier forts, but most other points of dispute were left to arbitration commissions. The treaty seemed mild-mannered, even subservient. When Genet had asked for help for America's old ally, the administration had rebuffed him; now the administration had sent Jay to our old enemy, cap in hand, to secure only a few tiny deals.

There were anti-treaty rallies in every American city; Jay said he could have walked the length of the country at night, guided by the light of his own image burning in effigies.

The Senate ratified Jay's Treaty, and Washington signed it. But its opponents tried a last maneuver: declaring it unconstitutional. The Constitution said that all treaties were "the Supreme Law of the Land" (Article VI). But it also gave Congress (Article I, Section 8) the power "to regulate Commerce with foreign Nations." Jay's Treaty included several articles regulating Anglo-American trade. Perhaps it could not do so without the approval of the House as well as the Senate.

Once again, Marshall rallied Richmond to support the Washington administration. In April, he organized an all-day meeting that drew four hundred people. Enemies of the treaty complained that the meeting was packed with ringers: federal officeholders, British merchants and their clerks, apprentices, schoolboys. Marshall described the discussion as "very ardent and zealous," capped by a resolution "that the welfare and honor of the nation required us to give full effect to the treaty" as ratified.

MARSHALL HAD RETURNED to the House of Delegates, seemingly by accident. The previous spring, he had gone to vote, when someone at the polling place said he should be a candidate himself. He refused and left to go to court, where he had business. But in his absence, his name was listed as a candidate, and that night he was told that he had won.

The source of the story is Marshall himself, but it is hard to believe. How could even a man as intermittently indolent as he was be so inattentive at a time of such political passion?

When a resolution challenging Jay's Treaty's constitutionality came before the House of Delegates in the spring of 1796, Marshall was all attention. He prepared a speech focusing on the Constitution's words and on the law of nations concerning commercial treaties. When he finished, he recalled, a bit smugly, "there was scarcely an intelligent man in the house who did not yield his opinion." The anti-treaty forces prevailed in the Virginia legislature (not enough intelligent men, evidently), though in the U.S. House of Representatives, an effort to scuttle the treaty was narrowly defeated.

Marshall, age forty, had become the most prominent defender of the Washington administration in Virginia. This brought on him the baleful gaze of Thomas Jefferson. Jefferson had left Washington's cabinet at the end of 1793. Even as a private citizen, he could not bring himself to attack Washington directly, perhaps not even in his own mind. Instead, he spun a myth, which he propagated in his correspondence: an aging Washington was being manipulated by Hamilton.

Jefferson attacked Washington's supporters with gusto. Marshall seemed to draw from him a note of special scorn. As early as 1792, Jefferson wrote Madison that "Hamilton has plied him [Marshall] well with flattery." Marshall was dealing with the archenemy, and he must be vain and gullible—why else would he succumb to flattery?

Three years later, Jefferson complained (to Madison again) that Marshall's "lax lounging manners have made him popular with the bulk of the people of Richmond." Jefferson's swipe at Marshall's manners is telling; after a taste of the high life in Paris, Jefferson had returned gratefully, and proudly, to the simple life of a Virginia gentleman. He left Washington's cabinet, he wrote, "to plant my corn, peas etc. in hills or drills as I please." But no one did the simple life more simply than John Marshall. All the more reason for Jefferson to dislike him.

Marshall's politicking earned him the approval of the administration and its supporters. Hamilton corresponded with him; Marshall's description of the ardent and zealous pro-treaty meeting in Richmond is from a letter to the New Yorker. Washington offered once again to make Marshall U.S. attorney for Virginia; once again, he declined.

M ARSHALL APPEARED BEFORE the national political class in person early in 1796, when he argued *Ware v. Hylton* before the Supreme Court in Philadelphia. The Court sat in a new brick building originally designed to be City Hall, next to Independence Hall on Chestnut Street. It would be Marshall's only appearance before the Court as a lawyer. This time, he lost his case. The most emphatic opinion, by Justice Samuel Chase, adhered firmly to Article VI: treaties were "the supreme Law of the Land . . . any Thing in the . . . Laws of any State to the Contrary notwithstanding." Marshall had argued that Virginia's 1777 law shifting obligations to the state loan office had relieved Hylton of his debt. But the Treaty of Paris, according to Chase, annihilated Virginia's law.

Marshall did well for himself outside the courtroom, however, meeting northern supporters of the administration. "I was delighted with these gentlemen," he wrote, and they with him.

I N SEPTEMBER 1796, Washington announced that he would retire from public life at the end of his second term, the following March. His farewell address, printed in a Philadelphia newspaper and reprinted everywhere, warned Americans against "the baneful effects of the spirit of party." In vain. The country had had, for at least six years, two full-fledged parties: the supporters of the administration, calling themselves Federalists; and its critics, calling themselves Republicans. For the first time, this division would be reflected in a presidential election.

The Federalist candidate to succeed Washington was Vice President Adams; his Republican opponent was Jefferson. Sixteen states would cast electoral votes—the original thirteen, plus Vermont, Tennessee, and Kentucky (now separated from Virginia). France tried to influence the contest. It interpreted Jay's Treaty as a rapprochement with its enemy Britain and therefore a hostile act. Pierre Adet, France's minister to the United States (Genet was long gone), declared publicly that diplomatic relations between the two countries would be broken unless a friendlier president— meaning Jefferson—were elected.

States did not choose their presidential electors on the same day, or in the same way: in some states, the legislatures made the choice; in others, it was done by the people, voting in electoral districts. Marshall carefully followed the results as they trickled in. In December, he wrote one Federalist a gloomy letter concluding that Adams could not win. He was wrong. Adams swept New England, New York, New Jersey, Delaware, and seven of Maryland's eleven electoral votes. Jefferson swept South Carolina, Georgia, Kentucky, and Tennessee and all but swept Pennsylvania, Virginia, and North Carolina, losing only one electoral vote in each. But Adams's single votes in those three states made the difference: his total was seventy-one, Jefferson's sixty-eight.

The Constitution (Article II, Section 1) did not recognize presidential tickets—how could it have, when no one had anticipated a two-party system? Each elector cast two votes; the candidate with the most would become president, the candidate with the second-most vice president. In 1796, South Carolina diplomat Thomas Pinckney and New York senator Aaron Burr were the Federalist and Republican vice presidential candidates, respectively, but electors wasting votes on favorite sons left them trailing far behind. So the new president would be Adams, and the new vice president his rival, Jefferson.

Political strife would continue, and Marshall would continue to take part in it.

Chapter 4

DIPLOMAT, CONGRESSMAN, SECRETARY OF STATE

O NE AFTERSHOCK OF THE 1796 ELECTION WAS FELT IN May 1797, two months into the new administration. A letter Thomas Jefferson had written a year earlier to a Florentine friend, Philip Mazzei, appeared in the press. In it, Jefferson assailed the "Anglo-Monarchico-Aristocratic party" in America, then went on to say "I should give you a fever" if he were to name "men who were Solomons in council and Sampsons [*sic*] in combat, but whose hair has been cut off by the whore England." Abusing Federalists as pro-British monarchists was standard Republican rhetoric, but invoking Solomon and Samson went a step further: Solomon had been the king, Samson a judge of Israel. Jefferson had taken the final political step—he had symbolically but unmistakably attacked George Washington. The Mazzei letter put Federalists in a fever; John Marshall would never forget it.

France took Adams's election as one more hostile act on top of Jay's Treaty and responded by plundering American shipping. Hundreds of American ships bound for Britain were captured by French privateers and millions of dollars of property seized or destroyed.

Adams proposed sending James Madison, Jefferson's right hand and best friend, to France to negotiate a treaty that would resolve tensions. Perhaps a Francophile American could get a good agreement. But Madison, loyal Republican, refused Adams's offer. The Federalists were in power; let them solve America's problems. In the spring of 1797, Adams decided instead to send a commission of three.

Charles Cotesworth Pinckney was a wealthy South Carolina planter, a veteran of the Revolutionary War, and a signer of the Constitution. Having polished his horsemanship at an academy in Caen before the war, he was the only one of Adams's commissioners who spoke French. Elbridge Gerry, a Marblehead merchant, was a veteran of Massachusetts politics and a signer of the Declaration of Independence. More important than any of his formal qualifications, he was an old friend of Adams.

The third commissioner was John Marshall, making his first and only trip abroad. His politicking and his legal skills had impressed Federalist leaders; giving an important assignment to a Virginian would boost the party locally. Marshall had an interview with the president in July. He found Adams "candid" and "good-tempered," while Adams thought Marshall "very sensible" and "learned"—sentiments that would never waver. Marshall sailed for Europe that month.

He had another motive for going to Europe besides helping his country. The previous December, as a member of the House of Delegates, he had brokered a political solution to one of the ongoing controversies over the Fairfax Grant. Fairfax's heirs would surrender to the state their claim to any land that had not already been sold. In return, Virginia would give up its claim to land that had been reserved for the family's personal estate. Since this was the very land John and James Marshall and their brother-in-law proposed to buy, the legislative deal removed a potential impediment to their purchase.

Marshall and his relatives still needed to come up with the purchase money, however. Marshall's ship was bound for Amsterdam, where he would stay one month before going on to Paris. Amsterdam was one of the world's centers of banking; perhaps he would find potential lenders there. Or if the commissioners signed a treaty quickly, he might be able to find some in London on his way home. Whatever salary he earned as a diplomat would also come in handy.

Such mingling of public and private time was common in the eighteenth century (and in others, perhaps, as well). Marshall and his colleagues soon found themselves in much deeper waters ethically.

ALL THREE AMERICANS were in Paris by the first week in October. They had a fifteen-minute interview with the foreign minister, Charles-Maurice de Talleyrand-Périgord, a sometime Catholic bishop turned politician. Talleyrand's manners, according to Marshall, were "polite and easy," though nothing important was discussed.

Then, silence. Talleyrand became inaccessible. In his place, several unofficial go-betweens appeared: Jean-Conrad Hottinguer, a Swiss-born banker; Pierre Bellamy, a Hamburg merchant said to be a "confidential friend" of Talleyrand; and Lucien Hauteval, a planter from Santo Domingo. They presented themselves as fixers; as with many fixers, their proposed remedies involved a lot of cash. They told the Americans that if they wanted a treaty, France would have to receive a loan up front and that French officials expected "something for the pocket" besides.

France's current government was an elaborate ramshackle known as the Directory (Talleyrand was one of the five ruling directors). The Directory had ended the worst domestic bloodletting of the Revolution and unleashed conquering generals on

France's unfortunate neighbors. But it was beset by both radicals and royalists at home and torn by the squabbles and machinations of the directors themselves. A sense of their own fragility made the directors and everyone connected with them greedy. Talleyrand had spent a bad patch of the Revolution in exile in New York, where he befriended Alexander Hamilton. The Frenchman was astonished when he saw the former treasury secretary working in his law office at night. Why hadn't he lined his pockets when he had managed his country's finances? Talleyrand and his colleagues would not now make that mistake.

The Americans were astonished by the French demands. Public service could ease the path of opportunity, but naked bartering was beyond the pale. Pinckney, when asked point-blank for money, exclaimed, "No, no, not a sixpence!" When the Americans refused to pay up, the French resorted to bullying. Hottinguer threatened them with the "power and violence" of France, while Bellamy warned that "the French party in America"—the Republicans—would blame them if they came home empty-handed.

That fall, the commissioners sent two long letters to Timothy Pickering, Adams's secretary of state, describing what was happening. All three Americans endorsed the letters, but Marshall was the author. He packed the letters with detail, highlighted by skillful shifts of his tone of voice. Sometimes he employed baffled innocence; after recounting one of Bellamy's demands for money, "we told him," wrote Marshall, "that we supposed it to be impossible that either he or [Talleyrand] could imagine that such a proposition could require an answer." Sometimes Marshall was slyly observant; Hottinguer, on another occasion, "asked if our government did not know that nothing was to be obtained here without money? We replied, that our government had not even suspected such a state of things. He appeared surprised." At all times, Marshall presented a picture of American earnestness and good faith, versus French contempt, stubbornness, and chicanery.

In January 1798, the commissioners, again speaking through Marshall, sent Talleyrand a dignified reproof for the manner in which they and the United States were being treated; if they could not be heard officially, they would have no choice but to demand their passports and go home. Marshall sailed at the end of April.

His letters had only arrived in Philadelphia the month before (transatlantic communication in the age of sail was a leisurely affair). The documents, which were coded, then had to be deciphered. When they finally became public—Hottinguer, Bellamy, and Hauteval being identified by the letters X, Y, and Z—they caused a political explosion.

France's treatment of the commissioners was worse than the misbehavior of Genet five years earlier. He had been one man, on his own abroad, making excessive demands. Now the French state, in the persons of its foreign minister and his cronies, was extorting and threatening before it would even hear Americans out. Federalists were jubilant—all their bad opinions of France seemed confirmed.

Jefferson blamed the bad news on the bearer of it, calling the XYZ Affair a "dish cooked up by Marshall." So it was; it can hardly be supposed that he was unaware of the political effect his letters would have. But all his ingredients had been supplied by the French.

When Marshall arrived in America in June, he was a hero. When he went to Philadelphia to report to Adams and Pickering, he was greeted with bells ringing, cannons firing, and three troops of cavalry. At a banquet packed with congressmen and other worthies, he was toasted. Pinckney's "No, no, not a sixpence," which Marshall had immortalized, was transformed into the slogan "Millions for defense, not one cent for tribute." Marshall "has raised the American people in their own esteem," wrote President Adams.

Vice President Jefferson felt constrained to make a courtesy call at the tavern where Marshall was staying, but he missed him.

Jefferson left his card with a note: "Thomas Jefferson presents his compliments to General Marshall. [Marshall had been named a general of the state militia in 1793.] He had the honor of calling at his lodgings twice this morning, but was so lucky as to find that he was out on both occasions." In front of the word *lucky,* Jefferson added the prefix *un.* Marshall later said of this slip of the pen that "Mr. Jefferson came very near writing me the truth."

Marshall had not been able to stop in London to prospect for lenders, but he was paid almost $20,000 for his long mission—a hefty sum. Minus expenses and his secretary's salary, he netted over $13,000—more than half the president's annual salary, almost three times the vice president's. The money went to pay the first installment of what he and his relatives owed on their Fairfax purchase.

MARSHALL HAD FAILED in one duty, however. His wife's nerves had been tried in his long absence. Since 1786, when Polly had lost one newborn and miscarried, she had borne four more children. Two of them—an infant son and an almost-three-year-old girl—had died in 1792, only two months apart; Marshall wrote Polly a poem of condolence, asking her to think of her love for the survivors and of the wisdom of Providence. When Marshall sailed for France, she had been pregnant once more—a fraught condition. She gave birth to a boy in January 1798 and named him for his missing father.

From Paris, Marshall wrote her, sometimes charmingly: "Scarcely a night passes in which during the hour of sleep I have not some interesting conversation with you or concerning you." One of his letters, however, gave distress. After expatiating on the amusements of Paris—"this gay metropolis"—he added that he had taken lodgings "in the house of a very accomplished, a very sensible, and I believe a very amiable lady." The lady, forty years old, was the Marquise de Villette, a noblewoman who had been discovered and married off in her youth by the aged Voltaire. Now a widow, she kept a bust of the philosopher in her house, before which she burned incense.

Was Marshall attracted to her? She to him? Elbridge Gerry was charmed with the marquise, but he was a little fifty-three-year-old man with an unusually large head. Marshall was forty-two, sloppy, but strong and bright-eyed. To apply Marshall's argument from *Commonwealth v. Randolph*, if he had felt an unseemly interest in the marquise, would he have written so warmly to his wife? Polly was not consoled by such arguments. Her husband's gushing letter, which arrived after the birth of John Jr., threw her into a depression. She moved from Richmond to be with her sister in Winchester.

After Marshall came home, he tried to make it up to her. Take cold baths and exercise, he advised. "Give you back to yourself and me." His simplicity in this matter of the heart was simpleminded.

M ARSHALL HAD MADE a national name for himself. Time now for him to get back to his law practice and the dependable income it afforded. But George Washington changed the course of his life.

The first president, who had warned against the spirit of party in his farewell address, had at last become a partisan himself. France's latest provocation and the unwillingness of hard-core Republicans, even now, to recognize it as such were insupportable to him. Federalism in Virginia, the country's largest state, needed bucking up. In September, Washington summoned Marshall and Bushrod Washington to Mount Vernon to order them to run for Congress.

Bushrod Washington was the son of George's elder half brother Augustine; his unusual first name was his mother's maiden name.

He had known Marshall since 1780 when they had both taken George Wythe's law lecture at William and Mary. Later, Bushrod had served with Marshall in the Virginia Ratifying Convention (pro-ratification, of course). Though he was now only thirty-six years old, he had earned a reputation as an excellent lawyer, reading so hard that he lost his sight in one eye.

As with many incidents in Marshall's life, the trip to Mount Vernon acquired the trappings of fable. According to one story, when he and Bushrod arrived and opened their bags, they found only ragged clothes and a bottle of whiskey, their luggage having accidentally been switched for that of some wagoners. According to another story, Marshall felt so beleaguered by Washington's urgings that he resolved to escape by leaving Mount Vernon at the crack of dawn. But his old commander in chief rose before he did and accosted him on the mansion's piazza with a last appeal.

What Marshall himself remembered was that he explained to his host that he could not run for Congress because of the necessity of "attending to my pecuniary affairs." Marshall went on to say, "I can never forget the manner in which he treated this objection." Washington had left Mount Vernon to fight the Revolution and to serve as president; he had now pledged to leave it once again to lead the army in case of a French invasion. "I saw him," Marshall remembered, "consenting, under a sense of duty, to surrender the sweets of retirement. . . . My resolution yielded to this representation."

SINCE NEW CONGRESSES did not meet until December of odd-numbered off-years, midterm elections were held very late by modern standards. Marshall's occurred in April 1799. The district he contested was centered on Richmond. The incumbent, John Clopton, was a Republican, like most of the voters; Marshall would have to rely on his personal popularity. Republican journalists sniffed that he danced around bonfires and spent lavishly on barbecues; very likely he did.

Election Day in Virginia was a public festival, with voice voting; the candidates themselves were present at the county courthouse. "It was usual, when a vote was cast," wrote a Virginian recalling the contest, "for the candidate in question to return thanks. Sometimes, 'I thank you, sir.' Sometimes, 'May you live a thousand years.' . . . Liquor in abundance was on the court green for the friends of either party. A barrel of whiskey for all, with the head knocked in, and the majority took it straight. . . . Sick men were taken in their beds to the polls; the halt, the lame and the blind were hunted up, and every mode of conveyance was mustered into service." Marshall eked out a win.

He entered Congress at a stormy time. The great Federalist surge that followed the XYZ Affair was almost immediately diluted by crosscurrents. Anticipating hostilities with France, Federalists in Congress raised military spending—and taxes to pay for it. They struck at enemies at home with laws allowing the president to deport aliens he deemed dangerous and the federal courts to prosecute libels on the federal government. The Alien Act was never invoked, but prosecutions under the Sedition Act landed heavily on almost a dozen Republican journalists. Vice President Jefferson and Madison responded with anonymous resolutions, passed by the legislatures of Kentucky and Virginia, assailing the constitutionality of both laws.

President Adams, meanwhile, heard from Elbridge Gerry, who had remained in Paris after Marshall and Pinckney left, hoping against hope to come to some arrangement with Talleyrand. Gerry's willingness to endure almost any slight in pursuit of peace had vexed his fellow commissioners, but Gerry understood Adams's deepest desires better than they did. When Talleyrand indicated that he was finally ready to negotiate in earnest—France had suffered military reverses and felt the need for fewer enemies—

Adams chose three new commissioners to go to Paris and try again, a move that split his party between peacemakers and hard-liners. (One of the new commissioners was Oliver Ellsworth, chief justice of the Supreme Court, willing, like John Jay before him, to take a diplomatic holiday.)

In December 1799, Federalism, and the United States, suffered a heavy blow. George Washington died of an inflammation of the throat at age sixty-seven. The congressman who delivered the news to the House was John Marshall. He borrowed the most famous line of his eulogy from another Revolutionary War veteran, Henry Lee (great writing is often great borrowing): Washington, Lee and Marshall said, was "first in war, first in peace, and first in the hearts of his countrymen." He had been, and would always remain, first in the heart of John Marshall.

Marshall navigated these events with a combination of attention to the mood of his home state and loyalty to the president. When running for Congress, he declared that he would not have voted for the Alien or Sedition Acts and favored letting them lapse—the popular position in Virginia. He supported Adams when the president wanted to stand firm against French bullying, and he supported the president when he wanted to reach out once more to make peace.

Marshall's longest speech in the House concerned a knotty legal and international matter. In 1797, the crew of a British frigate, HMS *Hermione,* enraged by a cruel captain, had mutinied, slaughtered most of the officers, and taken the ship into a Spanish port in Venezuela. Two years later, one of the crew, Thomas Nash, was found in Charleston, serving on an American schooner. Britain demanded that he be extradited (Jay's Treaty allowed both countries to reclaim persons suspected of committing murder or forgery in their jurisdictions). Nash protested that he was an American, Jonathan Robbins of Danbury, Connecticut. The local judge bucked the case to the State Department. President Adams approved Nash/Robbins's extradition, whereupon he was given to the British, who hanged him.

Congressional Republicans made the case an inverse of the Genet and XYZ Affairs: Federalists truckling, via Jay's craven treaty, to Britain, at the cost of an American sailor's life. The testimony of Danbury officials that no Jonathan Robbins had ever lived there, and the condemned man's gallows confession that he was indeed Nash, complicated this narrative. So the Republicans made instead a constitutional case: the president had assumed powers rightly belonging to the judiciary. Whoever Nash or Robbins was, he had deserved an American trial, as per Article III, Section 2: "The judicial Power shall extend to all Cases, in Law and Equity, arising under this Constitution, the Laws of the United States, and Treaties."

After weeks of acrid debate in the House, Marshall rose to speak. His speech was long, detailed, and learned, but it made three broad points. Nations have jurisdiction over their own warships; therefore, a murder on a British frigate was to be tried, under Jay's Treaty, by Britain. American courts could not try Nash because the judicial power did not cover everything. Article III, Section 2 gave federal courts power over "cases"—controversies in courts of law. "If the judicial power extended to every *question* [Marshall's emphasis] . . . it would involve almost every subject proper for legislative discussion [and] almost every subject on which the executive could act. The division of power . . . would exist no longer, and the other departments would be swallowed up by the judiciary." The president, finally, was the right man to make the decision on Nash's fate because the president "is the sole organ of the nation in its external relations and its sole representative" in foreign affairs. Congress may guide him—as in fact it had when the Senate ratified Jay's Treaty.

After Marshall was finished, anxious Republicans crowded around Albert Gallatin, the smart Genevan immigrant who was one of their champions in the House, asking him to rebut. "Answer it yourselves," Gallatin told them. "I think it is unanswerable." A Republican motion to censure Adams failed.

Washington's death seemed to have the effect of unleashing the inner demons of Federalism. In May 1800, Adams summarily fired James McHenry and Timothy Pickering, his secretaries of war and state. He accused them of resisting his rapprochement with France and of being beholden to Alexander Hamilton, whom Washington had insisted be second in command of the enlarged army. (Adams had disliked Hamilton for years.) Hamilton responded with a long pamphlet assailing Adams's "ill humors and jealousies."

Marshall stayed loyal to Adams. At the same time, he retained the good opinion of all these quarreling men. A diagram of the affections of Federalist leaders as the eighteenth century closed would describe something like this: The late George Washington had thought well, if seldom, of Adams; admired Hamilton's ability; and tolerated Timothy Pickering (Washington had reluctantly made Pickering secretary of state in his second term, which was why Adams kept him in the job). Adams admired Washington, with a trace of envy; loathed Hamilton; and detested Pickering. Hamilton esteemed and relied on Washington, disdained Adams, and was friendly enough with Pickering. Pickering had contempt for Washington and Adams and adored Hamilton. Yet Marshall liked all these men and was liked by all of them—a tribute to his good nature and lack of rough edges.

Adams asked Marshall to fill McHenry's shoes, which he refused. But when Adams asked him to succeed Pickering, Marshall agreed (two refusals would have been rude, and secretary of state was the more important position).

Serving as Adams's secretary of state was no easy job. In June 1800, the federal government moved to its new capital city on the Potomac—a site picked by Hamilton, Jefferson, and James Madison years earlier, when they were still speaking to each other. Adams and Marshall boarded in a hotel together for a week in June, then Adams went home to Massachusetts to nurse his sick wife. Marshall ran the executive branch in his absence and helped draft Adams's last message to Congress in November when the president returned to work.

One vexed issue that fell to Marshall was the seemingly unending question of American debts to British creditors. Jay's Treaty had established a five-man commission to settle all disputes, but the American members had pulled out, convinced that the British were giving too many judgments in Britain's favor. Marshall instructed the American minister in London to propose a lump-sum payment, covering all debts—the model for the ultimate solution, which would finally be reached in 1802.

Always in the background, when it was not in the foreground, was the presidential election of 1800. Charles Cotesworth Pinckney's indignant refusal to be extorted had made him Adams's running mate. Jefferson and Aaron Burr were once again the Republican candidates, Burr having been assured that this time he would not be humiliated by electoral votes wasted on favorite sons.

In states that left the choice of electors to their own legislatures, local elections decided the result. The Federalists experienced an early setback when New Yorkers voted in a Republican state legislature. By year's end, Adams had carried New England, New Jersey, and Delaware as he had in 1796. Pennsylvania, Maryland, and North Carolina split their electoral votes, with the Republicans sweeping South Carolina, Georgia, Tennessee, Kentucky, and Virginia (no lone vote there for Adams this time). The final tally was seventy-three electoral votes each for Jefferson and Burr, sixty-five for Adams, and sixty-four for Pinckney (one Federalist having wasted a vote on John Jay). In addition, the Republicans were assured of majorities in both houses of the new Congress.

Jefferson and Burr were a victorious ticket. But since the Constitution took no notice of tickets, they had tied. The beaten Federalists took heart. According to Article II, Section 1, the tie between the two Republicans would have to be broken in the lame-duck House, with each state's delegation voting as a unit. The Republicans controlled eight states, the Federalists six; two were evenly divided. The partisan breakdown was thus 8–6, with two states abstaining, thanks to their internal deadlocks. Since a majority of state delegations was necessary to pick a winner, if Federalist congressmen held firm for Burr, they could prevent the election of Thomas Jefferson.

And then? Some Federalists toyed with the idea of passing a last-minute electoral law that would provide for an acting president (presumably some Federalist) to serve in case no president should be chosen before the new term was to begin. Such a blatant trick would drive Republicans to revolt and so was not a serious option.

But suppose that Burr or his friends could pry loose enough Republican congressmen to make him, with Federalist support, the choice of the House? Burr, forty-four, had served with distinction in the Revolution, and his family background was respectable (his maternal grandfather was the great Puritan preacher Jonathan Edwards). Perhaps he was the better man, since Jefferson was so obviously worse.

Alexander Hamilton did not think Jefferson was worse. He wrote a series of vehement letters to leading Federalists, arguing from long acquaintance with Burr in New York politics that he was unprincipled and corrupt.

Marshall, who received one of Hamilton's appeals, replied on New Year's Day 1801. His objections to Jefferson, he wrote, were "almost insuperable." He decried Jefferson's "foreign [i.e.,

French] prejudices." He shrewdly speculated that by seeming to weaken the presidency, Jefferson would in fact "increase his personal power." Marshall predicted that Jefferson would be a populist demagogue, professing to follow the lead of the incoming Congress while directing it behind the scenes.

Marshall's most damning judgment was his last. "The morals of the author of the letter to Mazzei cannot be pure." Jefferson had attacked the greatest Man on earth, in a private letter to a foreigner, no less. Unpatriotic, unforthright, anti-Washington: he was triply steeped in infamy. It would never be possible for Marshall to respect him.

He deferred to Hamilton's characterization of Burr. "Believing that you know him well . . . my preference would certainly not be for him." He repeated, however, that he could not "bring [himself] to aid Mr. Jefferson." Marshall would stay neutral.

Marshall had enough to do without plunging into electoral scheming. Adams's second team of commissioners to France had successfully negotiated a treaty, which arrived in Washington in December 1800. Like Jay's Treaty, it was not perfect, but it seemed good enough to ratify (the two nations reaffirmed their friendship, though American shippers had to write off their losses). The lame-duck Federalist Senate, however, at first rejected it; Marshall had to massage its passage.

There was other news from France, which did not at first touch him directly. Oliver Ellsworth, the chief justice and temporary diplomat, was only fifty-five years old, yet he was afflicted with kidney stones and gout. His voyage out had exhausted him, and he feared his return would exhaust him still more. He informed President Adams, also in December, that he was retiring from public life.

Time was running out on the Adams administration. It was imperative to tap a new chief justice before a Republican, even a tractable one like Burr, could fill the slot. Marshall recommended that Adams promote Justice William Paterson, who had been on the Court since 1793. Congressional Federalists also liked this idea. Adams instead nominated the first man who had held the job, John Jay, who was then concluding a second term as governor of New York. The Senate confirmed him.

Jay, however, turned the job down. The federal judiciary, he wrote Adams, speaking from painful experience, was "defective," lacking in "energy, weight and dignity."

Years later, Marshall recalled what happened next. "When I waited on the president with Mr. Jay's letter, declining the appointment, he said thoughtfully, 'Who shall I nominate now?' I replied that I could not tell. . . . After a few moments hesitation, he said, 'I believe I must nominate you.'" Marshall's reaction was to bow in silence.

Senators who still liked Paterson balked for a week, but Marshall was confirmed on January 27, 1801; he was sworn in eight days later, in the presence of three of his fellow justices (the remaining two were out of town). Over the next five days, the Court attended to some business, heard some arguments, and adjourned on February 10. So began Marshall's tenure as chief justice.

I N THE HOUSE, Federalists continued to plot and scheme, but on February 17, after thirty-six ballots, they finally allowed Thomas Jefferson to be elected president.

Marshall administered the oath of office to his cousin on March 4.

Section II

BELEAGUERED
CHIEF JUSTICE

Chapter 5

THE CASE OF THE
MISSING COMMISSION

I N 1801, WASHINGTON WAS LESS A CITY THAN AN IDEA.
Pennsylvania Avenue was a muddy track. Hunters shot snipe
on Capitol Hill; cows grazed the Mall, which was bisected by
a marshy stream, Goose Creek, grandly (humorously?) called the
Tiber. Only three thousand people lived there, one hundred of
them government employees, six hundred of them slaves. Georgetown, across Rock Creek to the west, was an actual place. So was
Alexandria, down the Potomac on the Virginia side. Washington
was no place.

The Supreme Court had the most meager accommodations
of any branch of government. The shell of the president's mansion had been completed, and on Capitol Hill, the Senate and the
House had chambers to meet in, though the entire building was
far from finished. No structure had been reserved for the nation's
top court, however. It met in a committee room of the Capitol,
underneath the House, thirty feet by thirty-five feet, with two
windows and a fireplace. The architect of the Capitol himself
called the space "meanly furnished, very inconvenient." This was
where John Marshall was sworn in on February 4.

The federal court system had been organized by the Judiciary Act of 1789. One senator who disliked the bill complained that it had been "fabricated by a knot of lawyers." The Supreme Court was to be composed of five associate justices and one chief justice. They met twice a year, in February and August, for sessions that lasted initially about ten days. Under the Supreme Court, in decreasing order of importance, were three circuit courts and thirteen district courts (expanded to fifteen when North Carolina and Rhode Island belatedly ratified the Constitution).

The Supreme Court made several important decisions in its first decade. *Ware v. Hylton* (1796), the case that John Marshall had lost as an advocate, upheld the supremacy of treaties. *Hylton v. United States* (1796) brought Richmond merchant Daniel Hylton before the Supreme Court a second time, in this case for challenging a luxury tax on carriages that had been devised by Alexander Hamilton when he was treasury secretary. Hylton maintained that the law was unconstitutional, since Article I, Section 9 approved direct taxes—such as income taxes—only when they were apportioned according to the population of the states; yet no effort had been made to calculate a ratio of Virginians to their carriages. Hamilton, who had returned to private life, defended his law himself, arguing that the carriage tax was an excise—a tax on a product, permitted by Article I, Section 8. The Supreme Court upheld the law—and, incidentally, implied that it could uphold, or strike down, laws.

Chisholm v. Georgia (1793) earned the Supreme Court a rebuke. During the Revolution, Georgia had bought supplies on credit from a South Carolina merchant, Robert Farquahar. The state had refused to pay him, however, on the grounds that he was a loyalist. After Farquahar died, his executor, Alexander Chisholm, also from South Carolina, sued, as Article III, Section 2 allowed him to ("The judicial Power shall extend to all cases.... between a State and Citizens of another State."). The Court ruled for him and provoked the wrath of states from Georgia to New Hampshire. In only two years, the Eleventh Amendment—the first after the Bill of Rights—made states immune from suits brought by the citizens of other states.

The Court also declared what it would not do. On various occasions, other branches of government turned to it for help, the Senate asking it for advice on a bill concerning judicial procedure, Congress wanting it to rule on the pension claims of invalid veterans, and President Washington posing it several questions on international law during the Genet affair. The Court refused each of these requests. It was not to become a jack-of-all-trades. Its business, as Marshall had argued in his speech on Thomas Nash, was with cases.

And yet an air of triviality clung to the Court. Two of its first chief justices had been considerable men—John Jay (who served from 1789 to 1795), spymaster, diplomat, coauthor with Hamilton and James Madison of the *Federalist*; and Oliver Ellsworth (who served from 1796 to 1800), a first-class legal mind who had been one of the knot of lawyers who set the judiciary system up. Yet both men took months-long leaves of absence to negotiate treaties.

Between their tenures lay the embarrassing term of John Rutledge. Rutledge, like Charles Cotesworth Pinckney, belonged to one of the grand families of South Carolina. He had served as an associate justice from 1790 to 1791, then in the summer of 1795 received from President Washington a recess appointment to return to the Court as its chief. He took the oath of office and sat for the Court's August term. But when the Senate met in December, it refused to confirm him. Rutledge had spoken against Jay's Treaty, which roused the ire of Federalists; they also questioned his sanity: he was "a driveller and a fool," wrote one. That was the end of his chief justiceship.

Reporting of the Court's decisions was slipshod. Alexander Dallas, a Philadelphia lawyer, recorded and published them as a private venture, but his reports came out years late and covered only half the cases the Court took on. When Alexander Hamilton was asked by a potential client about a particular decision, Hamilton had to advise him to go to Philadelphia and Washington and ask the lawyers there what had happened.

The task of riding circuit, which the Judiciary Act of 1789 required justices to perform, symbolized the indignity of their station. The circuits were enormous, covering many hundreds of miles. Mishaps ensued. One justice wrote his wife of an accident on the southern circuit: "I was going on at my ease, when part of the rein getting under [the horse's] tail, he ran away, the [carriage] struck against a tree, and overset, throwing me out, and one of the wheels went over my leg. . . . Fortunately, the hurt was only a swelling in my ankle that subsided next day." Another justice fell into the Susquehanna River one February when he tried to cross it over the ice. In private, Chief Justice Jay called his office "intolerable."

At the end of the Adams administration, the Court's load was lightened. In Adams's November 1800 address to Congress, which Marshall helped write, the president asked it to expand the federal judiciary, to make "the administration of justice . . . convenient to the people." A new Judiciary Act, which became law in February 1801, created sixteen new circuit court judges in six circuits, dispersing the judicial system more widely about the country and sparing the justices of the Supreme Court the chore of riding circuit themselves.

When Marshall joined the Court, the most senior of his colleagues was sixty-nine-year-old William Cushing of Massachusetts. His career as a judge went back to colonial times; he came to his first session of the Court, in 1790, wearing a full English wig. Jefferson compared the look to "rats peeping through bunches of oakum [rope fiber]." Cushing quickly got measured for a smaller peruke.

Samuel Chase, who would turn sixty in April, had been a Maryland lawyer and politician. Physically imposing—he was tall, large-headed, and florid (his nickname was "Bacon Face")—he had a temperament to match: sharp, opinionated, quick to take offense.

William Paterson, fifty-five, born in northern Ireland, was raised in New Jersey and had served the state in a variety of offices. Paterson, New Jersey, the town at the falls of the Passaic River that Hamilton hoped would become a manufacturing dynamo, was named in his honor.

Alfred Moore of North Carolina, at forty-five and the same age as Marshall, was only four foot five, and his head, wrote one contemporary, "was large for his body, after the manner of dwarfs." Yet he, like Marshall, had been an officer in the Revolution, present at the first siege of Charleston and the battle of Guilford Court House.

The youngest justice was thirty-nine-year-old Bushrod Washington. Though he and Marshall had acceded to his uncle George's demand that they run for Congress from Virginia, a vacancy on the Supreme Court appeared shortly after their visit to Mount Vernon, and President Adams had tapped young Washington to fill it.

These were all capable jurists. When Paterson was a U.S. senator, he had helped Ellsworth plan the Judiciary Act of 1789; much of the draft is in Paterson's handwriting. When Chase bore down on a legal problem, he was both incisive and deep. Bushrod Washington, wrote one of his colleagues, "read to learn, and not to quote."

They were also all, like Marshall, of one mind politically—staunch Federalists, embracing Washington's and Adams's fiscal and foreign policies. Chase indeed had taken time off from the Court to campaign for Adams's reelection (this, and numerous other indiscretions, would come back to haunt him).

Every Federalist understood the political cast of the judiciary. The Judiciary Act of 1801 entrenched it. The Federalist-dominated Congress that passed it was not just reforming an overtaxed system; it was multiplying offices for party members. Some of the appointments were nepotistic as well as partisan; a separate law, in addition to the Judiciary Act, created a circuit court for the District of Columbia, thus providing judgeships for William Cranch, a nephew of Adams, and John Marshall's brother James. Marshall had advised Adams on all these appointments.

The mellowest explanation of this lame-duck potlatch was given by Gouverneur Morris, then serving as a senator from New York, in a letter to a Republican friend. "That the leaders of the federal party may use this opportunity to provide for friends and adherents is, I think, probable, and if they were my enemies I should not condemn them for it. . . . They are about to experience a heavy gale of adverse wind. Can they be blamed for casting many anchors to hold their ship through the storm?"

A gale indeed. Thomas Jefferson was now president. The new Senate would have eighteen Republicans (up from eleven) to fourteen Federalists (down from twenty-one). The new House would have sixty-five Republicans (up from forty-nine) to forty Federalists (down from fifty-six). The judiciary was Federalism's last bastion.

The Republican Party bore a powerful grudge against the judiciary. Federalist judges had enforced the Sedition Act zealously. Swelling the judiciary's ranks only strengthened the grudge. Republicans nicknamed the new appointees "midnight judges."

THE REPUBLICAN COUNTERATTACK came slowly. President Jefferson said nothing about the judiciary in his inaugural address on March 4. In a letter to Charles Cotesworth Pinckney, written that very day, Marshall called the speech he had just heard "well-judged and conciliatory." The incoming Republicans, he added, "are divided into speculative theorists and absolute terrorists. With the latter I am not disposed to class Mr. Jefferson."

Jefferson did not show his hand until December, when he sent his first annual message to the newly assembled Congress. "The judiciary system of the United States," he wrote, "and especially that portion of it recently erected, will of course present itself to the contemplation of Congress." In a private letter, Jefferson revealed what he expected Congress to contemplate doing: "Lop . . . off the parasitical plant engrafted at the last session."

Lopping began January 1802, when congressional Republicans brought forward a new Judiciary Act, undoing the expansions of the act of 1801; if it passed, the newly made judgeships would disappear, and the justices of the Supreme Court would have to ride circuit once more (in six circuits, however, not three—meaning that each justice would cover less ground, but cover it alone).

The Senate debated for the month of January, the House through February. The arguments were often intelligent and principled and cut deeper than the size of the federal court system to the very structure of the government. Gouverneur Morris feared a domineering Congress. Removing a judge's job seemed to him the same as removing a judge from a job, which would violate the Constitution (Article III, Section 1: "The Judges, both of the supreme and inferior Courts, shall hold their Offices during good Behaviour"). If Congress did such a thing, he said, then "the Constitution is whatever they choose to make it." In the House, Virginia Republican John Randolph of Roanoke, a twenty-eight-year-old cousin of both Jefferson and Marshall, argued that domination by Congress was no bad thing: "The decision of a Constitutional question must rest somewhere. Shall it be confided to men immediately responsible to the people, or to those who are irresponsible?" Intelligence and principle were all for show. The

Judiciary Act of 1802 passed both Senate and House on party-line votes and became law in March.

Congress did more; in April, it eliminated the summer sessions of the Supreme Court. The immediate effect of this measure was that the Court would not be able to rule on the constitutionality of the new Judiciary Act until February 1803. An alarmed Federalist asked, while the new schedule was being debated, whether Congress could not as easily adjourn the Supreme Court for ten or twenty years. But Republicans passed the measure briskly.

Marshall's first reaction to the new Judiciary Act was similar to Morris's. He doubted its validity and wrote his fellow justices, asking their opinions.

Chase agreed with him in a long, vehement letter. "My conscience must be satisfied, although my ruin should be the certain consequence. . . . The distinction of taking the *office* from the *judge,* and not the *judge* from the *office,* I consider as puerile and nonsensical." If dismissing the new circuit court judges was wrong, then asking Supreme Court justices to ride circuit in their places compounded the wrong. "If one person exercises an office to which another has *legal title,* he is a *wrong-doer,* and ought to be removed, and the injured person ought to be restored to his office. Shall a *judge* be a *wrong-doer* [Chase's emphasis]?" He wanted the Court to meet informally in August, the month of its canceled session, to decide how to respond.

But Cushing, Paterson, and Washington advised accepting the new act. Cushing saw it as a reversion to the Court's old practice. (Moore's opinion, if he wrote one, has not survived.)

Marshall bowed to the majority. "I shall hold myself," he wrote Cushing, "bound by the opinion of my brothers." The chief justice did not call an August conclave, and the Court did not meet again until February 1803.

Before then, Marshall had a chance to review what Congress had done. According to the provisions of the new Judiciary Act, he had to preside at circuit courts in Richmond and Raleigh, North Carolina. His duty in Raleigh was enlivened by his forgetting to pack a pair of pants. To make matters worse, local tailors were too busy to supply the lack. He had to sit in judgment, covering his legs with his robe. This was careless, even for Marshall; he must have wanted badly not to go.

One case that came before him in Richmond in December 1802 challenged the new Judiciary Act. John Laird, the Maryland agent of a Glasgow merchant house, had sued two Virginians, Hugh Stuart and Charles Carter, for failure to make good on a bond. The case had begun the year before in a district court, which the new act had subsequently abolished. The defendants now argued that the case should not be transferred to the circuit court because the act that annihilated its original venue was "unconstitutional and void." Marshall ruled that the defendants' plea was "insufficient" and found for Laird. Stuart would appeal to the Supreme Court.

In this first, arm's-length clash with President Jefferson, Marshall behaved in a manner that was suggestive of his early career and prophetic of the remainder of it. He had opinions, but he listened to the opinions of his fellows, even if they disagreed. This time he deferred to theirs; many times to come, they would defer to his. The Marshall Court would be as fraternal as the Quoits Club.

JEFFERSON AND HIS followers had struck at the judicial system. A case that came to the Supreme Court for judgment in February 1803 gave Marshall and his fellows a chance to return the blow.

William Marbury Jr. had been born into a family of planters in Piscataway, Maryland, on the Potomac a few miles downriver from Alexandria. By his generation, the land was worn out, and he looked for opportunities in the new capital city. He became a purchasing agent for the Navy Department, speculated in real estate, and served as a director of a local bank. In December 1800, he bought a handsome brick house in Georgetown (the house is now the Ukrainian embassy).

Marbury was a Federalist; he would name one of his sons after Alexander Hamilton. On February 17, 1801, when the House of Representatives finally broke its deadlock in favor of Thomas Jefferson, a jubilant Republican crowd demanded that Marbury put candles in his windows to celebrate. He refused, according to a local newspaper, "in the most resolute manner."

The Adams administration's blizzard of judicial patronage appointments did not overlook so loyal a partisan. The law that created a federal circuit court for the District of Columbia also authorized the president to nominate justices of the peace for the District. This was an honor rather than a career. Justices of the peace served for five years; they had the power to settle cases of up to twenty dollars in value; they earned no salary, only a percentage of the fines they collected. Adams tapped forty-two justices of the peace, three-quarters of them Federalists, including William Marbury.

Adams's nominations had to be sent to the Senate for confirmation, returned to him to be signed, sealed with the Great Seal of the United States, and delivered. The job of overseeing these tasks fell to the secretary of state, who was, until the very end of the Adams administration, John Marshall. Adams had asked Marshall to stay at his old job for one last month even after he began his duties as chief justice. (Such stopgap double-dipping happened occasionally; Jefferson's new attorney general, Levi Lincoln, would also serve as acting secretary of state until James Madison, detained by family business in Virginia, returned to the capital to fill the position full-time.)

Marshall had to work fast. The law authorizing the new legal establishment for the District passed on February 27, a Friday. Nomination, confirmation, and delivery had to be accomplished before Inauguration Day, March 4, the following Wednesday. Marshall's burdens were made heavier by the fact that he had loaned one of his State Department clerks (he only had two) to president-elect Jefferson to help him prepare for his new office. For years, Jefferson's family told a story that Marshall worked in the State Department processing appointments until midnight, March 3, when Levi Lincoln, pocket watch in hand, ordered him in the name of the new president to stop. Marshall supposedly said that he was allowed to take nothing on his way out but his hat. The wry line certainly sounds like Marshall, though the story also has the ring of fable. James Marshall later declared that on that last night, his brother asked him to deliver a batch of signed and sealed commissions, but James, unable to carry them all at once, had left some behind at the office. Among them was William Marbury's.

President Jefferson found the commissions lying on a desk when he visited the State Department the day after his inauguration, and he forbade their delivery. He would not be Adams's and Marshall's postman. If the commissions had not been sent out, then, he reasoned, the Federalist appointees had not in fact been appointed. "If there is any principle of law never yet contradicted," Jefferson explained years later, "it is that delivery is one of the essentials to the validity of the deed."

So matters rested until the December 1801 session of the Supreme Court. The Court met the week after Jefferson gave his annual message to Congress, with its oblique but portentous paragraph on the judiciary. Charles Lee, who had served as attorney general in the Washington and Adams administrations, appeared before the Court as counsel for Marbury and three other

Federalist justices of the peace manqué. Lee presented affidavits from his clients that told a tale of frustration. They had asked Secretary of State Madison for their commissions; he had bucked them to Jacob Wagner, his chief clerk; Wagner had said they should inquire of Attorney General Lincoln; Lincoln had been of no help.

Lee asked the Court to issue a writ of mandamus to Madison, directing him to produce the commissions.

A writ is a court order; *mandamus* is Latin for *we command*. Blackstone defined the writ of mandamus as a command requiring "any person . . . to do some *particular* thing therein specified, which appertains to [his] office and duty." The Judiciary Act of 1789, whose procedural provisions had been untouched by the Acts of 1801 and 1802, gave the Supreme Court the power to issue writs of mandamus to inferior courts and to federal officeholders. Lee wanted the Court to make Madison do his duty.

The eminence of the plaintiffs' lawyer and the high position of their intended target showed that more was at stake than whether William Marbury could pass judgment on nineteen-dollar disputes in the District of Columbia. The Federalist Party was trying to put the secretary of state in the wrong. Marbury's case was an effort to show that the Jefferson administration was lawless and had been so since day two.

Republicans knew what Federalists were up to. This was why Madison had brushed off Marbury and his fellows. In fairness to Madison, he had other matters to deal with: a war with Moslem pirates in the Mediterranean; rumors that Spain had secretly ceded the Louisiana Territory to France. But one thing he refused to deal with was a Federalist effort to entrap him.

The Court asked Madison to show cause why he should not be served with a writ of mandamus, and the case was slated to be continued when the Court next met, in the summer of 1802.

Before then came the new Judiciary Act and the law canceling the Court's summer session. The politicians locking horns over these issues were aware of Marbury's suit and its significance. One Republican senator denounced it as "a high-handed exertion of judiciary power . . . invading" the business of the executive branch. Marbury pressed his case in January 1803 by petitioning the Senate to provide proof, from its own records, that he and his fellow litigants had indeed been confirmed. The Senate, in a party-line vote, turned them down.

So it was that William Marbury's case arrived before the Supreme Court on February 10, 1803, almost two years after his commission had been left on a State Department desk. Four justices were present in their committee room—Cushing and Moore were home, sick. Madison had not attended the initial hearing in December 1801, and he was not there now. No lawyer represented him; Attorney General Lincoln was in the room, only as an observer. Madison and the Jefferson administration did not wish to dignify Marbury's suit by their participation.

Charles Lee once again represented the plaintiffs. To establish the fact that the commissions had existed, he called three witnesses—Wagner the clerk, his assistant David Brent, and Lincoln. All were reluctant to speak. Wagner, "at this distance of time," could not remember much. Brent remembered seeing two commissions, Marbury's and one other. Lincoln asked for Lee's questions to be written out and for a day to consider them. When this had been done, he said that he had seen the commissions but could not say whose they were, and he would not say what had happened to them. Lee finished his presentation of evidence with an affidavit from James Marshall explaining his bungled delivery of the night of the March 3.

There was an element of comedy in this elaborate effort to prove the existence of documents to a panel of justices headed by a man who, as secretary of state, had himself handled them. But the law cannot take shortcuts.

Lee then made his argument. The president, Lee stressed, was not on trial. This was politically false but legally true. Madison, Lincoln, and the clerks held their jobs in "two capacities"—as agents of the president and as governmental officers. As presidential agents, they carried out his policies and desires. These, said Lee, the court could not examine. But as officers of the government, they had duties that were independent of the president's will. Delivering legally executed commissions was one of those duties. The appointment of a justice of the peace "is complete" once he has been nominated and confirmed and his commission signed. "The president has then done with it; it becomes irrevocable." Then all officials, from the secretary of state to the lowliest clerk, must see that the commission is delivered. And if they failed, the Supreme Court could order them to produce the missing document. The Court "can refuse justice to no man," Lee concluded.

Over the next two weeks, the Supreme Court heard arguments in other cases. Justice Moore finally made it to Washington, but Justice Chase was immobilized by an attack of gout, which forced the Court to conduct its business in the parlor of Stelle's Hotel on Capitol Hill, where all the justices were staying, so that he could attend. There, on the morning of February 24, Marshall announced that he would read the opinion of the Court in *Marbury v. Madison*.

This was a still-new innovation. Before Marshall's chief justiceship, whenever the Court passed judgment on a case, each justice read his own opinion, one after the other. Marshall began the practice of unanimous opinions, whenever possible, delivered, as often as not, by him. His fellow justices remained free to give individual opinions, concurring with the majority decision or dissenting from it. On rare occasions, Marshall would deliver an opinion with which he partly disagreed; at other times, also rare, he would openly dissent. But he strove to make the Supreme Court an organism, like a coral reef. He wanted its judgments to be oracular.

The rhetoric he employed was that of an oracle: authoritative, inescapable. Marshall's manner seemed to be artless. His voice from the bench, as described by William Wirt, a young lawyer who heard it at this time, was "dry and hard." The easy humor he lavished on Richmonders and the poetical spirit he had shown the Ambler girls was nowhere in evidence. But he spoke with focus and breadth. He made every point clearly and directly, without losing a view of his entire subject, and he moved through points and subject to his conclusions with seemingly irresistible force. His "intellectual elevation," wrote Wirt, "enabled him to look down and comprehend the whole ground at once. . . . His eloquence consists in the apparently deep self-conviction and earnestness of his manner." As he spoke, "the dawn advances in easy but unremitting pace."

Marshall began by noting the "peculiar delicacy" and "real difficulty" of the case. This would become a characteristic opening gambit of his, always, in retrospect, ironic. Whenever Marshall spoke of delicacy or difficulty, he was sure to follow with a wagonload of legal granite.

Marshall presented a simple, three-step outline of the case. Did William Marbury have a right to his appointment? If he had, did the law offer him a remedy when the appointment was not forthcoming? If it did, was that remedy a writ of mandamus from the Supreme Court?

Marshall answered the first question by walking through every stage of making a presidential appointment. (He knew them well.) He concluded that "when a commission has been signed by the president, the appointment is made." Lee was right, Jefferson wrong. Marbury had been appointed and therefore had a right to his office.

When Marshall came to the second question, he quoted Blackstone: "Where there is a legal right, there is also a legal remedy . . . whenever that right is invaded." He added an American gloss: "The government of the United States has been emphatically termed a government of laws, and not of men. It will certainly cease to deserve this high appellation, if the laws furnish no remedy for the violation of a vested legal right."

He then made a distinction, suggested by Lee's argument that officers of the president served in "two capacities." They act, Marshall said, as his agents, a role in which they "can never be examinable by the courts." But when they perform "a specific duty . . . assigned by law, and individual rights depend upon the performance of" it, anyone "who considers himself injured has a right to resort to the laws of his country for a remedy." So far, so good for William Marbury.

The third question—was Marbury's proper remedy a mandamus issued by the Supreme Court?—led Marshall into a thicket of distinctions.

Marbury had sought a writ of mandamus under the Judiciary Act of 1789. Marshall quoted from it: the Supreme Court may issue writs of mandamus to "persons holding office, under the authority of the United States." James Madison, secretary of state, was clearly such a person.

But Marshall then turned to Article III, Section 2 of the Constitution, which assigned original and appellate jurisdiction to different courts. (Original jurisdiction is where cases begin; appellate jurisdiction is where they go once they have begun.) Marshall paraphrased: the Supreme Court had original jurisdiction in cases "affecting ambassadors, other public ministers and consuls. . . . In all other cases" it had appellate jurisdiction. (In the language of the Constitution, "public ministers" meant foreign envoys; Article II, Section 3 says the president "shall receive Ambassadors and other public Ministers.")

What was the problem? Issuing a writ of mandamus for a commission, said Marshall, was an act of original jurisdiction, like taking evidence or hearing testimony. Therefore, according to the Constitution, the Supreme Court could not issue one to James Madison, who was neither an ambassador, a foreign envoy, nor a consul, but a "person holding office."

The law and the Constitution disagreed. Either the law would have to be overruled, or the Constitution ignored.

Marshall folded into his argument a paean to the Constitution. "That the people have an original right to establish, for their future government, such principles as, in their opinion, shall most conduce to their own happiness, is the basis, on which the whole American fabric has been erected. The exercise of this original right is a very great exertion. . . . The principles, therefore, so established are deemed fundamental." Marshall had played a role in that great exertion; he would defend his, and the nation's, handiwork.

He concluded, "A law repugnant to the Constitution is void; and . . . *courts,* as well as other departments, are bound by that instrument."

Marshall's opinion was not only oracular, it was monumental: almost 9,400 words long. He carved it in stone: a large stone.

MARBURY V. MADISON overturned a section of a law passed by Congress. This was no novelty, either in theory or in practice. "Whenever a particular statute contravenes the Constitution," Alexander Hamilton had written in *Federalist* 78, "it will be the duty of the judicial tribunals to adhere to the latter and disregard the former." Marshall himself, in his speech on the judiciary at the Virginia Ratifying Convention, had said that if Congress made a law that infringed on the Constitution, judges "would declare it void." In *Hylton v. United States,* the Court had heard an argument challenging the constitutionality of Hamilton's carriage tax. Although it upheld the tax, it might conceivably have struck it down. Most telling, perhaps, was the acquiescence of Marshall's colleague, Justice Paterson, now. He had helped write the Judiciary Act of 1789. He had a dog in this fight—yet he concurred in Marshall's opinion.

Judged by the result, *Marbury v. Madison* was no victory for Federalism. William Marbury had not gotten his commission, and the Supreme Court, that Federalist bastion, had stripped itself of the power to issue a writ of mandamus to James Madison. But the bulk of the decision was a lecture to the Republicans who ruled the executive branch, instructing them that they had behaved badly—as a government of men, not laws.

Not all partisans recognized this immediately—the decision was forbidding—but some got the message. Hamilton's mouthpiece, the *New-York Evening Post,* ran an editorial headlined CONSTITUTION VIOLATED BY THE PRESIDENT. President Jefferson said nothing at the time, but the longer he thought about *Marbury v. Madison,* the less he liked it. Four years later, he told his attorney general that he wished it could be "denounced as not law."

William Marbury never pursued his suit further. His brief brush with high politics had evidently been enough for him. He died in 1835, remembered by his family and by legal historians.

A WEEK AFTER THE *Marbury* decision, the Court delivered its opinion in *Stuart v. Laird,* the commercial dispute that had become entangled in the politics surrounding the Judiciary Act of 1802. Marshall had rejected, on the circuit, Hugh Stuart's argument that the Judiciary Act of 1802 was unconstitutional, and he now withdrew from further judgment. So it was Justice

Paterson who read the opinion of the Court (a brief one—less than five hundred words). The judiciary's "acquiescence" in the new act "affords an irresistible answer. . . . The question is at rest, and ought not now to be disturbed." Marshall's decision was affirmed.

Marshall had held his Court together, picked his battles, and won the ones he had chosen to fight. New battles had already begun.

Chapter 6

IMPEACHMENT

J OHN MARSHALL'S FIRST YEARS ON THE COURT SAW MILE-
posts in his private life. His father died in Kentucky in June
1802, just months after Marshall polled his fellow justices
about the Republicans' new Judiciary Act; his next-to-last son
was born in February 1803, the day after the Court began hearing
final arguments in *Marbury;* the baby died in October (yet another blow for Polly).

These events passed out of the public view, and thanks to
Marshall's carelessness with letters, or some late-in-life act of
destruction, no record of his reactions to them survives. But he
was engaged in an act of personal piety that was also an act of
political warfare.

George Washington's will had left Mount Vernon and his papers, after the death of his widow, to his nephew, and Marshall's
colleague, Bushrod. He and Marshall planned to write a biography of their idol, making use of the documentary trove. But
thanks to Bushrod's weak eyesight, the burden of composition
fell to Marshall.

He embarked with high hopes that were entirely unrealistic,
expecting to produce four or five volumes, of four to five hundred
pages each, in less than a year. He and Bushrod counted on sales

of 30,000, with royalties to each of them of $75,000. Today this would be a sale of 1.8 million, with royalties of $1 million.

Marshall could be a hard worker and write to deadline. But the task of composing a life from original sources was beyond anything he had ever done, especially since he decided to begin with a survey of American history beginning with John Cabot's voyage of discovery in 1497; "Mr. Washington," as he is called, does not get born until the beginning of volume 2. The first three volumes of *The Life of George Washington* appeared in 1804; volume 4 would come in 1805, volume 5 in 1807. The publisher was able to sell seven thousand sets (the price, three dollars per volume, was high). Marshall and Bushrod made $19,500 apiece; Marshall's share covered the last installment of the Fairfax purchase.

The modern art of biography had been pioneered in England by Samuel Johnson and James Boswell, who used anecdotes and dialogue to bring their readers into the presence of their subjects. Even in America, Mason Weems, a Maryland bookseller who was one of the publisher's agents taking advance orders for Marshall's work, was pioneering the art of popular biography, with a life of Washington, first published in 1800. Weems's story of Washington's life was a single volume, enlivened with tales of his hero's youth (made up, it is true, by Weems himself) that lodged themselves in the American mind and that remain there still ("I can't tell a lie, Pa; you know I can't tell a lie. I did cut it"—the cherry tree, of course—"with my hatchet").

The oracular style that Marshall used on the bench smothers his biography. The war makes the best reading, told occasionally by Marshall as a modestly footnoted eyewitness, recounted at other times by comrades—Lafayette, Daniel Morgan—who shared their testimony with him.

As Marshall's story moved into the 1790s, his volumes became a brief for Federalism. Federalists were warmly praised. "To talents equally splendid and useful," Alexander Hamilton "united a patient industry, not always the companion of genius." John Jay showed "sound judgment . . . unyielding firmness . . . inflexible integrity." "No American had reflected more profoundly on the subject of government" than John Adams.

Marshall's treatment of Thomas Jefferson's clashes with Hamilton over his financial system was full and fair. Yet Marshall harped on Republican Francophilia, on all that the party was willing to praise and to swallow. Marshall's Republicans were patriots—French patriots: "The ardent patriot cannot maintain the choicest rights of his country with more zeal than was manifested in supporting all the claims of the French republic upon the United States."

Marshall's biography provoked a response from Jefferson—a collection of letters and jottings, anecdotes and rumors, that he called *Anas* (Johnson's dictionary defined *Ana* as a book of "loose thoughts . . . dropped by eminent men"). Jefferson did not publish the *Anas* in his lifetime but evidently hoped they would appear after his death, for he described them, in a prefatory note, as a rebuttal to Marshall: "testimony against the only history of that period which pretends to have been compiled from authentic and unpublished documents."

There is no question whose work, Marshall's or Jefferson's, is livelier. The *Anas* are scattershot, gossipy, paranoid, irresistible. The reader feels himself in the presence of a disreputable friend sharing disreputable confidences. "The St. Andrews club of New York (all of [them] Scotch Tories) gave a public dinner lately," Jefferson wrote in January 1800. "Among other guests A. Hamilton was one." The second toast after dinner was to George III. "Hamilton started up on his feet, and insisted on a bumper and three cheers." At the end of this item, Jefferson explained that he had it thirdhand.

A monument, like Marshall's *Life of George Washington*, may be respectable. But gossip, like Jefferson's *Anas,* is delicious.

Jefferson would win (posthumously) this battle of the books with Marshall. Meanwhile, another battle in their war had begun. Jefferson and his allies tried to purge the Supreme Court.

THE JUDICIARY ACT of 1802 had lopped the new growth of the federal courts. But could Congress prune further? According to the Constitution (Article III, Section 1), federal judges served "during good Behaviour." But the Constitution also gave Congress the power of impeachment. The House was to make the charge (Article I, Section 2), the Senate to try and convict (Article I, Section 3). Could the judiciary be cleaned out in this way?

Impeachments are trials of public officials conducted by a legislature. The most famous impeachment in recent history had been that of Warren Hastings, the architect of Britain's Indian empire, by Parliament. Although Hastings, accused of an array of crimes, was ultimately acquitted, Britain's greatest orators spent years denouncing him. Their eloquence cast a glow over the procedure.

In February 1803, just days before the Supreme Court heard *Marbury v. Madison*, Jefferson sent the House a sheaf of complaints concerning John Pickering, federal district judge for New Hampshire. Pickering (no relation to Timothy) had been a lawyer and a judge for decades and had written his state's constitution. But in recent years, he had lost his mind and taken to drink. His case, wrote Jefferson, was "not within executive cognizance," but perhaps the House "shall be of opinion" that it called for its attention. The House impeached the drunken judge and informed the Senate that his case would come its way in Congress's next session.

The Senate tried Pickering a year later in absentia, for he was so incapacitated that he could not appear in person. His trial posed a dilemma. Impeachment was the only way to get rid of him; the Judiciary Act of 1801 had included a procedure for substituting judges that had been used to sideline him, but under the Judiciary Act of 1802, that option was no longer available. Yet impeachment seemed unjust. The Constitution prescribed it for serious offenses: "Treason, Bribery, or other high Crimes and Misdemeanors." Drunkenness on the bench might be a misdemeanor, but was madness a crime at all?

But the most notable feature of Pickering's trial was that it was only a dress rehearsal. The Senate convicted him on March 12, 1804. Less than an hour later, the House voted to impeach Justice Samuel Chase.

Chase's impeachment had been coming for a long time, arguably all his adult life. He combined strong views and dramatic manners. As a young man, he burned a colonial official in effigy, and boasted that he had done so, while others "merely grumbled in your corners." He denounced a fellow delegate to the Continental Congress for treason and harassed Quakers during the Revolution for their pacifism. As a state judge, he ordered the arrest of two prominent Baltimoreans for leading a riot; when the sheriff said it would be impossible to take them in, Chase offered to do it himself: "I will be the posse comitatus."

Chase joined the Supreme Court in 1796. His new role did not teach him caution. He presided, as a circuit judge, over two of the most inflamed political trials of the Adams administration, behaving in both in a manner that enraged Republicans. In April 1800, John Fries, a Pennsylvania German, was tried in Philadelphia for leading a band of armed tax resisters in intimidating a federal marshal. The charge was treason, and as the trial opened, Chase defined the crime so broadly that Fries's lawyers refused to take part. Then, in June, journalist James Callender was tried in Richmond under the Sedition Act for libeling President Adams (Callender had called him, among other things, an aristocrat). When Callender's lawyers tried to tell the jury that they could pass judgment on the Sedition Act itself, Chase reproved them, and they too threw up their case as unwinnable in a court presided over by him.

The Republican sweep of 1800 boded ill for Chase. There were rumors as early as 1802 that the victors meant to immolate him. Then, in May 1803, Chase laid one more log on the stack that was rising around his feet. Judges in early America gave charges to grand juries (a custom based on English practice) that amounted to political speeches. Chase, riding circuit in Baltimore, opined that the Judiciary Act of 1802 and proposed changes to Maryland's laws would "*take away all security for property* and *personal liberty*. . . . Our republican constitution will sink into a *Mobocracy*, the worst of all possible governments" (emphasis, as always, Chase's).

Eleven days later, Jefferson wrote one of his allies in the House about Chase's "extraordinary charge. . . . Ought this seditious and official attack on the principles of our constitution, and the proceedings of a state, to go unpunished?" As he had done before when writing Congress, Jefferson professed simply to be raising questions. "It is better," he concluded, "that I should not interfere." The hint was enough. In January 1804, after months of consultation among its leaders, the House appointed a committee to examine Chase's conduct.

Marshall wrote his beleaguered colleague at the end of the month, offering to help him round up documents concerning the Callender trial, which was sure to be invoked against him. Then Marshall made an extraordinary suggestion: "I think the modern doctrine of impeachment should yield to an appellate jurisdiction in the legislature." The chief justice who had just ruled in *Marbury v. Madison* that the Court had a right to strike down laws passed by Congress was now proposing to let Congress strike down the decisions of the Court. Reversing a judge's decision would be better than removing him from office.

Marshall's letter to Chase flew in the face of his principles up to this point (and of his principles ever after). The completeness of the reversal was a measure of his fear. If Chase fell, the Republicans would not stop until they had impeached and removed the entire Supreme Court. At the end of his letter, Marshall alluded to the Bible (not a common thing for him). The verse he echoed was 2 Chronicles 10:10, from an account of Israelites asking Rehoboam to lower the taxes of his father, Solomon. "My little finger," Rehoboam answered, "shall be thicker than my father's loins. . . . My father chastised you with whips, but I will chastise you with scorpions." Jefferson and his party, Marshall believed, meant to rule with a heavy hand; better to let them overturn a few decisions, lest they do worse.

The Republicans were certainly chastising from strength. The election of 1804 was a rout. Jefferson had cut taxes, stayed out of European wars, and doubled the size of the country by buying Louisiana from France. He won every electoral vote except those of Connecticut and Delaware and two of Maryland's, while Republicans increased their margins in both the Senate and the House.

As in many triumphant parties, there was a difference of opinion about how to use its newfound powers. Some Republican leaders saw impeaching judges as simple political housekeeping. It "was nothing more," explained one Virginia congressman, "than a declaration by Congress to this effect: You hold dangerous opinions. . . . We want your offices, for the purpose of giving them to men who will fill them better."

Yet the Constitution plainly said that impeachment was to be for criminality. The charges that the House finally brought against Justice Chase in December 1804 arraigned him for specific offenses: his conduct in the Fries and Callender trials, his charge to the Baltimore grand jury, and several lesser matters. He was described as "highly arbitrary, oppressive and unjust," and condemned for "manifest injustice, partiality, and intemperance."

The charges were the work of the man who was to manage the House's case, John Randolph of Roanoke. Randolph had the look and sound of an obnoxious boy: a hairless chin and cheeks and a shrill voice that had never broken. Despite these traits, he awed congressional Republicans with his freewheeling eloquence, his sarcasm (what he himself called "the spice of the devil"), and his clear principles (he had begun to think that even his cousin Jefferson wavered). Randolph was unsuited to the task at hand in only one respect: he was not a lawyer.

The tone of the trial was set by the president of the Senate, Vice President Aaron Burr. Burr was in legal difficulties himself, having killed Alexander Hamilton the summer before. Since Burr had shot Hamilton in a duel, it was unlikely that any jury of gentlemen would convict him of a crime; the code duello would trump the law. Still, an indictment for murder hung over him.

The Jefferson administration came to his defense. Jefferson's allies in Congress petitioned the governor of New Jersey, where the duel had taken place, to quash the indictment. Burr's relations with Jefferson had been cool ever since their electoral deadlock in 1800—so much so that he had been replaced as Jefferson's running mate in 1804 by another New York politician, George Clinton. But Vice President–elect Clinton would not take office until March 1805. Jefferson's new friendliness toward the lame duck Burr showed how badly he wanted Chase removed from office.

Burr arranged the Senate chamber to look like a courtroom in an opera. His model was the House of Lords, where Hastings had been tried. The regular chairs of the senators were replaced by benches covered in crimson baize. Spectators and members of the House were given benches covered in green. The trial began on February 4, 1805, with Burr treating Chase severely, as if he meant the defendant to stand during his ordeal (Chase was almost sixty-four years old). He finally granted Chase a chair, though not a table.

As soon as the trial was under way, however, Chase's prospects brightened. He spoke well in his own defense and was supported by a team of five excellent lawyers, including the attorney general of Maryland, Luther Martin, an old friend. Of the witnesses called to testify to his alleged misdeeds, some let fall evidence in his favor. A juror in the Callender trial thought that Chase had been a fair judge: "It was my impression that [he] wished the prisoner to have a full hearing, that he might be acquitted, if found innocent, and found guilty, if really guilty."

The House managers of the case—Randolph and six other congressmen—made mistakes in law and bogged down in trivialities. To demonstrate Chase's intemperance, they argued that he had called Callender's lawyers "young gentlemen" (they were half his age), and Callender himself, outside the courtroom, "damned." Considering Chase's temper, these were mild expressions. Martin had fun with "damned"; in the south, he explained gravely, "it is in familiar use, generally introduced as a word of comparison, supplying frequently the place of the word 'very.'"

Marshall was summoned as a witness. He had attended the Callender trial in Richmond as a spectator, between his tenures as congressman and secretary of state. If Chase's brother justice could now be made to give evidence that was damaging to him, it would make a powerful impression. Marshall twisted away from questions as well as he could. When Burr asked him if Chase's conduct had been "tyrannical, overbearing and oppressive," Marshall answered, "I will state the facts." William Plumer, an ardent Federalist senator from New Hampshire, disliked Marshall's testimony. He looked for boldness, but the chief justice, he wrote in his diary, instead showed "too much caution—too much fear—too much cunning." Marshall showed all three. But, as in the case of *Commonwealth v. Randolph,* in which he had prepared the defense of an accused adulteress and murderess, he was trying to avoid impressions and conclusions and stick instead to details that might favor Chase, or at least seem not definite or serious enough to warrant a conviction.

On March 1, the Senate delivered its verdict. Uriah Tracy, a sick Federalist from Connecticut, was carried to the Senate chamber on a couch so that he could vote. He could have stayed in bed. On only three of the eight counts against Chase did even a majority of the Senate find him guilty, and on none of them were the House managers able to win the two-thirds necessary to remove him from office.

From a combination of Republican incompetence, Federalist courtroom savvy, and Marshall's tactical prudence, the impeachment option had run aground. Three days later, on March 4, Marshall, for a second time, administered the presidential oath of office to Jefferson. They had yet another clash coming.

Chapter 7

TREASON

I F THOMAS JEFFERSON COULD NOT SIMPLY SWEEP JOHN Marshall and his colleagues away, he could, if he were patient, slowly replace them.

The first vacancy in the Marshall Court occurred in February 1804 when Alfred Moore resigned because of ill health (he would live for six more years). In September 1806, William Paterson died, not quite sixty-one. Then, in February 1807, Congress, mindful of the westward march of population, created a new judicial circuit for Kentucky, Tennessee, and the new state of Ohio, and expanded the roster of the Supreme Court from six justices to seven.

Jefferson filled all these slots with Republicans, all of them younger than Marshall. Moore's replacement was William Johnson of South Carolina. A note in the administration's appointment files praised his "republican connections" and the "good nerves in his political principles." In for Paterson went Brockholst Livingston, a sprig of a Republican clan with roots in New York and New Jersey (his second cousin, Robert R. Livingston, had negotiated the Louisiana Purchase). Brockholst had established his Republican bona fides in the most dramatic way possible by killing a Federalist in a duel. No one mentioned the matter when the Senate confirmed him. To fill the new Supreme Court seat,

Jefferson asked the congressmen of the three westernmost states (all Republicans) to propose a nominee. They chose one of their number, which was unconstitutional (Article I, Section 6: "No Senator or Representative shall, during the Time for which he was elected, be appointed to any civil Office . . . which shall have been created . . . during such time"). So Jefferson tapped Kentuckian Thomas Todd.

In three years, the Court had shifted from six Federalists to four Federalists and three Republicans, without the drama of lopping or impeaching. And yet the Court continued to be Marshall's. Years later, Justice Johnson, the most independent of Jefferson's justices, tried to explain, in a letter to the man who appointed him, what had happened. Early in his tenure, Johnson wrote, "I disagreed from my brethren" on a case "and I thought it a thing of course to deliver my opinion"—in other words, to dissent. "But during the rest of the session I heard nothing but lectures on the indecency of judges cutting at each other, and the loss of reputation which [courts] sustained by pursuing such a course. . . . I therefore bent to the current."

Johnson, either to salve his own pride or to cater to Jefferson's suspicions, presented himself as a target of social pressure. No doubt social pressure was exerted within the Marshall Court. But the justices were also the beneficiaries of comradeship—of Marshall's bonhomie and of his insistence that they board together during their Washington sessions. This made for efficiency; they could discuss cases after hours, over dinner and over drinks. It also made for fellow feeling. Marshall, with confidence born of ease, encouraged discussion and deference and practiced what he encouraged. Giving the Court's opinion in *M'Ferran v. Taylor and Massie,* an 1806 case involving a Kentucky land deal, he admitted that he had some reservations about the decision, but added, "I am . . . perfectly content with that which I have been directed to deliver." Years later, in *Leef and Goodwin v. Schooner Rover and*

Moore and Hudgins, a circuit court case involving admiralty law, he wrote a fellow justice asking for advice, admitting that he lacked "much practice of that description." Johnson's reference to "brethren" was a caste-marker, a term that judges typically used of each other. Marshall sought to make brotherhood emotionally real.

Marshall's colleagues, finally, respected his power. He was charming, he was convivial, he was politic. But, as he had shown in his XYZ letters, his speech in Congress on Thomas Nash, and most relevantly his opinion in *Marbury v. Madison,* when he bore down, he seemed almost implacable. All the Jeffersonians felt the current of his mind and bent to it.

J EFFERSON'S SECOND TERM began in March 1805 under in- coming clouds: after a year of peace, Europe had slid back into war. The United States tried to stay out of it, despite rising tensions with Britain, France, and Spain, with whose empire Louisiana shared a boundary.

Then, in January 1807, the president delivered an electrifying message to Congress: the United States was under attack, from within. James Wilkinson, the commanding general of the army, had accused Aaron Burr, the former vice president, of a double-barreled plot to invade Mexico and break up the United States, peeling off everything west of the Appalachians.

Much of the proof, Jefferson admitted, was "rumors, conjectures, and suspicions," not "formal and legal evidence." But he said Burr's guilt was "beyond question." Two of Burr's underlings had been arrested by Wilkinson in New Orleans and were on their way to the capital, where they would be tried by "the highest judicial authorities."

Here was work for Marshall and the Supreme Court—two prisoners, accused of the greatest conspiracy in American history since Benedict Arnold's, and their mastermind, still at large but already condemned by the president.

Burr and Wilkinson were both veterans of the Revolutionary War. While Marshall was fighting his first battle in Virginia, they took part in a desperate, doomed invasion of Canada. After the war, Wilkinson moved to Kentucky, while Burr made a career in law and politics in New York City.

Temperamentally, the two could not have been more different. Wilkinson ("Wilky" to friends) was expansive, verbose, given to gaudy uniforms designed by himself. Burr's twin fetishes were correct manners and self-possession. He fancied himself a disciple of Lord Chesterfield, author of a famous set of elegant letters of amoral advice to his son. Burr's advice to his law clerks was to put nothing on paper: "Things written," he would say, "remain."

After rejoining the army in the 1790s, Wilkinson impressed both John Adams and Thomas Jefferson with his professionalism and his flattery. By 1797, he held the highest rank. He spent his time improving the army's many posts on the Ohio and Mississippi Rivers, from Pittsburgh to Fort Massac in southern Illinois, to Natchez. After Jefferson bought the Louisiana Territory, Wilkinson attended the raising of the American flag in New Orleans.

Burr joined the Republican Party in New York and rose high and fast. He knew how to get out the vote in the city's ethnic wards and how to cultivate high-level allies in and out of state. The electoral-vote deadlock in the election of 1800 was his high-water mark. Jefferson never trusted Burr after he refused to step aside, and he looked for opportunities outside ordinary politics.

In May 1804, Burr hosted Wilkinson at his home in Greenwich Village. Wilkinson, who addressed Burr in a letter as "*mon beau et chère diable*" (my handsome, dear devil), insisted on meeting after dark. He brought a trove of the latest maps of Spanish North America.

Spain had owned Louisiana until 1800, when it gave it to Napoleon, who sold it to the United States. But Spain still owned Texas and everything to the west and south. Much of this land was fertile and therefore valuable in itself. Far more valuable were the silver mines of northern Mexico.

Wilkinson had been involved in shady land schemes from the moment he moved to Kentucky, so much so that he was widely suspected of being a Spanish agent. Without question, he knew the lay of the land. If Burr ever found it necessary to begin a new life, Wilkinson would be a valuable partner.

Burr killed Hamilton, presided over the Chase trial, and then began traveling in the west. For two years, he went everywhere and saw everyone. He went down the Ohio and the Mississippi, all the way to New Orleans, then doubled back to Washington, DC, before setting out again. He met frontier politicians and Creole high society. He befriended a minor Irish aristocrat, Harman Blennerhassett, who owned an island in the Ohio River opposite northern Virginia (now West Virginia). And he spent four days at Fort Massac with Wilkinson.

At the same time, no one knew for sure what, if anything, Burr was about. He said he was interested in settling a tract of land, once owned by a Dutch baron, in what is now Arkansas. He sometimes said he was interested in invading Mexico. If the United States was at peace with Spain, such a plan would be criminal. But if the two countries were at war—and there were tensions over the disputed border of Texas—what patriot, dreaming of land and silver, could resist?

The U.S. attorney for Kentucky, Joseph Daveiss, thought Burr was interested in disunion. Late in 1806, he haled Burr before the federal district court in Frankfort, the state capital. But the grand jury refused to issue an indictment. Burr's friends celebrated with a ball in his honor.

Wilkinson ended all suspense by sending Jefferson the message, which reached the president in January 1807. In it, Wilkinson declared that "a deep, dark and widespread conspiracy" was afoot. To prove it, he enclosed a transcript of a coded letter to him from Burr, announcing that he and a band of "choice spirits" would descend the Mississippi, seize New Orleans, and move on to Mexico. "The gods invite to glory and fortune," Burr wrote. "It remains to be seen whether we deserve the boon."

Wilkinson put New Orleans under martial law and arrested suspects left and right; when a local judge tried to intervene, Wilkinson arrested him too. Two couriers of Burr—Samuel Swartout, a young friend from New York, and Erich Bollmann, a German doctor—were shipped as prisoners to Washington; Jefferson himself grilled Bollmann in the White House.

At last, the long period of rumors and countercharges, at once muffled and hysterical, was over. The drama that followed, though played out chiefly in the graver atmosphere of the courtroom, was no less hysterical.

BOLLMANN AND SWARTOUT sued for their freedom. After the DC circuit court ruled that they should be held to be tried for treason, they appealed to the Supreme Court.

Their cases—*Ex parte Bollman* (his surname would be consistently shorn of one *n* in court documents) and *Ex parte Swartout*— were heard in February 1807. (*Ex parte*—for the party—was the legal formula for an appeal for release from unjust imprisonment.) Marshall delivered the opinion of the Court, which was a rebuke to the prosecution. Marshall hewed to the Constitution's definition of treason, Article III, Section 3: it "shall consist only in levying war against [the United States], or in adhering to their enemies, giving them aid and comfort." Since the United States had no declared enemies at that moment—tensions with Spain had not come to a boil—the only possible treason could be levying war against it, and "to constitute that specific crime," said Marshall, "war must be actually levied." Plotting war and levying it "are distinct offenses."

The prosecution's main evidence against Bollmann and Swartout was Wilkinson's transcript of Burr's coded letter. For all its urgent flourishes—*the gods invite*—Marshall found it vague: its "language . . . furnishes no distinct view of the design of the writer." The subject seemed to be an invasion of Mexico— "a high misdemeanor," but not treason.

Marshall, finally, said that the prisoners should not be tried in Washington, DC. "At the place where the prisoners were seized by the authority of the commander in chief, there existed . . . a tribunal." Wilkinson had sent them away specifically because he believed the judges on the spot were biased, but Marshall would not allow a general to make such a decision.

He concluded by saying that, although the government could later charge Bollmann and Swartout with plotting to attack Mexico, he would now let them go.

Meanwhile, Aaron Burr, unaware of these events, had been floating down the Mississippi with sixty men in nine riverboats. This little fleet had been launched from Blennerhassett's Island; Burr had rendezvoused with it a few miles above Fort Massac. In mid-January, he was arrested at Bayou Pierre, between what is now Vicksburg and Natchez. Once again, a local grand jury set him free, but the territorial governor put a price on his head, and Burr took to the bush. He was recognized and apprehended north of Mobile and marched eight hundred miles overland to Richmond.

Burr was to be tried in Richmond because Blennerhassett's Island, whence his armada had set out, was on the Virginia side of the Ohio River, and thus in the Richmond circuit. This gave the prosecution something it had lacked in the trial of Bollmann and Swartout: a definite action, within the purview of a relevant court. It also meant that the two judges hearing the case would be the judge of the Richmond circuit, Cyrus Griffin, and the Supreme Court justice assigned to it—John Marshall.

THE TRIAL WAS held in the chamber of the House of Delegates. Spectators flocked to Richmond and overflowed the room. A bronze stove, unneeded in spring and summer, sat in the middle of the floor, blocking sight lines.

George Hay, the U.S. attorney for Virginia, moved to have Burr committed for treason and for the high misdemeanor of launching an attack on Mexico. When Hay cited Burr's flight as evidence of his guilt, Burr himself replied that he was simply trying to escape Wilkinson's martial law.

Marshall ruled on April 1 (Judge Griffin would be virtually a mute throughout the proceedings). He was struck, as he had been in the case of Bollmann and Swartout, by the lack of evidence for treason. "The assembling of forces to levy war [against the United States] is a visible transaction, and numbers must witness it. . . . Several months have elapsed, since the fact did occur, if it ever occurred. . . . Why is it not proved?"

The coded letter might prove the high misdemeanor of attacking Mexico, so Marshall set a bail of $10,000 for that offense. But he refused to commit the prisoner for treason, though he noted the prosecution could seek an indictment for it from a grand jury, if it supplied "the necessary testimony." He set May 22 as the date for the grand jury to meet.

Although the United States was already a vast country and Burr had traversed great tracts of it, its legal world was still very small. Joseph Daveiss, who had tried to indict Burr in Kentucky, was married to Marshall's youngest sister, Nancy. The foreman of the grand jury that was to decide whether to indict Burr now would be John Randolph of Roanoke, the prosecutor of Justice Chase. Randolph had finally repudiated his cousin Jefferson as a Republican in name only and begun a long political career as a solo gadfly. One sign of his singularity was his admiration for his cousin John Marshall and his distrust of the prosecution's narrative.

This narrative had several weak spots. Wilkinson's letter to Jefferson warned that Burr would storm New Orleans at the head of seven thousand men. Yet he had been arrested with sixty: enough to make a settlement in Arkansas, absurdly small for invading Mexico or breaking up the Union. The coded letter Wilkinson forwarded did not sound like its supposed author. It was florid; Burr was laconic. And when did Burr willingly write letters?

The muster at Blennerhassett's Island was the "visible transaction" the prosecution would seek to prove was treasonous. But Burr had been hundreds of miles away, in Kentucky, when his men gathered and set off. Marshall's decision in *Ex parte Bollman* gave the prosecution a handle; in defining treason, Marshall had said that "if war be actually levied . . . all those who perform any part, however . . . remote from the scene of the action," were traitors, as much as the men actually bearing arms.

The Jefferson administration now made a monumental effort to assemble "the necessary testimony." One hundred forty witnesses—from anyone who had observed anything suspicious at Blennerhassett's Island to anyone who had ever had a suspicious conversation with Aaron Burr—were called to establish his guilt.

Burr's efforts to defend himself, while smaller in scale, were also impressive. Burr was an excellent trial lawyer; he and Alexander Hamilton had met often in New York City's courts, sometimes arguing against each other, sometimes on the same side. He was assisted by six other lawyers, the most memorable being Luther Martin, defender of Justice Chase. Martin was a mass of peculiarities, beginning with his alcoholism. Like his friend Chase

("Bacon Face"), he had a nickname: "Lawyer Brandy Bottle." Two decades earlier, he had represented Maryland at the Constitutional Convention, where he gave a two-day speech that bored his fellow delegates, then left in disgust without signing. He wore lace ruffles at his wrists, an antiquated fashion, but because he seldom changed them they were ever soiled. Yet he had wide legal knowledge, iron lungs, and passionate devotion to his clients—as with Chase, so now with Burr.

The grand jury sat for a month. The prosecution's case, it became clear, hinged on Wilkinson and his credibility. Was Burr's coded letter Wilkinson's first inkling of such a monstrous plot? Summoned from his New Orleans headquarters, he confronted Burr face-to-face in the House of Delegates. In his memoirs, Wilkinson recalled that Burr looked away, "sinking under the weight of conscious guilt." But a young journalist from New York, Washington Irving, saw in Burr's face only "a slight expression of contempt."

Randolph thought Wilkinson must have been scheming with Burr until the last minute; he "is the only man I ever saw," Randolph wrote, "who was from the bark to the very core a villain." Randolph wanted to indict Wilkinson too, which the grand jury declined to do only by a narrow vote.

Burr enlivened the proceedings by asking the circuit court to issue a subpoena to President Jefferson for the original of the coded letter. Marshall had criticized the executive in *Marbury v. Madison*. Now he was being asked to reach into the executive's desk and retrieve a letter.

Marshall's decision on the motion to subpoena, given on June 13, combined courtesy and duty. He professed the highest regard for Jefferson's office, less only than his regard for the law. "The court," he declared, "would not lend its aid to motions obviously designed to manifest disrespect to the government." But the court's "judgement" had to be guided "by sound legal principles." These gave a defendant "the right of preparing the means to secure . . . a fair and impartial trial." The president was directed to produce the coded letter.

Along the way, Marshall made a slip when he said that the government "expected" the case to end in a guilty verdict. Of course it did; Jefferson had told Congress in January that Burr's guilt was "beyond question." But in a courtroom, prejudgments are not allowed—not even prejudgments about the prejudgments of others. Marshall apologized to the government's lead prosecutor, Hay, for the remark.

Marshall had a larger matter on his conscience: his ruling in *Ex parte Bollman* that "all those who perform any part" in an act of treason were also guilty. Had he defined treason too broadly? He wrote his fellow justices asking their advice.

T HE GRAND JURY indicted Burr and Harman Blennerhassett for treason and high misdemeanor. Their trial began in August. Marshall and Griffin would preside. The foreman of the jury—small world once again—was Edward Carrington, another brother-in-law of Marshall's.

The prosecution began its procession of witnesses. The first two were heroes. William Eaton had conquered Derne, a pirate stronghold on the North African coast, at the head of a force of Marines and native allies in 1805, and Commodore Thomas Truxton had captured a French frigate while serving in the U.S. Navy during the Adams administration. Both men said they had been approached by Burr to take part in his grandiose plans—Eaton said they embraced disunion, Truxton only invading Mexico—though they had nothing to say about Blennerhassett's Island. Next, a handful of locals testified to seeing twenty-some men on the island, with rifles and bullets (not unusual for men intending to settle the frontier).

Burr's lawyers then asked Marshall to stop testimony. If this was the only proof the prosecution had that Burr had levied war against the United States, then no treasonous act had been proved, and further testimony about his designs or hopes was irrelevant. The lawyers argued for days.

At this late date, the relative guilt of Wilkinson and Burr is hard to judge. Each seems to have expected the other to do the lion's share of work toward their joint goal, whatever it was. Wilkinson was the first to guess that his partner would let him down, and so he turned patriot.

Their scheme, however romantic, was unimportant. Both men were operators, out for themselves. But the time of freebooters and freelance adventurers had passed, as the piddling denouement of their enterprise proved. The wars and rebellions of the modern era would be the products of political action or popular sentiment, movements of states or peoples.

What mattered about the conspirators was what they caused Jefferson and Marshall to do.

Thomas Jefferson was determined to hang Aaron Burr and was enraged with anyone who frustrated his determination. He announced Burr's guilt before he was even apprehended. He interviewed Erich Bollmann, when the doctor was first delivered to Washington, under a pledge of confidentiality, then gave Bollmann's statement to the prosecution. He wrote Hay continuously during all phases of the Richmond trial. After one unusually vitriolic speech by Luther Martin, he suggested that Burr's lawyer be indicted as part of Burr's plot.

Why such vindictive, dishonorable, and illegal measures? Burr threatened one of Jefferson's great achievements: doubling the size of the nation without firing a shot. Jefferson, the poet of new beginnings ("it is the Right of the People . . . to institute new Government") had given the people a domain, stretching from the Mississippi to the Rockies, that was a clean slate, a few Spaniards and Frenchmen and numerous Indians excepted. But Burr, a sly pseudo-gentleman from New York, tried to plunge this second Eden into strife.

Jefferson had an extra reason to hate Burr. Jefferson knew that politics was dirty business, but he assumed that the dirt stuck to his enemies—the British, the Federalists. But Burr had been his Republican running mate and vice president. If not for the virtuous unanimity of congressional Republicans in the deadlocked election, Burr might have been the first Republican president. His career seemed to Jefferson a satire on democracy.

To expunge such a menace any steps were justified.

Marshall's antagonist was, as he had been for over six years, Thomas Jefferson. The president and his allies had amputated, purged, and repopulated the judiciary. Armed only with his own mind and the support of a few colleagues, Marshall had accepted the amputation, watched the purge fall short, and combated the makeover by converting Jefferson's appointees. When the opportunity arose, in *Marbury v. Madison,* he had rebuked the administration's high-handedness.

Marshall had no love for Aaron Burr. Yet now Jefferson was bending the law to destroy him.

Marshall's ruling on the defense's motion to stop testimony adhered, as had his earlier rulings, to the constitutional requirements for defining and proving treason: it had to be an act of levying war, proven by "the Testimony of two Witnesses to the same overt Act" (Article III, Section 3). The Constitution had defined it strictly because accusations of treason had been weapons of political warfare throughout English history; "Prosecutions for treason," Benjamin Franklin had observed at the Constitutional Convention, "were generally virulent."

Marshall's ruling—formally, his opinion on the law of treason in *United States v. Burr*—was immense: twenty-five thousand words. *Marbury* had been a monument; this decision was a monstrosity. Marshall made a parade of English legal authorities (Coke, Hale, Foster, Blackstone, East). This was confusing as well as tedious since he used them as often as not to raise difficulties, which he then decided it was unnecessary to untangle in the present case. He spent time parsing his decision in *Ex parte Bollman,* for reasons not apparent to the layman's mind: if no act of levying war had occurred on Blennerhassett's Island—and no solid testimony had established that any had—then it did not matter whether Burr had been "remote from the scene of the action," or holding Blennerhassett's hand.

One passage stood out for clarity and force. "If it be said," said Marshall, "that the advising or procurement of treason is a secret transaction which can scarcely ever be proved in the manner required . . . the answer which will readily suggest itself is, that the difficulty of proving a fact will not justify conviction without proof." In that last clause, Marshall approached his old idol Alexander Pope in concision and wit.

Another passage showed the stress under which Marshall labored, from the pressure the Jefferson administration had brought to bear on the case: "No man is desirous of placing himself in a disagreeable situation. No man is desirous of becoming the peculiar subject of calumny. No man, might he let the bitter cup pass from him without self-reproach, would drain it to the bottom." By comparing himself to Christ at Gethsemane, Marshall made a rare slip into bathos. He recovered and went on.

"But if he has no choice in the case; if there is no alternative presented to him but a dereliction of duty or the opprobrium of those who are denominated the world, he merits the contempt as well as the indignation of his country who can hesitate which to embrace." In this sentence, he spoke with the voice of Captain Marshall, the young volunteer.

He ruled that further testimony would be stopped, since there had been no proof of an overt act of levying war by two witnesses.

THE JURY ACQUITTED Burr of treason the following day. A subsequent trial on the high misdemeanor of invading Mexico also sputtered out. Burr was burned in effigy in Baltimore, along with Marshall and Luther Martin. Jefferson wrote Hay that "this criminal is preserved to become the rallying point of all the disaffected and the worthless of the United States." He wanted the testimony of all the witnesses, called or uncalled, laid before Congress, "that they may provide the proper remedy for the past and the future." What would that be? An amendment to the Constitution redefining treason? Jefferson was so angry he could not say.

And then—nothing. Other crises intervened to distract the president (tensions with Britain, rather than Spain, became much worse). It was also true of him that his wrath could blow over as fast as it could blow up. If this quality was not a virtue, it was at least the softening of a vice.

Marshall wrote a district court judge that the Burr case had been "the most unpleasant . . . which has ever been brought before a judge in this or perhaps in any other country which affected to be governed by laws."

It had been more than unpleasant for Polly Marshall. The trial had sucked up all the air in Richmond and all of John's attention. A woman who had come to dislike company and strangers found herself in a city swarming with them, all focused on Burr, her husband, and their interminable proceedings. After this time, she became a recluse—witty in private, according to Marshall, but unwilling to go out or to receive guests at home.

BURR SPENT SOME years in Europe and more back home in New York. He made no effort to settle in Arkansas. Wilkinson, after his military career ended, served as an envoy to Mexico.

Long after they and Marshall had died, material in foreign archives showed that Wilkinson had been a paid agent of Spain since 1787 and that Burr had asked both Spanish and British diplomats for help in dismembering the United States (they had turned him down). The philosopher Jeremy Bentham, whom Burr befriended while he was in England, recalled Burr telling him that he had planned to become emperor of Mexico, "and if his project had failed [there], he meant to set up for a monarch in the United States."

Courts deal with the cases presented to them; many cases leave a lot out.

Chapter 8

CORRUPTION AND CONTRACTS

Thomas Jefferson's last year in the White House, 1808, was an unhappy one. Britain had been preying on American ships, removing contraband cargo bound for France and deserters from its own navy. (Thomas Nash had been forfeit after a consul's request; now British captains were simply seizing men on the high seas.)

Jefferson's response to these provocations was to stop all American foreign trade. The Embargo, as his policy was known, imposed misery on the commercial East Coast and ate into his popularity.

The Republican Party, however, remained strong. For the election of 1808, the Federalists nominated, as they had in 1804, Marshall's XYZ colleague Charles Cotesworth Pinckney. Federalists in Virginia, however, were so few—"a small and oppressed minority," Marshall described them in a letter to Pinckney—that they felt unable to make any mark except by backing a least-bad Republican. There were two Republicans on offer in Virginia: Secretary of State James Madison and Marshall's old schoolfellow James Monroe. Since Monroe was a long shot (the Republican

Party nationally was for Madison), helping him in Virginia might cause mischief.

Nothing worked. Federalist strength in Congress increased slightly, but Madison swept Virginia and all or most of the electoral votes of eleven other states to follow Jefferson in the White House.

Marshall, however, still dominated the Supreme Court.

At the end of 1809, he performed a lawyerly service for a prominent fellow Federalist. Gouverneur Morris wrote him concerning one of his earliest cases, *Commonwealth v. Randolph*. Nancy Randolph, the defendant's cousin, sister-in-law, and alleged mother of their murdered newborn, had now, after years of social ostracism and poverty, moved to New York and become Morris's housekeeper and bride-to-be—a reversal of fortune as astonishing as any in a novel of Fielding or Smollett. Before Morris tied the knot, he wrote Nancy's former lawyer to ask what reputation she had in Virginia.

Morris cast his request as a party matter. He was "connected with so many worthy" Federalists, Republicans might use his wife "to affix a stigma on any one of us." Marshall told him not to worry. Nancy Randolph had her enemies, but the circumstances of her case "were ambiguous, and rumor, with her usual industry, spread a thousand others which were probably invented by the malignant." Two days after getting Marshall's answer, Gouverneur and Nancy were married.

So the chief justice and the draftsman of the Constitution disposed of gossip, for the good of Federalism.

Shortly thereafter, Marshall took up a case, brewing for several years, that would advance Federalist views of contracts and of the power of states.

W EAKEST AND POOREST of the original thirteen states was Georgia, a colonial-era dumping ground for convicts that, by the end of the eighteenth century, had some coastal rice plantations, one city—Savannah—and debts.

Georgia was rich in one thing: land—thirty-five million backcountry acres, stretching from the Chattahoochee River to the Mississippi. The tract took its name from one of the many streams that wound through it, the Yazoo. If the state could sell the Yazoo country, it would balance its books.

Any purchase would be a speculation. The current residents were Indian tribes; the largest, the Creeks, were led until his death in 1793 by Alexander McGillivray, a half-Scottish chief who had sided with Britain in the Revolution. Spain was a near and perhaps hostile neighbor: besides Texas and Mexico, she owned Florida, whose Gulf Coast panhandle then stretched as far west as Baton Rouge. But land-buying was a mania in early America, especially when the odds were long; if you bought at the bottom, your profits could be enormous.

The State of Georgia sold the Yazoo tract in January 1795 to four land companies formed for the occasion. The price was $500,000 (or 1.5 cents per acre). The well-connected men behind the purchase included two U.S. senators, two congressmen, and Justice James Wilson of the Supreme Court (Bushrod Washington would occupy his seat five years later).

The state legislators who approved the deal were well rewarded for their complaisance; the going rate for a yes vote seems to have been $1,000 (one state representative who voted aye for only $600 explained that he was "not greedy").

One Georgia politician disapproved of the sale. James Jackson had come to Georgia from England as a teenager before the Revolution. He fought in the state militia and was elected in 1789 to the House of Representatives, where he quickly distinguished himself. One of his speeches, against Alexander Hamilton's financial program, was delivered in such a bellowing tone that the Senate, meeting one floor above the House, closed its windows to "keep out the din." Another speech, a defense of slavery against a petition presented by Quakers, inspired a satire by Benjamin Franklin: Franklin put Jackson's arguments in the mouth of a Moslem pirate, endorsing the enslavement of Christians. Jackson himself admitted that he was a man of "violent passions," though he claimed that his "natural good temper" always prevailed.

In March 1795, Jackson began to attack the Yazoo sale. It is possible that he was a disappointed speculator; one of his closest friends had put in an inflated bid of his own, perhaps with the intention of being bought off by the ultimate purchasers. But if speculation fails, outraged virtue sells equally well in the American market, and this was the stance that Jackson now adopted.

The sale, he said, had been an "abominable act," "invalid and unconstitutional." The legislators who approved it had not only been bribed but coerced by threats and bullwhips. A "virtuous minority," which had balked, "were every moment in dread of their lives." The only recourse of the people of Georgia was to elect new representatives, including Jackson himself, who would overturn the sale.

The voters responded favorably, and a Repeal Act, passed in February 1796, declared the sale, and any claims arising from it, null and void. The act of sale was burned in a public ceremony in the state capitol. At the climactic moment, an old man stepped from the crowd and declared that "the fire in which the records of corruption were to be destroyed should come from heaven. . . . He drew from his bosom with trembling hands a sun glass, and in this way burned the papers." More practically, the Repeal Act directed that any mention of the sale be expunged from the state's record books, and any officer of the state who acted as if the sale had been valid be fined $1,000. The new legislators wanted to kill the sale and prevent anyone from trying to resurrect it in a Georgia court.

The Yazoo purchasers, meanwhile, were not idle. As soon as they could, they flipped their tracts. In February 1796, eleven million acres were sold to the New England Mississippi Land Company for over a million dollars—a profit of 650 percent. The New Englanders hoped later to resell, for a similar profit, themselves.

But all potential profits depended on the security of the original sale. The purchasers accordingly sought legal advice, and they went to the top of the profession—former treasury secretary Alexander Hamilton, then practicing law in New York City.

In a trim little opinion of five hundred words, Hamilton gutted the Repeal Act. He simply dismissed the argument, so fervently made by Jackson and his allies, that the sale was invalidated by the corruption that greased it; he would not, he wrote, "pretend . . . to judge of the original merits or demerits of the purchasers."

He then presented reasons why a valid sale could not be undone. Legislatures can make new laws at will; that is their job. But they may not "revoke" a previous "grant of property." To do so would violate "natural justice and social policy." It would be wrong; and committing such a wrong would have pernicious effects (who would trust a state's word, if it could summarily take it back?).

The Repeal Act was not only unjust and unwise; it was unconstitutional, said Hamilton, citing Article I, Section 10: "No State shall . . . pass any . . . Law impairing the Obligation of Contracts." Hamilton knew this clause well, for he was probably responsible for putting it in the Constitution. (There had been a brief and inconclusive discussion of contracts in the home stretch of the Constitutional Convention, but the contract clause first appeared in the final draft, prepared by the Committee of Style, on which Hamilton sat.) The contract clause, he wrote now, "must be equivalent to saying, no state shall pass a law revoking, invalidating, or altering a contract." The original sale was a contract. Therefore, the Repeal Act was unconstitutional, and "the courts of the United States . . . will be likely to pronounce it so."

Hamilton's opinion was published in a pro-Yazoo pamphlet.

This was the voice of Federalism, from its intellectual leader. But the Yazoo purchasers included many northern Republicans. One of the largest shareholders in the New England Mississippi Land Company was Gideon Granger, a Connecticut lawyer who in 1801 became Thomas Jefferson's postmaster general. As such, he was responsible for the efficiency of the mails. But he was also, and even more importantly, responsible for the efficiency of the Republican Party. Doling out postmasterships was one way of rewarding party loyalists; defending the Yazoo purchasers would be another.

In 1803, the Jefferson administration offered a compromise as a pragmatic solution to the Yazoo controversy. Everybody would get something. Georgia would get over a million dollars; the Yazoo purchasers would get five million acres; the federal government would get the other thirty million. All the compromise lacked was the approval of Congress.

Denying it, however, became the passion of representative John Randolph of Roanoke, self-appointed guardian of Republican Party purity. Randolph had many calls on his attention in the Jefferson years—impeaching Justice Chase; serving on Aaron Burr's grand jury. But stopping the Yazoo compromise consumed him. To him, it epitomized amorality and self-dealing: typical for Federalists, unthinkable for good Republicans.

Randolph railed at the deal on the House floor; he accused Granger of bribing members to pass it; at one dinner, he broke a wineglass on a pro-Yazoo congressman's head and threw a bottle at him. Encouraged no doubt by the strange euphony of the word, he made Yazoo an all-purpose epithet. If anyone disagreed with him about anything, he might stare his rival down, point a finger, and declare, "You are a Yazoo man."

Randolph was able, by sheer vehemence, to keep the Yazoo compromise bottled up for years.

Blocked in Congress, the New England Yazoo purchasers turned to the courts for relief. They faced several obstacles. The Repeal Act froze them out of Georgia's courts, while the Eleventh Amendment blocked Georgia from being sued in federal courts by citizens of other states (New England states, for instance). But Article III, Section 2 offered an opening: "The Judicial Power shall extend . . . to Controversies . . . between Citizens of different States." In 1803, Robert Fletcher of New Hampshire sued John Peck of Massachusetts in the Massachusetts Circuit Court. Fletcher had paid Peck $3,000 for fifteen thousand acres of Yazoo land that, Fletcher now claimed, Peck had not rightfully owned. Fletcher accordingly wanted his money back.

The two litigants let their case roll over, from term to term, for several years. Then, in 1807, the Circuit Court ruled for Peck: the original sale was valid, the Repeal Act was not; Fletcher could not recover his money. Fletcher appealed to the Supreme Court, which heard the case in 1809. But there was yet another delay, thanks to a technical error by one of Peck's attorneys. *Fletcher v. Peck* came before the Court for the second, and last, time in February 1810.

Fletcher was represented by Luther Martin, the defender of Justice Chase and Aaron Burr; Peck, by Robert Harper, the man who had published Hamilton's opinion on the case back in 1796, and by Joseph Story, a new man at the Supreme Court bar. Story was a thirty-year-old lawyer from Marblehead, Massachusetts, bespectacled and already balding, with a pleasant face; politically, he was the very sort of man John Randolph deplored—both a former Republican congressman and a paid lobbyist of the New England Mississippi Land Company.

Justices Chase and Cushing missed the case due to ill health. Marshall gave the opinion of the Court.

He began with what he called "a question of much delicacy," which he decided, as he always did with such questions, decisively.

Did the sale of 1795, as Jackson had proclaimed up and down the state, violate Georgia's constitution? Not for any reason that Marshall could find. A judge may not strike down a law "on slight implication and vague conjecture," but only when he "feels a clear and strong conviction" of its "incompatibility" with a constitution. Marshall had struck down a federal law in *Marbury;* in *Fletcher,* he refined the guidelines for doing so.

Next, he reasoned his way through the case as Hamilton had. Was the original sale invalidated by corruption? Marshall began in a tone of saddened idealism: "That corruption should find its way into the government of our infant republics and contaminate the very source of legislation . . . are circumstances most deeply to be deplored." But courts could not be the moral referees of other branches of government: "If the majority of [a] legislature be corrupted, it may be doubted whether it be within the province of the judiciary to control their conduct." Fletcher and Peck, the men now before the Court, were third parties, downstream from the original offense. "It would be indecent, in the extreme" to use their case to assess the level of political honesty in a state.

Was the Repeal Act proper? Could a legislature revoke a sale it had authorized? Doing so, Marshall argued, would be impractical. Legislatures may repeal any law they have made. "But, if an act be done under a law, a succeeding legislature cannot undo it. The past cannot be recalled by the most absolute power." It would also be unjust. "The nature of society and of government . . . prescribed" that "the property of an individual, fairly and honestly acquired, may [not] be seized without compensation." Marshall's argument from natural rights was not as eloquent as those made by his cousin Jefferson, in the Declaration of Independence and elsewhere, but it was equally forthright.

Marshall then turned, as Hamilton had, to the Constitution, and here he came into his own. "The validity" of the Repeal Act "might well be doubted, were Georgia a single sovereign power.

But Georgia . . . is a part of a large empire, she is a member of the American union; and that union has a Constitution, the supremacy of which all acknowledge, and which imposes limits to the legislatures of the several states, which none claim a right to pass."

He turned to Article I, Section 10 and singled out three such limits: "No state shall pass . . . any Bill of Attainder, ex post facto Law, or Law impairing the obligation of Contracts." Bills of attainder imposed penalties on the families of criminals, ex post facto laws criminalized acts that were legal when they were committed; the contract clause was relevant to *Fletcher v. Peck*. Why did the Constitution include such prohibitions? Marshall recalled the atmosphere of the ratification struggle. "The framers" wanted "to shield themselves and their property" from the reckless law-making of the postrevolutionary period. The provisions Marshall cited "may be deemed a bill of rights for the people of each state."

This sweeping argument echoed Hamilton's and went beyond it. When Marshall invoked the Constitution, he also invoked the nation that had adopted it. He made the Constitution the voice of the nation.

He audaciously redefined the Bill of Rights. The first ten amendments, which we know by that name, were not so called in Supreme Court decisions until long after Marshall died. But it was understood at the time they were proposed and debated that they constituted a Bill of Rights. Several of the amendments recalled, or even quoted, provisions in the bills of rights of states, or the English Bill of Rights of 1689. Marshall was now saying that the Constitution already guaranteed rights before the first ten amendments were passed.

Marshall brought his argument to a close: "The state of Georgia was restrained, either by general principles which are common to our free institutions, or by the particular provisions of the Constitution," from passing the Repeal Act.

Fletcher's complaint against Peck's sale was dismissed.

Justice Johnson, in a concurring opinion, joined Marshall in rejecting the Repeal Act, but in his conclusion, he introduced an acrid note. "I have been very unwilling to proceed to the decision of this cause at all. It appears to me to bear strong evidence . . . of being a mere feigned case."

Johnson was right that it had been arranged beforehand. Fletcher was a land speculator in his native state; Peck, a director of the New England Mississippi Land Company. The two men had not pushed their case when it seemed that Congress might ratify a Yazoo deal; only after John Randolph had blocked that option did they move. In the twentieth century, it was discovered that Fletcher's original filing was altered to make sure that the value of the acreage he had been sold exceeded the legal minimum necessary for a lawsuit to be appealed to the Supreme Court. (Congress had set this standard to winnow out frivolous suits.) Collusion may have extended to Fletcher's lawyer, Martin, who made what was for him an unusually weak argument. He also appeared so drunk one day that the Court had to adjourn until he sobered up.

Marshall himself suspected the case's artificial genesis. When it was first argued before the Court in 1809, he had remarked that it seemed "manifestly made up for the purpose of getting the Court's judgment on all the points" at issue.

Fletcher was not the first arranged case to have been brought before the Court. Daniel Hylton's 1796 challenge to the constitutionality of the carriage tax had been welcomed by the federal government and by Hamilton, the tax's author. To bring Hylton's penalty over the legal minimum for an appeal, he and the government agreed, absurdly, that he owned 125 carriages. (No one in the English-speaking world, except possibly George III, owned 125 carriages.) The Court would hear other arranged cases during Marshall's tenure. Johnson's language—*mere feigned case*—makes *Fletcher* sound frivolous, but it and other such cases were arranged precisely to settle important points.

Johnson dropped his objection as soon as he made it. "My confidence . . . in the respectable gentlemen who have been engaged for the parties, has induced me to abandon my scruples." Johnson trusted Harper, Story, and Martin (drunk or sober) not to trifle with him.

The decision of the Court heartened congressional supporters of the Yazoo deal. Randolph continued to fight them until he lost his own seat in an intra-party dispute about foreign policy. In 1814, Congress finally passed Jefferson's compromise.

Jefferson's political instincts had been ratified, though he still complained, in retirement at Monticello, of the "twistifications" of Marshall's reasoning in *Fletcher v. Peck*. Well might he complain. Marshall had guaranteed New England Republicans a return on their investments, and he had enabled the party, at the cost of enraging ideological diehards like John Randolph, to broaden its base nationally. In doing so, however, he had chastened the power of the states; *Fletcher* ostentatiously respected the acts of one Georgia legislature but brushed away those of another. And he had also defended contracts, the cement of industry and commerce.

Jefferson and his allies were not antibusiness per se; the Republican Party appealed to new men, including entrepreneurs and investors. Granger, Story, and the New England Yazoo purchasers typified that class. But Republicanism also appealed to populists and demagogues like James Jackson, who believed that the people had the power to undo contracts made by bad people (i.e., the demagogues' enemies of the moment). In defending contracts, Marshall (and Hamilton) wanted to instill in Americans a sense of discipline and responsibility: let the buyer beware, because all sales are final.

Jefferson was not wrong to think that Marshall would continue to rule in this fashion.

Section III

MAGISTERIAL CHIEF JUSTICE

Chapter 9

A SMALL COLLEGE

J AMES MADISON SHOULD HAVE BEEN A PRESIDENT MORE TO John Marshall's liking than Thomas Jefferson. Madison had been the Constitution's champion at the Virginia Ratifying Convention, and Marshall ever after acknowledged his "superior talents." But the all-dominating issue of Madison's first term was America's steady slide to war with Britain, which he approved, and which Marshall and all Federalists bitterly opposed.

Britain and Napoleonic France had been at war since 1803. Both countries had seized American ships bound for their enemies, although Britain, with the world's greatest navy, had seized the most. Jefferson's attempted remedy, the Embargo, had hurt only Americans, not their tormentors, and had been repealed by his own party after a year. Congress then offered to impose a new embargo on the enemy of whichever belligerent stopped molesting the United States first. In 1810, France announced that it would meet Congress's terms—dishonestly, for its depredations continued. But Madison seized on France's supposed change of heart to focus American anger on the Republican Party's ancient enemy, Britain. Congress declared war in June 1812, with every Federalist voting against it.

In July, Marshall wrote a frankly political letter to Robert Smith. The recipient was as interesting as Marshall's subject. Smith's brother, Samuel, was a senator from Maryland. Although Samuel was a Republican, he spoke for Baltimore's merchants, who resented the party's trade restrictions. Robert himself had served as Madison's secretary of state until the preceding year, when Madison fired him for incompetence. Marshall unburdened himself to this well-connected, disaffected Republican with both political and personal grudges against the administration.

"Although I have for several years forborne to intermingle with those questions which agitate and excite the feelings of party, it is impossible that I could be inattentive to passing events." He dismissed France's pretensions to friendliness as "offensive and contemptuous." He dreaded war. "All minor considerations should be waived. . . . All who wish peace ought to unite."

Unite for what? Benjamin Stoddert, another Marylander who had been John Adams's secretary of the navy, had an idea. The year 1812 was an election year, and "there is," Stoddert wrote, "but one man to be thought of as the candidate . . . of all who were against the war. That man is John Marshall." A Marshall candidacy could break the Republicans' lock on Virginia, and, with the votes of northern Federalists, take the White House.

Stoddert pitched his idea to Federalists in Maryland and New York and published it in a Georgetown newspaper.

Marshall's personal popularity had won him elections in Richmond, despite the political opinions of his neighbors. But to buck the sentiment of the entire state was a hopeless prospect, and Marshall, however tempted he may have been by the enthusiasm of such as Stoddert, knew it. He ended his letter to Smith with resignation. "It is not however for me to indulge these feelings."

Federalists instead backed New York governor DeWitt Clinton, a renegade Republican willing to run with their support.

Clinton made a strong showing and Federalists picked up seats in the House, but Madison was reelected and the war continued.

Marshall the patriot had put himself in a false position. Britain's behavior on the high seas had been more offensive and contemptuous than France's; the British governor general of Canada maintained an arc of Indian allies, from the Shawnees in Indiana to the Creeks in the Yazoo country, who threatened the peace of the American frontier. But years of combating French arrogance and Republican fecklessness had narrowed Marshall's vision.

One consequence of the war and its long run-up was a string of Court cases involving ships that had fallen afoul of America's restrictive trade laws. (The case with the most winning name was *United States v. 1960 Bags of Coffee*—cargoes as well as the ships that carried them could be brought before the Court.) This load of litigation, involving questions of fact, U.S. law, and maritime law, sharpened the Court's analytical skills: a side benefit of the country's distress.

MARSHALL ESCAPED THE perplexities of war with a journey into the wilderness. The Virginia legislature tapped the chief justice to survey a route for a canal linking the James River and a tributary of the Ohio.

The assignment was a plunge into his family's past; his father's first job had been surveying for Lord Fairfax. It was also a plunge into George Washington's past. Before he became president, Washington was obsessed with trans-Appalachian canals; one guest at Mount Vernon reported that Washington's enthusiasm "completely infected me with the canal mania."

Marshall and his party set out in September 1812. Their trip over the mountains took six weeks (during which Marshall turned fifty-seven). His report, submitted in December, had touches of an adventure story, with glimpses of "lofty and ragged mountains," "awful and discouraging" rapids, and "the labor of removing stones" from streambeds "and of dragging the boat over those which could not be removed." Yet Marshall breathed a spirit of optimism. A canal would "cement more closely the union of the eastern with the western states" (perhaps Marshall remembered the intrigues of Burr and Wilkinson). It would benefit the entire nation: "By the augmentation of the wealth and population of a part . . . the whole would be more powerful" (an old Federalist theme: "The veins of commerce in every part" of the United States, Alexander Hamilton had written, "will be replenished [by] a free circulation of the commodities of every part").

It was all in vain. New York had already leaped ahead of Virginia. An alliance of local Federalists and Republicans, led by Gouverneur Morris and DeWitt Clinton, had planned a canal to link Lake Erie to the Atlantic via the Mohawk and Hudson Rivers. Their pathway to the interior was flatter and easier, and their state, thanks to its innovative banking sector, was better able to pay for a great public project. The produce of the Ohio Valley would flow into New York City, not Virginia.

Marshall's dreams of infrastructure were as misguided as the efforts to draft him into partisan politics. His service to his country would be done on the bench.

His journey to the mountains had not interfered with his circuit duty in Raleigh and Richmond or with the 1813 session of the Court. John Jay and Oliver Ellsworth had not scrupled to cross the Atlantic during their tenures as chief justice. Marshall knew where his most important duty lay.

TWO NEW JUSTICES had joined the Court on the eve of the War of 1812, bringing the number of Republican appointees up to five, out of seven. Yet both became dependable Marshall allies, one discreetly, the other spectacularly.

Justice Chase, age seventy, had died in June 1811 and was succeeded by another Marylander, Gabriel Duvall. Three years older than Marshall, Duvall had been a Jefferson elector in his first two presidential runs; after Jefferson won, he had given Duvall a job in the Treasury Department.

If Republicans expected him to buck the current of the Court, however, they were mistaken. Duvall was a quiet man—he told one of his fellow justices that he had never lost a night's sleep in his life—who became quieter as he aged and deafness set in. Marshall praised him for his "cordiality." He was one of those justices, like Livingston, Todd, and Johnson (except when he was complaining about it), who accepted the Marshall Court as it was.

Justice Cushing had died, age seventy-eight, in September 1810, but finding a successor for him was an onerous process. Two men that Madison nominated turned the job down; a third was rejected by the Senate.

Former president Jefferson took a lively interest in filling the vacancy. He had, he thought, a personal stake; he was being sued for the stupendous sum of $100,000 by Edward Livingston, a former political ally in New Orleans, from whom the federal government had, at Jefferson's direction, seized a swath of built-up alluvial land along the Mississippi River. (Livingston had also been an ally of Burr's, which may have prompted the seizure.) Under the legal doctrine of that day, Jefferson himself could be held personally liable for actions he had ordered, and Livingston had brought a suit in Marshall's Richmond circuit. There, Jefferson believed—or on appeal to the Supreme Court, unless a loyal Republican could be appointed—Marshall would surely rule so as to bankrupt him. Marshall's "mind," Jefferson wrote, is "of that gloomy malignity which will never let him forego the opportunity of satiating it on a victim." Marshall, in fact, let the opportunity go; he dismissed the suit on the grounds that the Richmond circuit lacked jurisdiction.

But Jefferson wanted a Republican appointee for the good of the country as well as himself. When Madison, after three strikes, considered naming Joseph Story, the Yazoo lawyer who had since become speaker of the Massachusetts House, Jefferson was alarmed. He questioned Story's Republicanism (Story had been lukewarm on the Embargo); he tried to warn the young man about Marshall. "When conversing with Marshall, I never admit anything," Jefferson lectured. "So great is his sophistry you must never give him an affirmative answer or you will be forced to grant his conclusion. Why, if he were to ask me if it were daylight or not, I'd reply, 'Sir, I don't know. I can't tell.'" But Madison, with war looming, needed all the goodwill in New England he could muster, and he sent Story's name to the Senate, which promptly confirmed him in November 1811.

Story became one of the most active and prolific justices in Supreme Court history. He wrote voluminously and interested himself in every aspect of the law: legal education (he taught at Harvard), legal journals, publishing and publicizing Supreme Court decisions. He was busy, gregarious, and garrulous. His love of his job shone in a letter he wrote his eight-year-old son from Washington:

"Now you will ask what I am doing in this City—I will tell you. I believe you know that I am what they call a Judge, and that I sit in a court room to hear lawyers . . . well—six other Judges sit with me, and after we have heard all they have to say, we then tell them what we think ought to be done; and then it is done—and this is very hard work, for sometimes they puzzle us with very odd and strange questions."

Above all, Story loved John Marshall. "I love his laugh," he wrote after hearing him for the first time as a Yazoo lobbyist. "I am in love with his character, positively in love," he wrote at the end of Marshall's life. The difference in their intelligence—Story's, restless, staccato, incessant; Marshall's, slow and massive—and the difference in their ages—twenty-four years—made for a filial relationship.

Marshall appreciated having such a disciple. They functioned as a team—on the bench, as a legal team; off it, sometimes as a comic team. It was an established custom of the Court that the justices could have wine at their boardinghouse dinners only if it were raining (evidently to cheer themselves up). Marshall would ask "Brother Story" to look out the window and say what the weather was. If Story reported that the sun was shining, Marshall would answer, "Our jurisdiction extends over so large a territory . . . that it must be raining somewhere." Evidently, Jefferson was right about Marshall and daylight.

Even as Marshall was a paternal figure for Story, so the younger man was an auxiliary son to Marshall. In 1800 and 1805, Polly had given birth to two boys who lived—their last children. Marshall gave them and all his sons good educations, sending his two eldest to Princeton and the rest to Harvard. When they entered adulthood, he gave them farms in Fauquier County and slaves to work them. Yet none would be as accomplished as their father. The most problematic was his namesake, John Jr., who would be kicked out of Harvard for "immoral and dissolute conduct." After that, Marshall got him a job at a Philadelphia merchant house, which did not work out either. John Jr.'s problem was chronic drunkenness. He evidently imitated his father's conviviality too literally. Marshall thought that his father, Thomas, had been his "only intelligent companion" while growing up; Story could be the intelligent companion of his maturity that his own children could not supply.

As a justice, Story performed a service for the Marshall family when he gave the Court's opinion in *Martin v. Hunter's Lessee,* an 1816 case spawned by a still-unresolved claim to the Fairfax Grant. Although the case became an important jurisdictional clash between federal and state courts, the Marshalls' stake in it was relatively small—a 788-acre parcel in the northern Shenandoah Valley. John Marshall recused himself from the case, though he advised Story on his opinion, and "concurred in every word."

Among the legal subjects that Story interested himself in was reporting the Court's decisions. In 1803, William Cranch, John Adams's son-in-law on the District of Columbia circuit, had taken over the job from Alexander Dallas. Like Dallas, he published his reports on his own, as a private venture (he complained that doing so had cost him $1,000). His volumes, like Dallas's, were late and incomplete. Story lobbied Congress to create a salaried post, reporter for the court. In 1817, the job went to Story's candidate, Henry Wheaton, a lawyer and sometime journalist, who better understood deadlines.

Wheaton was hampered by the fact that while the decisions of the justices were written down, the arguments of the lawyers were not. He had to take notes himself or ask the lawyers for summaries; if that failed, he would, like Thucydides, write up an argument "as it ought to have been argued."

The Court at last left the meanly furnished committee room in which it had met since 1801. In 1810, as the Capitol neared completion, it was assigned a chamber beneath that of the Senate. This room was furnished with mahogany tables, six stoves, seven chairs for the justices, and nineteen yards of carpeting for their chairs' seats. In 1814, the British occupied Washington and burned its public buildings. The Court became a refugee, meeting first in the house of its clerk, then in a meager room in a still-standing portion of the Capitol. But in 1819, it was restored to its re-created quarters. Attending its sessions became something of a social occasion. Good lawyers were good performers, and the high society of Washington, such as it was, came to hear them. On one occasion, counsel stopped speaking when Dolley Madison and a party of ladies arrived and recapped the argument for their benefit.

The Supreme Court had acquired somewhat impressive chambers and somewhat complete records of its doings. It had esprit de corps. It had Marshall. Now it would enjoy an unusual thing—stability. From 1812 to 1823, the personnel of the Court did not change. (The only comparable period was 1994–2005, between the retirement of Justice Blackmun and the death of Chief Justice Rehnquist.)

The country changed. In 1815, the war with Britain ended in what Americans called victory. And who could blame them? Despite many disasters, the nation that had beaten Napoleon had not beaten them. The army that burned Washington was repulsed from Baltimore. British fleets were beaten on Lake Erie and Lake Champlain. Britain's Indian allies were destroyed; a British army of hardened veterans was mauled before New Orleans.

The war destroyed the Federalist Party. Friends and allies of Marshall—Timothy Pickering, Gouverneur Morris—had been so demented by their opposition to the war that they had hoped for defeat and expected the secession of a purified Federalist north. (If Marshall ever challenged their opinions, no hint of it survives.) Peace with victory mocked every Federalist prediction. Federalists had nothing to say, and no one to hear them if they had.

As a political force, Federalism had failed. James Monroe, running to succeed Madison in 1816, carried all but three states; four years later, running for reelection, he would win all but one electoral vote.

But Federalist principles still had value. So John Marshall thought. As the last Federalist left standing, he would apply them to the country's problems.

A NEW HAMPSHIRE politician, William Plumer, exemplified one possible response to the collapse of the Federalist Party: he switched sides. He had gone to the Senate as a Federalist in

1802, where he took a hard line, dismissing Jefferson as an "infidel"; Burr, after the death of Hamilton, as a "murderer"; and Marshall's careful testimony in the trial of Justice Chase as cowardly.

But the increasing un-patriotism of his party as war approached caused him to join the Republicans, who in gratitude elected him governor. (In Massachusetts, John Quincy Adams, eldest son of Marshall's patron, had made the same switch, for the same reason.) In 1816, Plumer's new position and his new principles brought him into a confrontation with Dartmouth College.

Dartmouth's first president, the Reverend Eleazar Wheelock, had begun his career as an educator in Connecticut, training Christian Indians to become evangelists. His first pupil, a Mohegan named Samson Occom, toured Britain in 1766–7, where his preaching so impressed George III and the 2nd Earl of Dartmouth (nicknamed "Psalmsinger" for his piety) that they gave money to support Wheelock's efforts. In 1769, Wheelock opened a second institution, a college for white students, in Hanover, New Hampshire, which named itself Dartmouth, even though the earl disapproved of Wheelock's new focus. Wheelock chose as its motto *Vox clemantis in deserto,* "a voice crying in the wilderness" (from Isaiah 40:3 and John 1:23). The college's royal charter provided for a president—Wheelock—and twelve trustees, who would choose the professors, their own successors, and future presidents. When Wheelock died in 1779, the trustees tapped his son John to replace him.

The college was staunchly Calvinist and, once America achieved independence and partisanship, staunchly Federalist. Still there was internal dissension. John Wheelock was a Presbyterian; most of the professors and the trustees were Congregationalists (the two churches were both children of Calvin, but Presbyterianism had a more hierarchical organization). A majority of the trustees came to resent the younger Wheelock as a dynast. In 1815, they fired him and brought in a new president. Wheelock turned for help to Governor Plumer, who was happy to assist.

The governor asked the state legislature, dominated by fellow Republicans, to "render this important institution more useful to mankind." This they did by passing a law that changed its name from Dartmouth College to Dartmouth University, increased the number of its trustees from twelve to twenty-one, and set over them a board of overseers, all the newcomers to be picked by the state government.

Plumer saw himself as opening the college to all points of view. "I would select those men only for office who are best qualified, without regard to the religious sect or political party to which they are attached," he explained blandly. But opening a Federalist institution to Republicans would make it more Republican—in effect, changing (and controlling) its point of view.

From his aerie in Monticello, Jefferson wrote Plumer, cheering him on. "The idea that institutions established for the use of the nation, cannot be touched nor modified, even to make them answer their end . . . may perhaps be a salutary provision against the abuses of a monarch, but is most absurd against the nation itself." Monarchs were bad, but the nation, especially when it was governed by Republicans, could do no wrong.

John Wheelock became president of the university. William Woodward, secretary and treasurer of the old college, stuck by him. The professors and students who rejected the new order moved to a hall over a store in a nearby building, where they continued to hold classes.

The old trustees, meanwhile, sued Woodward for Dartmouth's charter, seal, and record books. So the struggle became a case in court. In 1817, New Hampshire's Superior Court of Appeals ruled for Woodward. Dartmouth, it held, was a "public corporation"; education was "too intimately connected with the public welfare and prosperity" to be left "in the hands of a few." Therefore, the State of New Hampshire had been within its rights to take Dartmouth over. The trustees appealed to the Supreme Court, which heard the case in March 1818.

The lead lawyer for the trustees was a Dartmouth graduate (class of 1801), Daniel Webster. He had been elected to the House of Representatives as a Federalist in 1812; he would become, after moving to Massachusetts, one of the greatest of all senators. At this stage in his life—age thirty-six—he was making his mark as a lawyer.

Physically, Webster was striking rather than attractive. He had a large head, black hair and eyebrows, black eyes, and a dark complexion; his childhood nickname was Black Dan. When he spoke, he was slow to get going, but once he did he could be overpowering, even frightening. The English author Thomas Carlyle compared his eyes to "anthracite furnaces needing only to be blown. . . . I have not traced so much of silent berserker rage . . . in any other man."

Webster made a masterly argument, logical and passionate by turns. When he gave it to Henry Wheaton to be printed, he left out the peroration, dismissing it as "stuff and nonsense," but a man who had heard it when he was young recalled it three decades later. After finishing his arguments, Webster had paused, then spoke directly to Chief Justice Marshall. "Sir, you may destroy this little institution; it is weak; it is in your hands. . . . It is, sir, as I have said, a small college. And yet, there are those who love it."

Did Webster actually say this? No one else who was present remembered it, though two eyewitnesses recalled the courtroom being deadly silent or in tears as Webster concluded.

The day after arguments were finished, Marshall announced that the case would be carried over to the 1819 term, since the justices disagreed or had not formed opinions.

Webster then showed his second great skill, as a juridical politician, distributing copies of his argument throughout the northeast. One went to James Kent, a New York judge widely respected in legal circles. Kent had at first been persuaded by the judgment of the New Hampshire Superior Court, but Webster's argument swung him to the side of the trustees. Kent shared his new view of the case with Justices Johnson, who was traveling in New York, and Livingston. Webster also sent multiple copies of his argument to Justice Story, who had of course already heard it, but written reminders never hurt. Story needed no reminding, for, although he was an old friend of Governor Plumer's, he was already on the trustees' side.

Dartmouth's new regime, alarmed by Webster's eloquence, now hired a lawyer who was then even more famous, William Pinkney of Baltimore. When the Supreme Court next met in February 1819, Pinkney planned to move that the case be reargued—not an unusual request when justices were still in doubt—and he spent an entire week with a Dartmouth official to master every detail of its history. But on the first morning of the new term, before Pinkney could speak, Marshall announced that the justices had made their decisions, and he began reading his own opinion.

Trustees of Dartmouth College v. Woodward was another moderately long Marshall decision—almost nine thousand words. There is some repetition and hairsplitting in the late middle of it, but it moves clearly toward its conclusions. Marshall "reasoned along from step to step," wrote Webster, "in his own peculiar way." Not *peculiar* in the sense of strange but *peculiar* to Marshall himself: stating principles, and "work[ing] them into a close, connected, and very able argument."

Marshall began with his by now customary invocation of "delicacy": he had under judgment a state law and a state superior court decision, the latter marked by "diligence," "ability, " and "integrity." He proceeded to sweep them all away.

The question before the Court was whether New Hampshire had violated the contract clause of the Constitution, Article I, Section 10: "No State shall . . . pass any . . . Law impairing the Obligation of Contracts." Some contracts, Marshall admitted, were clearly outside its purview; states could write divorce laws and alter or abolish their own agencies. The contracts protected by the Constitution were those "which respect property" and "confer rights."

Did Dartmouth's 1769 charter fall under those categories? Marshall described the college as "a private eleemosynary institution" (*eleemosynary* means *charitable*, from the same root as the word *alms*). Its endowment came from private individuals; even George III and the Earl of Dartmouth contributed as themselves, not as officers of the state.

Did its charitable purpose—education—bring it, as Plumer and Jefferson thought, under the control of the state? "That education is an object of national concern, and a proper subject of legislation," wrote Marshall, "all admit." But, he went on, "is education altogether in the hands of government? Does every teacher of youth become a public officer, and do donations for the purposes of education necessarily become public property . . . ?" To ask the question in such a fashion was to dispose of it. Marshall's query was its own reductio ad absurdum.

Did the very fact of incorporation give the state an entrée into Dartmouth's affairs? Here Marshall's opinion became subtler. He defined a corporation as "an artificial being," possessed of "individuality" and "immortality." It was artificial because it was "a creature of law"; it had individuality because it performed actions that the individuals who made it wanted done; it had "immortality" because it survived its creators and its employees. Despite the state's role in setting up a corporation, "it is no more a state

Marshall served under George Washington at Valley Forge in the winter of 1777–78. *(Museum of the American Revolution)*

Washington signed the Constitution in September 1787. Marshall supported ratification at the Virginia Ratifying Convention. *(National Archives)*

Marshall and Alexander Hamilton were both at the Battle of Monmouth, 1778 (Hamilton wears the feathered hat).

(Washington Rallying the Troops at Monmouth by Emanuel Leutze, 1853, on display at University of California–Berkeley. Photo by Keegan Houser.)

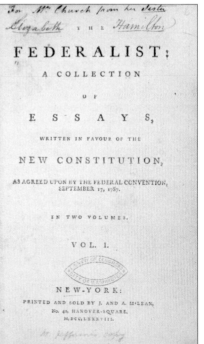

Marshall ordered an early printing of the *Federalist*, Hamilton's pro-Constitution PR campaign.

(Library of Congress)

Thomas Jefferson and Marshall were second cousins,
once removed. They detested each other.

(Metropolitan Museum of Art)

Charles-Maurice de Talleyrand-Périgord, wily French diplomat, dueled diplomatically with Marshall. *(Metropolitan Museum of Art)*

As president, Andrew Jackson opposed
Marshall as strongly as Jefferson, and more successfully.

John Marshall, in middle and
old age: at fifty-three …

(Library of Congress)

… and at seventy-five.

*(Chester Harding [American,
1792–1886], John Marshall
[1830], oil on canvas, Boston
Athenæum)*

Mary (Polly) Marshall. John called her "the solace of my life." *(Courtesy of Preservation Virginia)*

The Georgetown home of William Marbury, Federalist (now the Ukrainian Embassy). *(Jibran Khan)*

Justice Samuel Chase, Marshall's colleague, impeached by
Jefferson's allies in Congress. *(New York Public Library)*

Aaron Burr was
prosecuted for treason
by the Jefferson
administration.

(New York Public Library)

The seal of Dartmouth College, established in 1769.

(Seal of Dartmouth College in the College's Collis Center. Photograph by Kane5187.)

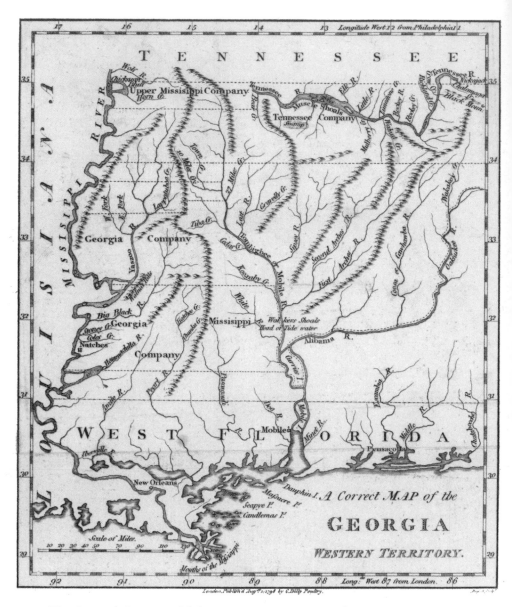

The State of Georgia sold the Yazoo country to speculators,
then annulled the sale.

*(A Correct Map of the Georgia Western Territory,
courtesy of the Birmingham Public Library)*

A note of the second Bank of the United States.

(Courtesy of National Numismatic Collection, National Museum of American History)

Robert Fulton's steamboat, also known as *Clermont*.

*("Robert Fulton's 'Clermont,' First Vessel Ever Propelled by Steam."
From the New York Public Library.)*

Was the slave trade against the law of nations,
as well as the law of nature?

(Library of Congress)

How debtors were treated before the advent of
bankruptcy laws. *(Metropolitan Museum of Art)*

Sequoyah, inventor of the Cherokees' unique system of writing.

Dred Scott, the subject of
Chief Justice Roger Taney's most famous ruling.

(Pictorial Press / Alamy Stock Photo)

Abraham Lincoln's first inauguration, sworn in by Taney.

(Bettmann / Getty Images)

instrument than a natural person exercising the same powers would be."

Was the State of New Hampshire entitled to control Dartmouth because it was located there? Marshall dismissed the idea. "The particular interests of New Hampshire never entered the mind[s] of the donors." They were interested in educating youth; Eleazar Wheelock might have stayed in Connecticut or relocated to Vermont for all they cared.

Marshall, more audaciously, dismissed the intentions of the framers of the Constitution. "It is more than possible," he wrote, that the authors of the contract clause had other contracts in mind besides colonial-era college charters. (Marshall knew from his own memory what those contracts had been: colonial-era debts, which Americans had been loath to pay.) Marshall went beyond originalism to the text; if "the case" now before the Court was "within the words of the rule," it "must be within its operation likewise." The framers had their intentions, but the words in which they expressed them might give rise to new, different intentions. The originalism of the Constitution's history and the originalism of its words could diverge. In *Dartmouth,* Marshall followed the words.

Marshall disposed of a few more points. Was Dartmouth's charter tainted because it had been issued by a king? Marshall said no; Eleazar Wheelock was the prime mover, not George III; he had picked the original trustees, and they had picked their own successors. Had New Hampshire, in the language of the contract clause, "impaired" the charter by changing it? Marshall answered yes indeed; under the law passed in 1816, "the will of the state is substituted for the will of the donors. . . . This system is totally changed."

Marshall found the state's acts "repugnant to the Constitution," and reversed the state court's judgment.

His fellow justices offered an unusual number of opinions—perhaps because of their months apart from each other—though the majority agreed with Marshall's. Washington and Story wrote their own opinions; Livingston concurred with all three, and Johnson concurred with Marshall's. Duvall dissented silently; Todd was absent due to illness.

When news of the Court's decision reached Hanover, the townspeople fired celebratory cannon; the administrators of the university gracelessly ceded the chapel and the school's lone building to the college. Governor Plumer, who found the decision "unfortunate," retired from politics that June. Years later, when Plumer was ninety years old, the Sons of New Hampshire honored him with a banquet, at which he was toasted by Senator Daniel Webster.

In *Fletcher v. Peck,* Marshall had defended contracts by invoking both natural rights ("general principles common to our free institutions") and the contract clause ("particular provisions of our Constitution"). In the *Dartmouth* case, he relied on the contract clause alone, giving it all the force a votary of natural rights might wish.

Marshall was not privy to Governor Plumer's correspondence with Thomas Jefferson. If he had been, he might have taken satisfaction from defying one of Jefferson's most dearly held beliefs. After writing Plumer that republican nations did not need to be protected against the abuses of monarchs, Jefferson went on: "Lawyers and priests"—by which he meant all Christian clergy, favorite villains of his—"suppose that preceding generations held the earth more freely than we do; had a right to impose laws on us, unalterable by ourselves; and that we, in like manner, can make laws, and impose burthens on future generations, which they will have no right to alter: in fine that the earth belongs to the dead, and not the living."

Jefferson here echoed a passionate letter he had written over a quarter century earlier to his dearest friend, James Madison, in which he had wrestled with the obligations of generations over time. "I set out on . . . ground which I suppose to be self-evident, 'that the earth belongs in usufruct to the living;' that the dead have neither powers nor rights over it." (*In usufruct* is a legal phrase meaning *for the use of.*) "The portion occupied by an individual ceases to be his when himself ceases to be, and reverts to the society." Not so fast, said Marshall; the living can create corporations, artificial immortal beings, to carry their will, backed by their donations, into the future. Jefferson thought he was siding with life against death; Marshall thought he was defending rights against power.

Marshall wrote that the founders might not have been thinking about colonial-era college charters when they wrote the contract clause. Was he thinking about the blizzard of business corporations that would alight on America in the next few decades when he wrote his *Dartmouth* decision? By 1830, there would be 1,900 business corporations in New England alone. The *Dartmouth* decision did not start the torrent, but it blessed it.

Scholars debate how much Marshall, a sixty-three-year-old man who had spent most of his life on farms or in courtrooms, knew of America's economic ferment. Maybe little. But Marshall was an admirer of Alexander Hamilton; Hamilton, who may have midwifed the contract clause, had been eager to jump-start American business. Many Federalists were, as Jefferson complained, lawyers and priests. But some of them saw, and willed, America's economic future.

The same month that the Court decided *Dartmouth,* it would hear arguments on a centerpiece of Hamilton's handiwork.

Chapter 10

BANKERS AND EMBEZZLERS

J OHN MARSHALL HAD COVERED ALEXANDER HAMILTON'S financial program, and the fights it provoked, in his *Life of Washington*.

After pushing for the federal government to assume the debts of the states, Hamilton called in 1790 for the creation of a national bank. The Bank of the United States would receive an initial infusion of government credit and provide the government short-term loans to cover its operations. But it would be run as a private institution, guided not by politicians but by the self-interest of its directors. The Bank would be in Philadelphia, with a twenty-year charter.

Thomas Jefferson and James Madison opposed the Bank as unnecessary and unconstitutional. It was unnecessary, they argued, because loans from existing banks and taxes could supply all the federal government's needs. It was unconstitutional because chartering a bank was not one of the enumerated powers of Congress in Article I, Section 8.

Hamilton pointed to the utility of public banks abroad, especially in England and Holland, and argued that the last of Congress's enumerated powers—"To make all Laws which shall be necessary and proper for carrying into Execution the foregoing

Powers"—justified chartering one here. The Constitution permitted Congress to collect taxes, borrow money, regulate interstate commerce, and pay armies and navies—all tasks that a Bank would make easier.

Marshall, in his biography of Washington, described the dispute as it played out in Congress, which passed a bank bill in February 1791, and in Washington's cabinet, where Jefferson urged the president to exercise his veto, and Hamilton rebutted with a long countermemo defending his brainchild. The debate, wrote Marshall, "was supported on both sides with ability, and by that ardor which was naturally excited by the importance" of the contest. Marshall's discussion was detailed and evenhanded; the only sign of his own preference was that, in a long footnote, he expanded his summary of Madison's and Jefferson's arguments but quoted several pages of Hamilton's memo word for word.

Washington heeded Hamilton, and the Bank of the United States was chartered in March 1791 and eventually housed in a handsome neoclassical building on Third Street, a few blocks from Independence Hall. After the capital moved to Washington, the Bank remained in Philadelphia.

When Jefferson became president in 1801, he considered abolishing Hamilton's financial system, even as he pared back the judiciary. He asked his treasury secretary, Albert Gallatin, to comb the government's books for proof of fiscal skullduggery (he believed Hamilton had been crooked as well as misguided). Gallatin reported back that Hamilton "made no blunders, committed no frauds," and left "the most perfect system ever formed." Although the Republicans slashed taxes and military spending, reversing Hamilton's and Washington's policies, they kept the machinery of Hamilton's system intact.

As the 1811 expiration of the Bank's charter approached, Gallatin lobbied for it to be renewed. President Madison had by then also come to support the Bank. But his and Jefferson's old arguments from twenty years earlier still had power in the Republican Party. When the Senate split evenly on the question of recharter, Vice President George Clinton (DeWitt's uncle) broke the tie in the negative on the grounds that "the power to create corporations is not expressly granted" by the Constitution.

When the Madison administration subsequently declared war on the world's greatest superpower, it had no means to pay for it. At the nadir of the War of 1812, the government had to scrape by on loans from wealthy immigrants—Stephen Girard, a one-eyed French merchant in Philadelphia, and John Jacob Astor, a German fur trader in New York. After the war ended, Girard and Astor urged the creation of a second Bank of the United States.

Congress created the new national bank in April 1816, and it began operations the following year. Girard was one of the directors; the Bank picked as its president William Jones, a Republican politician. Headquartered, like its predecessor, in Philadelphia, it opened branches in fourteen states and Washington, DC.

When Hamilton envisioned the first Bank, there were only three other banks in the country. By 1816, there were almost 250. Local banks and their backers feared the second Bank's competition.

Gallatin concluded that Hamilton made no blunders, but the second Bank made several. Jones, who had been an able secretary of the navy under Madison, turned out to be a poor financier. He began his tenure with a policy of easy credit, extending loans via the Bank's branches. Girard, the Bank's largest stockholder, thought this reckless and left the board of directors in disgust. In the summer of 1818, deciding that he had gone too far, Jones suddenly tightened credit, causing a financial panic.

The Bank was attacked on several fronts, even before the full measure of Jones's incompetence was revealed. Two brand-new states, Indiana and Illinois, wrote provisions in their constitutions forbidding banks not chartered by themselves from operating within their borders. Kentucky and Ohio passed punitive laws, levying taxes of $50,000 or more on the Bank's local branches (each state had two). Other states passed more modest levies for raising revenue. A Maryland law required out-of-state banks to pay either a stamp tax on every note they issued or a yearly tax of $15,000.

The Bank and the State of Maryland agreed to a suit that would test the law's constitutionality (the governor called the case "an amicable arrangement"). James McCulloch, the Baltimore branch's cashier, paid out some unstamped banknotes to George Williams, one of the directors. The Baltimore branch had, of course, not paid the $15,000 tax. For this offense, McCulloch was tried and convicted in Baltimore County Court and the state court of appeals. *McCulloch v. Maryland* came before the Supreme Court in February 1819. (Marshall, who owned seventeen shares of stock in the Bank, had sold them in January so as to have no interest in the case.)

Like *Dartmouth v. Woodward, McCulloch v. Maryland* raised a question of state power: Could the State of Maryland treat a federally chartered corporation as it did its own legal creations? In doing so, the case revived a constitutional question of the Washington administration: Was this particular corporation, the Bank of the United States, lawful?

The gravity of the case attracted top legal talent. Daniel Webster, fresh from his victory in *Dartmouth*, appeared as one of the Bank's lawyers, but their star was William Pinkney, his intended opponent in *Dartmouth*. A former Federalist, Pinkney had served the Madison administration as a diplomat and as attorney general. He was smart, erudite, and eloquent. He seemed to know everything, and he always displayed all that he knew. Justice Story said his argument in *McCulloch* was worth a trip from Massachusetts to hear it. Pinkney was also acerbic, arrogant, and vain. He bullied opposing counsel, laced himself into corsets, and used cosmetics on his face.

There was a reason for Pinkney's hard, bright surface. His father was a Tory who lost everything in the Revolution. Pinkney got his start in the law by sweeping out law offices. Thanks to his talents, he rose fast and was sent, while still in his thirties, on a mission to Britain to settle Revolutionary War claims. While there, he attended a dinner with Pitt, Fox, and other luminaries, who, in the way of Oxbridge-educated aristos, discussed a passage of Euripides. When they turned to the young American for his opinion, Pinkney told them that he was there to learn rather than to speak. "I resolved," he added, telling the story years later, "to study the classics." What he did not say, years later or at any time, was, *I will never be shamed again.*

The lead lawyer for Maryland was Luther Martin, just turned seventy-one, arguing his last important case (he would suffer a stroke in August). In assessing the constitutionality of the Bank, he invoked his own past as a delegate to the Constitutional Convention, quoting a line from an account of the siege of Troy that Virgil gave Aeneas, but modestly altering it: *quorum pars minima fui*—"in which I played a small part." Pinkney caught the allusion and pitched it back to Martin, quoting the original correctly: *quorum pars magna fui*—"in which I played a large part." Pinkney thus praised Martin's service and displayed his own learning all at the same time.

Marshall read his opinion on March 6, three days after arguments ended. It was endorsed by all the other justices with no concurrences or dissents. It was even longer than *Dartmouth,* over eleven thousand words. Marshall had written fast and made good use of several of the points made by counsel.

Marshall carved his opinion into two large questions: Did Congress have the power to create a Bank of the United States? If it had, did the State of Maryland have the power to tax it?

Marshall began with a creation story of the Constitution. It was, he wrote, an "act" of the people, "ordained and established," as the Preamble put it, in their name, and "submitted" to them, to be debated and voted up or down.

Marshall told this story to combat a competing story—the compact theory, which held that the Constitution, like the Articles of Confederation before it, was a contract among states. None of Maryland's lawyers had advanced such an argument, but Thomas Jefferson's Kentucky Resolutions, protesting the Alien and Sedition Acts two decades earlier, had. Marshall admitted that the conventions that ratified the Constitution had met state by state—"Where else," he asked, "should [the people] have assembled?" But it was the people, not the states, who had made the final decision, and it was on their authority that the Constitution rested.

Marshall concluded this thought with the most resonant paragraph he ever wrote. "The government of the Union . . . is, emphatically and truly, a government of the people. In form and in substance it emanates from them. Its powers are granted by them, and are to be exercised directly on them, and for their benefit."

Eleven years later, Webster, then a senator, debating Robert Hayne, a partisan of the compact theory, would sharpen Marshall's thought, defining the federal government as "the people's government, made for the people, made by the people, and answerable to the people." Thirty-three years after that, Abraham Lincoln, in the midst of a war against the compact theory in arms, would make yet another epitome, vowing "that government of the people, by the people, for the people shall not perish from the earth."

But it was Marshall who first formed the spinal column of prepositions; his list is longer than Webster's and Lincoln's and clothed with greater substance. He wrote like an anatomist, and an anatomical illustrator, simultaneously analyzing and illuminating the living structure of America's government.

Next, Marshall made a pair of observations about the federal government and the Constitution. The federal government, "though limited in its powers, is supreme within its sphere of action." (He cited the second paragraph of Article VI: "This Constitution, and the Laws of the United States which shall be made in Pursuance thereof . . . shall be the supreme Law of the Land.") But not all of the supreme precepts of the Constitution were spelled out; some—many?—had to be deduced. A document that contained "an accurate detail" of all its powers and all the means of executing them "would partake of the prolixity of a legal code, and could scarcely be embraced by the human mind. . . . We must never forget that it is *a constitution* we are expounding." Constitutions are not compendiums of all laws; they are large-scale maps with a lot of necessarily blank space. Using them can require the skills of a navigator.

Marshall turned at last from these generalities to the case at hand. The power to charter a bank was nowhere specified in the Constitution. If the federal government had it, it had to be deduced from other powers. The source indicated by Hamilton in 1791 was the "necessary and proper" clause of Article I, Section 8.

But was a federally chartered bank indeed necessary for fulfilling other functions? Jefferson and Madison had argued that the United States could get by without one. The government could, for example, borrow money from state and local banks.

Marshall's answer tracked the answer that Hamilton had given President Washington. *Necessary* did not mean *absolutely necessary*. "*Necessary*," wrote Hamilton in 1791, "often means no more than *needful, requisite, incidental, useful* or *conducive to*." "The word 'necessary,'" wrote Marshall now, "means 'needful,' 'requisite,' 'essential,' 'conducive to,' in order to . . . facilitate the execution of the powers of government."

If a federally chartered bank was conducive to fulfilling a specified power, then it was lawful under the Constitution.

Hamilton: "If the end be clearly comprehended within any of the specified powers, and if the measure have an obvious relation to that end, and is not forbidden by any particular provision of the constitution—it may safely be deemed to come within the compass of the national authority."

Marshall: "Let the end be legitimate, let it be within the scope of the constitution, and all means which are appropriate, which are plainly adapted to that end, which are not prohibited . . . are constitutional."

As he had in *Fletcher v. Peck,* the last Federalist channeled Federalism's premier legal mind.

Marshall had shown that Congress could erect a Bank of the United States. Could a state tax it?

To answer this question, Marshall invoked the "great principle" of Article VI, which he had already cited, and he did so in a way that was, for him, new. In *Dartmouth,* he had hewed to the letter of the contract clause. Now he composed an aria, in which the supremacy clause was depicted as if it were a force, like gravity or magnetism, radiating through the entire document.

The supremacy clause, he wrote, "so entirely pervades the constitution, is so intermixed with the materials which compose it, so interwoven with its web, so blended with its texture, as to be incapable of being separated from it."

This unfortunate paragraph was a rare stylistic excess on Marshall's part. Its rhetoric, so far from strengthening his argument, weakened it. The supremacy clause is definite enough as it is. To say that supremacy intermixed, interwove, and blended with the Constitution sounded like an admission that it was not actually there and had to be smuggled in via poetry.

What did the ubiquitous force of supremacy require? "It is of the very nature of supremacy," Marshall went on, "to remove all obstacles to its action within its own sphere." He then echoed a phrase Webster had used in his argument: "The power to tax involves the power to destroy." But if Congress's power to charter a bank was supreme, then no state could be allowed to possess a power that might destroy it.

Marshall was not interested in the lightness, or otherwise, of a state's tax—whether it was intended (as Maryland's was) to raise revenue or to be annihilating. Such a question, he wrote, would be a "perplexing enquiry . . . unfit for the judicial department."

Marshall was concerned to set bright, broad limits. If the Court did not do so in this case, then the federal government might be "prostrat[ed]," by state taxes, "at the foot of the states." States, he concluded, "have no power, by taxation, or otherwise, to retard, impede, burden, or in any manner control the operations of . . . laws enacted by Congress" to execute its constitutionally approved powers. Therefore Maryland's "tax must be unconstitutional."

M ARSHALL WAS CONVINCED his decision in *McCulloch v. Maryland* was important; he fussed over the printed version of it with Henry Wheaton, the Court reporter, making small changes to get it exactly right. Yet *McCulloch* did not immediately quiet either the critics of the Bank's branches or the partisans of the compact theory.

Early in 1819, before *McCulloch* was argued, the State of Ohio passed its punitive $50,000 tax on the Bank's branches, one in Cincinnati, the other in Chillicothe. The Bank was deeply unpopular in Ohio, which, like most of the west and south, had been hard hit by the contraction of 1818. The branches were given until September to pay; if they did not by then, tax collectors were authorized to search their premises and seize the money (hence the law's nickname: "crowbar law").

On the eve of the deadline, the Chillicothe branch sought an injunction from the federal circuit court, which sat in the same

town, forbidding Ralph Osborn, the state auditor, from breaking into its vault. By mistake, however, the branch served him
with the petition for the injunction, instead of the injunction
itself. Osborn went ahead and dispatched three minions who,
in the words of the branch's cashier, hopped the counter "in a
ruffian-like manner" and took $120,425 in coins and banknotes,
which they piled into a wagon and drove to the state capital,
Columbus. (The leader of the raid kept $2,000 as his fee.)

Osborn was now served with a real injunction, forbidding him
from disbursing the money. Two of his tax collectors were arrested
for trespassing, with their bail set at the gaudy sum of $200,000.

The matter assumed the calmer form of a legal case: *Osborn
v. Bank of the United States,* which reached the Supreme Court
in 1824. Osborn's lawyers argued that the case should have been
tried in state not federal courts, since it was a criminal matter
of trespass; that it violated the Eleventh Amendment, since the
real target of the Bank's suit was the State of Ohio, not Osborn
the auditor; and that Marshall's decision in *McCulloch* was not
relevant, since the Bank was in fact a private institution, run for
the profit of its shareholders.

Marshall rejected every argument. Federal courts had jurisdiction over the creation of federal law; the Eleventh Amendment
did not apply, since Ohio was not named in the indictment;
McCulloch did apply, since the Bank, whatever its private activities, was "a public corporation, created for public and national
purposes." The crowbar law was "certainly much more objection-
able" than Maryland's tax, and "therefore void."

Only Justice Johnson dissented, and only on the issue of
jurisdiction.

Ohio, after such a bold start, meekly accepted the Court's
verdict. Osborn's trespassing tax collectors had already been released, on a technicality (the officer who had arrested them had
not himself been properly sworn in).

A constitutional attack on *McCulloch,* meanwhile, had been mounted in Marshall's hometown. Thomas Ritchie lived a block away from Marshall and was a fellow member of the Quoits Club. He was also the editor of the *Richmond Enquirer,* a Republican newspaper of pure Jeffersonian principle. Marshall's decision, he editorialized in March 1819, should be "controverted and exposed." He published two sets of critical essays by Virginia jurists William Brockenbrough and Spencer Roane, Marshall's sometime classmate at William and Mary. They wrote under pseudonyms, Brockenbrough as Amphictyon (a legendary Athenian king, whose name was Greek for *neighbor*), Roane as Hampden (a hero of the Parliamentary side in the English Civil War, for whom a college in Virginia had been named). But everyone in Virginia soon figured out who wrote the essays. Jefferson wrote Roane that "I subscribe to every tittle of them."

Marshall decided to respond. To preserve his anonymity, he confided only in Justice Washington, who acted as his literary agent, placing his manuscripts. Marshall's first reply, as "A Friend to the Union," ran as two essays in a Philadelphia newspaper. But the publisher made a hash of them, transposing the middle of each into the other. Marshall returned as "A Friend of the Constitution," with nine more essays, printed correctly this time, in the *Alexandria Gazette.*

Marshall's rhetoric was notably sharp. He wrote of his critics' "zealous and persevering hostility," and their "deep rooted and vindictive hate." Journalism was not Marshall's forte; he preferred the intimacy of fellowship or the height of the bench. He was also stung by the criticism of neighbors; Brockenbrough and Roane, like Ritchie, lived almost in his lap.

Marshall made passing comments on how the Supreme Court should rule. "The great duty of a judge who construes an instrument," he wrote, "is to find the intention of its makers." This was to be sought in "the nature of the instrument, the words that are employed" and "the object to be effected." This described a wider search than he had undertaken in *Dartmouth,* narrower than his rhapsody to the supremacy clause in *McCulloch.*

He fought, as his opponents did, over the past, he and they alike scoring old points and calling old fouls. (Politics in post-revolutionary societies always looks backward.) Roane recited the sins of Federalism—the Sedition Act, Justice Chase's orations to grand juries; Marshall countered with the hypocrisies of Jefferson and Madison, wielding the federal government's power to embargo trade with countries they disliked or to fight wars they approved.

Marshall reviewed Jefferson's and Hamilton's dispute over the constitutionality of the first Bank. His source was his own *Life of Washington;* he called Hamilton's argument "masterly."

Over and over again, he defended his creation story of the Constitution against the compact theory. For Roane, the Constitution was the Articles of Confederation, somewhat boosted: a "league" of states, "as was the former confederation," the only difference being "that the powers of this government are much *extended.*"

Marshall denied it. "Our Constitution is not a compact [of states]. It is the act of a single party. It is the act of [the] people of the United States ... adopting a government for the whole nation. ... The powers of this government are conferred for their own benefit, are essential to their own prosperity, and are to be exercised for their good, by persons chosen for that purpose by themselves."

Could such a government overstep its proper bounds? Marshall thought not. It would never annihilate the states. "No person in his senses," he wrote, "ever has, ever will, or ever can" think so. Nor would the judiciary ever extend the federal government beyond its proper limits. Judges, wrote Marshall, "have no personal interest in aggrandizing the legislative power." He did not ask whether they had a personal interest in aggrandizing the judicial power. Only time could show whether Marshall's confidence was justified.

Marshall had a specific fear in mind as he wrote: that the Virginia legislature, inspired by Ritchie, Brockenbrough, and Roane, would officially criticize the *McCulloch* decision and call on other states to do likewise. Such a motion passed in the lower house, though it died in the state senate.

Marshall's differences with his fellow Virginians remained, however. He would soon give them yet more reason to attack him and the Court.

B ACK IN MARYLAND, the *McCulloch* decision had been followed by a scandalous coda. Two weeks after Marshall delivered his opinion, James McCulloch and two officials of the Baltimore branch were revealed to have loaned $3 million to themselves out of the Bank's till for speculations that had gone bust. McCulloch personally had lost almost half a million.

Yet Maryland had no laws against embezzlement. The three were tried for conspiracy, a hard charge to prove when what they had conspired to do was not criminal. Tried in a local court, they were acquitted.

Under new management—Jones the president had retired in January 1819—the Bank would free itself from incompetents and rascals. This was none of Marshall's business. Scoundrels crossed his path in *McCulloch* as they had in *Fletcher,* but he was concerned with upholding the principles of Federalism and rebuking the ambitions of the states.

Chapter 11

JEWISH LOTTERY RUNNERS

J OHN MARSHALL WAS VIRGINIA'S MOST EMINENT LEGAL
personality. Yet the Virginia bench supplied some of his
most active enemies. The bitterest was Spencer Roane, the
Hampden of the *McCulloch* wars. A judge of the state court of
appeals since 1794, Roane had, as one lawyer who knew him put
it, "strong passions and morose manners . . . and could not endure a superior."

Roane disliked Marshall's business dealings as well as his
principles. Roane ruled against the Marshall family in every suit
related to the Fairfax Grant that came before him, condemning
their "rapacity." Marshall had brokered a compromise between
the Fairfax purchasers and the state in 1796, but miscellaneous
overlapping claims kept percolating up through the courts.

One of Roane's decisions, dismissing James Marshall's claim
to a tract in the Shenandoah Valley, was appealed to the Supreme
Court in 1813. The Court overturned it, and brusquely "commanded" Virginia to obey its "instructions." Roane and his fellow
judges, bristling, declared that the Court had no appellate power
over them. The Court thought otherwise; when the case went
back to them in 1816 as *Martin v. Hunter's Lessee,* Justice Story
ruled with a Marshallian hymn: "The constitution of the United

States was ordained and established . . . by the people," who had a right "to make the powers of the state governments, in given cases, subordinate to those of the nation."

Two negative rulings were twice as galling as one. Virginia found a new occasion for anger in the activities of a family of Jewish businessmen from Baltimore.

THE COHENS CAME to America from Oberdorf, in the upper Danube valley, a region scoured by the Thirty Years' War and the War of the Spanish Succession. First to arrive in the New World was Jacob Cohen in 1773; his younger brother, Israel, followed within a decade.

Jews were a tiny minority in late-eighteenth-century America, one-twentieth of 1 percent of the population, supporting a handful of synagogues strung along the Atlantic coast. Although several states had laws restricting office-holding to Christians, Jews encountered less everyday suspicion than Catholics. To the enlightened, they were exotics whom it was gratifying to welcome.

Leaders of the community made themselves generally useful. After living briefly in Pennsylvania, Jacob Cohen moved to Charleston, where he joined the militia during the Revolution. Before the end of the war, he moved again to Richmond, where he met both Marshall and Bushrod Washington, serving alongside Marshall as a trustee of the Masonic Hall and winning a seat vacated by Washington on the city council. Israel, who joined Jacob in Richmond, subscribed to a projected Academy of Arts and Sciences and signed a petition to the first Bank of the United States asking that it open a Richmond branch.

Israel died in 1803. Five years later, his widow moved with seven of their children to Baltimore. Three of the sons joined a volunteer artillery company in the War of 1812, and two of them,

Philip and Mendes, were in Fort McHenry during the British bombardment.

But the Baltimore Cohens were best known for the family business, which was financial services. The Cohens published periodic lists of the value of paper money in circulation. Neither the states nor the federal government issued paper money; Hamilton had condemned government currency as a "seducing and dangerous expedient." Banks, including the Bank of the United States, took up the slack. But the paper of some banks was good as gold, while the paper of others was bad as brass. The Cohens helped merchants keep track.

The Cohens also ran lotteries. Early American lotteries were not an ongoing tax on irrational hope but one-shots designed to raise money for specific purposes, from clearing rivers to building churches. As a Virginia legislator, Marshall had voted for several such measures; in the District of Columbia, Congress authorized the city of Washington to run lotteries "for effecting any important improvement." Washington would never become a great city, but it wanted at least to be a city, and in 1820, it began work on a city hall. The Cohens had acquired a good reputation in the lottery business by paying winners on time, and the city hired them to run a lottery, grandly called the National Lottery, to pay for it.

That June, Philip and Mendes Cohen sold six tickets—two half tickets, and four quarters—at the family firm's branch office in Norfolk, Virginia. In doing so, they became lawbreakers. Lotteries were so useful that states and cities resented competition; Virginia had passed a law forbidding any lotteries not authorized by itself. The Cohens were tried in Norfolk's borough court in September and fined one hundred dollars.

Immediately, this minor business infraction became a burning legal issue. William Pinkney and four other lawyers wrote a public letter assailing Virginia's law. Pinkney, a Marylander, and the Cohens knew each other; this, and the swiftness of Pinkney's response, suggest that the case was a contrived legal test. In October, the Cohens appealed to the Supreme Court, which agreed to hear their case.

When Marshall arrived in Washington for the Court's 1821 session, he wrote Justice Washington, who was home sick, urging him if he could to hear the Cohens' suit, "which has occasioned so much commotion in our legislature." Commotion indeed. Roane and his allies were unhappy with *McCulloch* and still smarting from *Martin v. Hunter's Lessee.* Following their lead, the legislature passed a resolution instructing state's counsel in the Cohens' case to argue only that the Court had "no rightful authority . . . to examine and correct" a Virginia court's decisions; on the merits, they were to say nothing at all.

Pinkney was the lead lawyer for the Cohens. "The supremacy of the national constitution and laws," he argued, "is a fundamental principle of the federal government. . . . To part with this leaves the Union a mere league." Virginia's lawyers all but threatened secession if the case went ahead: "The confidence of the people constitutes the real strength of this government. Nothing can so much endanger it as exciting the hostility of the state governments. With them it is to determine how long this government shall endure."

Marshall spoke for a unanimous Court on the question of jurisdiction on March 3. His opinion in *Cohens v. Virginia* was enormous, over fifteen thousand words, containing peaks of eloquence separated by wide thickets of detail. No less than in 1788, Marshall was fighting with fellow Virginians over the nature of the Union itself. He wanted to be both ringing and exhaustive.

He began with the Constitution's creation story. "The American states as well as the American people have believed a close and firm Union to be essential to their liberty and to their happiness. . . . Under the influence of this opinion . . . the American people, in the conventions of their respective states, adopted the present Constitution." Marshall here included the states in the process, but he gave, as he always did, pride of place to the people.

He looked to the future. Although "a constitution is framed for ages to come," it may, as Virginia's lawyers had suggested, be discarded. "But this supreme and irresistible power to make or to unmake resides only in the whole body of the people; not in any subdivision of them." In America as understood by Marshall, revolutions may happen, but not secessions.

He then plunged into a long grapple with Article III, the Eleventh Amendment, and the Judiciary Act of 1789, seeking to show that the Cohen brothers could appeal, beyond Virginia, for justice and that the Supreme Court was the venue for administering it. Marshall's reasoning on these points was intricate and at times slippery; for example, he took a plain statement (Article III, Section 2) that, in cases involving states, the Court's jurisdiction was original and concluded that it could also be appellate.

His best argument was not based on details but on general principle: "The Constitution gave to every person having a claim upon a state, a right to submit his case to the court of the nation. However unimportant his claim might be, however little the community might be interested in its decision, the framers . . . thought it necessary for the purposes of justice to provide a tribunal . . . in which that claim might be decided."

Marshall ended on the high note with which he began. He quoted two essays from the *Federalist,* which he called "a complete commentary on our Constitution," both of them by "a very celebrated statesman" (Alexander Hamilton). "What relation would subsist between the national and state courts" under the Constitution, Hamilton had asked. "I answer, that an appeal would certainly lie from the latter, to the supreme court of the United States. . . . The national and state [judicial] systems are to be regarded as ONE WHOLE" (Hamilton's caps).

The alternative, which Virginia was claiming, was that state courts had final say over the cases they tried. Hamilton likened such a system to a mythological monster. "Thirteen independent courts of final jurisdiction ... is a hydra in government, from which nothing but contradiction and confusion can proceed." Hercules had cut off the Hydra's many heads and burned the stumps of the necks to prevent new heads from growing; Marshall hoped to do the same to Virginia's judicial pretensions.

He gave his own commentary on the Constitution in a paragraph grander and more spacious than his paean to popular government in *McCulloch*. "In war, we are one people. In making peace, we are one people. In all commercial regulations, we are one and the same people. . . . America has chosen to be, in many respects, and to many purposes, a nation; and for all these purposes, her government is complete; to all these objects, it is competent."

Here he echoed not the words but the sentiments of George Washington's farewell address, which Marshall had quoted in its entirety in his *Life*. In it, Washington had defined the United States as "one nation," under a constitution "calculated for the efficacious management of [its] common concerns." He had also warned, as Marshall surely remembered, "there will always be reason to distrust the patriotism of those who . . . may endeavor to weaken its bands."

Virginia's objections to the Court's jurisdiction, Marshall concluded, "are not sustained."

THERE REMAINED THE nub of the case: Did the Cohen brothers owe Virginia one hundred dollars? Since the state disdained to argue the point, the Court gave the job to Daniel Webster. (Asking the New England Federalist to speak for Virginia was almost as insulting as letting the case go forward.) On March 5, Marshall spoke, once again for a unanimous Court, much more briefly. The object of the National Lottery, despite its name, was entirely local; Washington's city hall, unlike the president's house or the Navy Yard, was not a national building. Congress had given no hint that it wanted lottery tickets raising money to build such a structure to be sold nationwide. In the absence of any reason to overrule Virginia's lottery law, the Cohens were guilty as charged and would have to pay.

As in *Marbury*, Marshall had given a crust of substance to one side and a loaf of law to his.

Undaunted by their fine, the Cohens, as the years passed, opened a branch office in Richmond, went into banking, and ran for and won more local offices. At the end of the decade, Mendes made a grand tour of Europe and the Middle East, sailing up the Nile flying a star-spangled banner made of the shirts and handkerchiefs of the sailors on his boat.

VIRGINIA'S LEGAL AND political establishment was outraged by the *Cohens* decision. The *Richmond Enquirer* ran five essays by Roane, who this time used the name of Algernon Sidney, a seventeenth-century English republican executed during the reign of Charles II. The Constitution, Roane wrote, was a compact between "sovereign governments." Federal judges had no more say concerning state laws than "aliens and foreigners." Marshall's decision to the contrary imposed "the blind and absolute despotism" of "a tyrant over his slaves."

Roane railed at the passivity of Marshall's Republican-appointed colleagues. The chief justice was "honorably distinguished from you, messieurs judges. He is true to his former politics.... He must be equally delighted and *surprised* to find his *Republican* brothers going with him." Marshall's Republican brothers had long accepted his comradeship and his leadership; they did not rise to Roane's bait.

Back of Roane, cheering him on, was Thomas Jefferson. "The great object of my fear," the former president wrote Roane after Marshall's decision, "is the federal judiciary. That body, like gravity, ever acting, with noiseless foot and un-alarming advance, gaining ground step by step, and holding what it gains," was "engulfing" all in its path.

Marshall did rise to Roane's bait, at least in private, with comments as acrid as Roane's. "For coarseness and malignity of invective," he wrote Story, "Algernon Sidney surpasses all party writers who have ever made pretensions to any decency of character." Marshall declined to make any public answer to them, as he had done for the Hampden essays. But he and Story discouraged a Philadelphia legal journal from reprinting Roane's polemics. A quarantine was as effective as a response.

Marshall also intuited Jefferson's offstage role. Roane, he told Story, had been egged on by "the great Lama of the mountains" (or of Monticello). Marshall's diagnosis of his old enemy had not changed since his correspondence with Hamilton about the deadlocked election of 1800: Jefferson was a demagogue. "His great power . . . is chiefly acquired by professions of democracy. Every check on the wild impulse of the moment is [therefore] a check on his own power, and he is unfriendly to the source from which it flows. He looks, of course, with an ill will at an independent judiciary." More than state's rights, or even liberty, Jefferson honored the popular will. So did Marshall, but he honored it when it had united in the two great causes of his youth, the war for independence and the ratification of the Constitution. Jefferson wanted to ride the storms of the moment.

In 1822, Jefferson began an odd correspondence with one of Marshall's colleagues. Justice Johnson, emulous of Marshall's

Life of Washington, had written a life of Washington's great protégé, General Nathanael Greene. Marshall was encouraging and helpful to his brother justice, which damped whatever envy Johnson may have felt. The new author sent his finished book to Jefferson, and the two exchanged half a dozen letters.

They wrote as old people talk, a little past each other (Johnson was only fifty, but Jefferson was turning eighty). Johnson explained how the social structure of the Marshall Court discouraged dissents and concurrences. Jefferson expressed his distress over the Court itself, writing at length about "the slipperiness of the eels of the law"; about the *Cohens* decision, "hanging inference on inference, from heaven to earth, like Jacob's ladder"; about Roane's critique of it, which "appeared to me to pulverize [nearly] every word which had been delivered by Judge Marshall."

Jefferson's fight against the Court was taken up publicly by another Johnson, Senator Richard Mentor Johnson of Kentucky. Johnson had made his name in the War of 1812, commanding a unit of mounted riflemen at the Battle of the Thames in Upper Canada, where he was credited with killing the Shawnee chief Tecumseh. His deed was immortalized in a play, a poem, and a campaign jingle: *Ripsey Rampsey, Rumpsey Dumpsey, I Dick Johnson killed Tecumseh.*

In person, Johnson was warm and simple. "His hair wanders all abroad, and he wears no cravat," wrote one observer. "But there is no telling how he might look if dressed like other people." Politically, he was an idealistic populist, against imprisonment for debt, and for Sunday mail delivery (forbidding it, he believed, would be an establishment of religion).

Early in 1822, Johnson assailed the Marshall Court on the Senate floor. "Its decisions . . . assume the character of immutability. Like the laws of the Medes and Persians, they live forever, and operate through all time." (Daniel 6:8 speaks of "the law of the Medes and Persians, which altereth not.") Johnson called a roll of Court decisions overruling state actions, including *Fletcher,* *Dartmouth, McCulloch,* and *Cohens,* and offered a series of constitutional amendments, suggested by Roane, to limit judicial power: restricting the jurisdiction of the federal courts; limiting the tenure of federal judges or making them removable by votes in Congress; making the Senate a court of last appeal from the Supreme Court's judgments.

The following year, Johnson was back with another proposal— to increase the Court to ten justices and require a supermajority of seven for any decision striking down a law.

And then—nothing. Roane died, age sixty, in September 1822; none of Johnson's amendments became law. Jefferson, who never spoke out publicly during his retirement, was feeling the weight of his years; in one of his letters to Roane, he complained of "the decays of nature" and the "wane of the mind." And it was still as true of him as it had been after Burr's treason trial that, however high his anger blazed, prudence or mildness of temper or indolence of will could cool him off.

Virginia itself was no longer as important as it had once been. By far the most populous state in the Union throughout the eighteenth century, it had by the 1820 census fallen behind New York and Pennsylvania. James Monroe, the fourth Virginian president (only John Adams had come from somewhere else) still served, but there was no Virginian on the horizon to succeed him.

More significant than any relative loss of population or political clout, Virginia's mind was going dark. The intellectual ferment that had produced the Declaration of Rights, the Declaration of Independence, the Statute for Religious Freedom, and the *Federalist,* all wholly or partly by Virginians, had ceased. There remained John Marshall, but he was an internal exile in his own state.

One other cause cast both Virginia and the Court into the shade. In 1819, Missouri had applied for statehood—the second state to be carved out of the Louisiana Territory, the first entirely west of the Mississippi. Should it be a slave state or a free state? Its fate, it seemed, might determine the future growth of the country. The free states of the North wanted Missouri free, and in the House, they were numerous enough to prevail. Yet the slave states of the South would not tolerate the restriction, and they held the balance of power in the Senate. The fight became a naked clash of sections and principles, hopes and fears, abolishing all other partisan and intellectual distinctions. Marshall wrote hardly anything about it, and that obliquely (one letter of his refers to "asperities and jealousies between the states"); Jefferson, more candid or more shocked, called the Missouri fight "a fire-bell in the night." It took all the legislative wiles of Henry Clay to patch up a cluster of interrelated compromises in 1820–21, admitting Missouri as a slave state, pairing it with the Maine district of Massachusetts as a free state, and reserving most of the remainder of the Louisiana Territory for freedom. While that fire burned, and even after it was (for the time) extinguished, all other matters seemed dim.

Marshall's next important decision, after the controversy over Cohens had subsided, turned from Virginia to the commerce of the nation.

Chapter 12

STEAMBOATS
AND COMMERCE

H ENRY HUDSON HOPED THE NORTH AMERICAN RIVER that he explored in 1609 for 130 miles might offer a passage to Cathay. It did not. But the broad, straight waterway, which was eventually named for him, did offer easy access to the interior.

For almost two centuries, single-masted sloops were the best way of navigating the Hudson River between New York City and Albany (Alexander Hamilton wrote the first *Federalist* essay on such a ship, using a lap-top writing desk). With fair winds, a one-way trip typically took three days. If they failed, or were contrary, it could take two weeks.

All this changed forever in August 1807 when a steam-powered boat, prosaically named the *Steamboat*, left a New York City wharf, bound for Albany. It was long, flat, and homely, carried forty passengers and the equipment that propelled it, and moved at a speed of five miles per hour.

Its builder was Robert Fulton. In his youth, he had hoped to become a painter of miniatures and went to Europe to study his art. Instead, he followed his superior gifts at designing and tinkering and tested a paddle-wheeled boat, powered by a Watt steam engine, on the Seine. He could not be called its inventor; other steamboats had preceded his, including one built by another American, John Fitch, whose work Fulton knew.

But Fitch had no backers, took to drink, and finally killed himself. Fulton, however, found a backer in France.

Robert R. Livingston, a cousin of Justice Livingston, was a wealthy New York aristocrat with a knack for almost-greatness. In 1776, as a congressman, he had belonged to the five-man committee that produced the Declaration of Independence (John Adams, Benjamin Franklin, and of course Thomas Jefferson did all the work). In 1789, as a New York judge, he had administered the first presidential oath of office to George Washington (Washington, who gave top jobs to two other New Yorkers, Hamilton and John Jay, had none for him). And in 1803, as minister to France, he negotiated the purchase of the Louisiana Territory, though the credit went to James Monroe, who had joined his mission at the last minute.

Livingston had been interested in the possibilities of steamboats for years. When he joined forces with Fulton, his hour of greatness finally arrived. (The alternate name for the *Steamboat* would be *Clermont,* after Livingston's Hudson River estate.)

Five years after the *Steamboat*'s first Hudson River run, Gouverneur Morris, an old friend of Livingston's who lived in what is now the Bronx, described a summertime trip on it. We "embark in the steam-boat a few minutes before five, at which hour we leave the wharf, and proceed up Hudson's River against the wind. The lodging is so uncomfortable that I can stay in bed but a short time, though the evening is cool.

"Early [next] morning I come on deck, and find we are opposite to West Point; the wind still unfavorable, but our progress good, considering that the current is also adverse. . . . I remain on deck till we reach Albany, which is at midnight."

Morris spent the next day ashore doing business, then boarded the steamboat the following morning "at half an hour after eight. . . . There is a frequent ejection and collection of passengers from towns and places along the river. In the course of the day the engine receives an injury from a piece of wood thrown among the works by a careless servant. This retards our progress. Sit all night on deck, and get a little uneasy. Sleep in my chair.

"We enter the [Hudson] Highlands at sunrise, and breakfast below Haverstraw, having a fair wind and tide. When nearly opposite to [Harlem] the engine gets again out of order; but we have no longer any interest in it, for here I disembark."

Morris's round trip was thus less than five days, including an entire day ashore. The price, he noted, had been seven dollars, and half as much for his servant.

Fulton's know-how was good, Livingston's financial support was better, but the third thing the *Steamboat* needed to be lucrative was political protection. New Yorkers were charmed with the new contraption, but it would be most profitable for its builder and its backer if no other steamboats were allowed on the river.

This Livingston could also arrange. Over the years, he had dealt with everyone of consequence in New York politics. In the 1780s, John Fitch had secured a monopoly from the state legislature to run steamboats in New York waters; after he died, Livingston got it transferred to him. In 1808, the legislature guaranteed Livingston's monopoly for thirty years, a supplementary act in 1811 providing that the ships of competitors be impounded during any litigation.

For competition quickly sprang up. Fulton and Livingston built more boats and ran them in New York Harbor and Long Island Sound. But a group of Albany businessmen built two boats of their own, *Hope* and *Perseverance,* to challenge the monopolists' control of the river. Fulton and Livingston sued, and the case ended up in a state court in 1811, where the most important opinion was written by the state's most learned judge, James Kent.

As a young man, Kent had idolized Alexander Hamilton; years after the duel, when he saw Aaron Burr on the streets of New York, he shouted at him that he was a scoundrel. Burr answered suavely that the judge's opinions were "always entitled to the highest consideration." Kent's opinion in the New York State steamboat case cited *Federalist* 32, a Hamilton essay that laid out rules for deciding when the actions of states were constitutionally prohibited. Two were obvious: when a power to do something was given exclusively to the federal government, or when it was explicitly forbidden to the states. Hamilton deduced a third rule: if a state action "would be absolutely and totally *contradictory and repugnant*" to a federal power.

What federal power was the monopoly contradicting? It could only have been the power "to regulate Commerce . . . among the several States" (Article I, Section 8). Yet the monopoly's boats sailed within New York waters, and Congress had passed no law concerning them. Kent therefore found no constitutional impediment. He added that the steamboats of the monopoly had been "a triumphant success."

For good measure, the monopoly bought off the Albany group by letting it run boats on Lake Champlain.

Livingston died in 1813. Fulton followed two years later, tragically; he and the monopoly's lawyer, Thomas Addis Emmet, were crossing the frozen Hudson in February—a necessary winter activity in those bridge-less days—when Emmet fell through the ice; Fulton pulled him out, contracting a fatal case of pneumonia. But the monopoly was carried on by the dead men's heirs and associates.

One of these was Aaron Ogden, a former governor of New Jersey. Ogden began as a competitor of the monopoly, running a boat called *Sea Horse* from Elizabethtown, opposite Staten

Island, to New York. The monopoly took him to court, but in 1815, the contestants decided to join rather than fight; Ogden became a licensee of the monopoly, paying $600 a year to run in and out of New York waters.

The new licensee attracted a new competitor, Thomas Gibbons, a Georgia transplant who had moved north to pursue a variety of business ventures. At first, Gibbons was a partner of Ogden's, but in 1816, they had a grotesque falling out. Rumor had it that Gibbons's daughter had slept with her fiancé. Gibbons wanted all his family to join him in a public statement declaring the rumor to be false (apparently, it was not). When Ogden suggested that discretion would be wiser, Gibbons became enraged and appeared at Ogden's door brandishing a horsewhip. Ogden escaped out the back of his house and sued Gibbons for trespass.

This ended the partnership. Gibbons started running two steamboats of his own, the *Mouse* and the *Bellona,* from Elizabethtown to New York. His business manager was a young Staten Island ferryboat skipper, Cornelius Vanderbilt. Vanderbilt was uneducated—he had been on the water since he was eleven—but he was shrewd, bold, and resourceful: perfect for the game of cat-and-mouse that now ensued.

The monopoly fought back legally, slapping Gibbons's boats with injunctions. Vanderbilt evaded pursuers and process servers, hiding himself in a secret interior cabin whenever they caught up with him. "This day," he described one run-in, the monopolists "brought a suite againts all my men even the kook but caught no boddy." Gibbons also dispatched young Vanderbilt to Washington to hire, as counsel, Daniel Webster.

Gibbons challenged the monopoly in New York's courts, where the issue once more came before James Kent who, unsurprisingly, followed the logic of his own previous ruling and declared the monopoly constitutional. In 1820, Gibbons appealed to the Supreme Court.

The Court was slated to hear the case in its 1821 term, immediately after Marshall's final decision in *Cohens,* but postponed it because of a flaw in the New York preliminaries. The case was finally argued in February 1824.

A last-minute scheduling problem caught both lawyers and the Court off guard. *Gibbons v. Ogden* was listed twenty-ninth on the docket, or schedule of cases. But because none of the cases ahead of it in line were ready to be argued, Marshall announced on February 3, the first day of the session, that it would be heard on the following morning. Webster had been busy with congressional work (he was now a representative from Massachusetts). Marshall's announcement caused him to stay up all night, organizing his notes. Then he shaved, ate breakfast, and came to the Court ready to argue.

Hearing the case early also ensured that it would be heard at the very end of the long era of stability in the Marshall Court. In March 1823, Justice Livingston had died, age sixty-five, of pleurisy. Although a new justice, Smith Thompson, had been named by President Monroe and confirmed by the Senate, he missed the start of the 1824 session because of a death in his family. *Gibbons v. Ogden* was thus heard by six justices who had been together for twelve years.

Webster made a sweeping case for America's economic unity, protected by Congress under the commerce clause. New York State, he maintained, had indeed violated the Constitution, for "what is it," he asked, that the commerce clause regulated? "Not the commerce of the several states, respectively, but the commerce of the United States. Henceforth, the commerce of the States was to be an *unit*," a web of activity overriding state lines. "Its character was to be described in the flag which waves over it, E PLURIBUS UNUM."

Only Congress could oversee such a unit: "The higher branches of commercial regulation must be exclusively committed to a single hand." New York's grant of a monopoly was therefore out of order. "How could individual states assert a right . . . in a case of this sort, without manifest encroachment and confusion?"

Ogden's lawyers, including Thomas Addis Emmet, the man Fulton had saved from drowning, admitted that commercial regulations adopted by states "never can be in collision with [those of] Congress." But, they maintained, since Congress had passed no laws regulating steamboats, New York's grant of a monopoly collided with nothing. The state had simply filled a vacuum.

The lawyers had their say, other cases were heard; Justice Thompson arrived in Washington to join the Court. Then Marshall, who had begun to write his opinion on the steamboat case, had a fall in the boardinghouse the justices were staying in, dislocating his shoulder and suffering a mild concussion. As he recovered, he wrote a sweet letter to Polly. "Old men"—Marshall was sixty-eight—"do not get over sprains and hurts quite as quickly as young ones." He had, he went on, plenty of time on his hands as he recovered, which he spent recalling the episodes of their courtship, over forty years ago: "our little tiffs and makings up. . . . the lock of hair . . . all the thousand indescribable but deeply affecting instances of your affection or coldness which constituted for a time the happiness or misery of my life." They could "never be lost while recollection remains."

On March 2, Marshall, one arm in a sling, delivered his opinion in what one reporter called "a low feeble voice."

He began with a tribute to the "great names" of the New York bench who had upheld the monopoly. Surely, he was thinking of Kent, a legal scholar, a fellow Federalist, a fellow admirer of Hamilton. But then, Marshall dropped the hammer: "It is the province of this Court, while it respects, not to bow to [them] implicitly."

He repeated one of his standing principles: the Constitution meant what its words meant. "The enlightened patriots who framed [it], and the people who adopted it, must be understood to have employed words in their natural sense, and to have intended what they have said."

He then went to work on the word *commerce.*

Commerce was buying and selling, but it was more: "It is intercourse." (This word had as many meanings then as it has now, and one wag wrote at the time that he expected the Court would soon pass judgment on "our fornication laws.") For Marshall, *intercourse* meant *communication,* which included navigation.

"The commerce of the United States," he wrote, "is that of the whole United States. Every district has a right to participate in it. The deep streams which penetrate our country in every direction, pass through the interior of almost every state in the Union, and furnish the means of exercising this right. If Congress has the power to regulate it, that power must be exercised wherever the subject exists."

This paragraph recalled Webster's paean to the American economic unit. Webster certainly thought so; he boasted afterward that Marshall had taken in his argument "as a baby takes in its mother's milk." But Webster was not Marshall's only source for such thoughts. The expanse of the American market had been a theme of Federalist polemic—almost of Federalist poetry—for years.

"The veins of commerce in every part," Hamilton wrote in the *Federalist,* "will be replenished, and will acquire additional motion and vigour from a free circulation of the commodities of every part." Washington's farewell address had even used the word *intercourse.* "The *North,* in an unrestrained intercourse with the *South* . . . finds in the productions of the latter . . . precious materials of manufacturing industry. The *South,* in the same intercourse . . . sees its agriculture grow and its commerce expand. . . . The *East,* in a like intercourse with the *West* . . . finds . . . vent for the commodities which it . . . manufactures. The *West* derives from the *East* supplies requisite to its growth and comfort."

Marshall respected Webster, as he respected most of the lawyers who appeared before him; they all belonged to the great Quoits Club of the Supreme Court bar. But he had learned Webster's lesson earlier, and from greater teachers.

Marshall acknowledged that there was such a thing as "commerce which is completely internal": "carried on between man and man in a state . . . which does not extend to, or affect other states." Congress had no business with that.

But the Constitution had given the power to regulate the great web of American exchange to Congress.

Was it then true, as Webster had argued, that the states could play no role? Not even when Congress had failed to exercise its power?

Marshall came close to saying so—then drew back. "There is great force," he said, "in [Webster's] argument, and the court is not satisfied that it has been refuted." He then turned, however, to a comparatively minor point.

Early in his steamboat ventures, Thomas Gibbons had taken out a federal coasting license. Such a license, issued under a law passed by Congress in 1793, gave an American vessel immunity from fees levied on foreign ships. It was a tool used in protecting American shipowners from foreign competition. Gibbons's lawyers had argued all along that it also protected his steamboats from state laws, though Kent and other New York judges had ruled that it was simply a form of identification for revenue purposes.

Marshall now explicated the word *license*. "A license to do any particular thing is a permission or authority to do that thing." If the *Bellona* had a license that allowed it to navigate without paying certain taxes, that license also allowed it to navigate from Elizabethtown to New York.

All the New York legal decisions in favor of the monopoly, Marshall concluded, were "reversed and annulled."

MARSHALL'S DECISION IN *Gibbons v. Ogden* was like an elephant standing on one leg. He had sketched a panorama of a vast American market, liberated by Congress from petty obstacles and local privileges, but he based his decision instead on a piece of regulatory paperwork.

Justice Johnson made the point in a concurring opinion. Although the judgment in favor of Gibbons had his "entire approbation," he thought it should have rested on Congress's broad power to regulate navigation, not on Gibbons's coasting license.

Why did Marshall rule the way he had? The most obvious, and Marshallian, explanation would be found in his words: he wrote what he wrote because he meant it. He felt the "great force" of the concepts of a national market, and Congress's superintendence of it, but was also mindful that an act of Congress, creating the coasting license, had been defied.

Another factor in his limited ruling might have been politics. In *McCullough* and *Cohens,* Marshall had taken on powerful state interests and incurred sharp criticism. He did not shrink from doing either. But neither was he "fond," as he wrote Justice Story in another context, "of butting against a wall in sport."

One of the more lucrative items of interstate commerce was slaves. In the 1820s, slaves were being sold from the exhausted fields of Virginia to the rich cotton lands of Mississippi and Alabama (tracts of the old Yazoo territory, promoted to statehood in 1817 and 1819, respectively). The planter class would fear even a possibility of federal interference in their labor management.

New York had yet another interest of its own to protect. The Erie Canal, which beat Virginia's canal dreams to fulfillment, was nearing completion—built entirely with New York taxes and loans raised by New York banks. It lay entirely within New York State, but much of the produce it moved came from the old Northwest Territory, via the Great Lakes. New York would not welcome Congress taking an interest in its great project.

The Marshall who had thrown bones to the losing side in *Marbury* and *Cohens* might have wanted to avoid further fights now.

Five years after *Gibbons v. Ogden*, Marshall would hear another case involving navigation, *Willson v. Blackbird Creek Marsh Company*, which showed his circumspection even more clearly.

In 1822, the Delaware legislature licensed a company to dam and bank Blackbird Creek, a stream that flows into the Delaware River about twenty miles south of Wilmington. The land there is low and flat, and the lawmakers believed that property values would rise if the creek's surroundings were made less marshy. One of the lawyers of the dam's builders called Blackbird Creek a "sluggish reptile stream . . . which, wherever it passes, spreads its venom and destroys the health" of everyone in the neighborhood. (We think differently of such streams: Blackbird Creek is now an eco-spot, part of the Delaware National Estuarine Research Reserve.) The owners of a sloop, the *Sally*, had their own opinion of Blackbird Creek, considering it a navigable stream, "in the nature of a highway," and ordered their crew to rip up the piles and cut through the dam. The Blackbird Creek Marsh Company sued for trespass and was upheld in local and state courts. In 1829, the owners of the *Sally*, who had a federal coasting license, argued their case before the Supreme Court, invoking *Gibbons*.

In a short opinion (under a thousand words), Marshall ruled that, "under all the circumstances of the case," Delaware could authorize the damming of Blackbird Creek. Evidently, he considered local public health one of those "minute interests" that, Hamilton had argued in *Federalist* 17, "can never be desirable cares" for the federal government. The *Sally*'s coasting license was not allowed to supersede it.

However odd its shape or limited its scope, Marshall's decision in *Gibbons v. Ogden* had a powerful effect. Twelve days after he gave it, the *United States,* a steamboat from New Haven, Connecticut, sailed into New York Harbor, firing a salute and cheered from the wharves. By the end of 1825, the number of steamboats using the harbor had risen from six to forty-three. Cornelius Vanderbilt struck out on his own, first with steamboats, then with railroads, eventually becoming the wealthiest man in the United States.

In 1849, Congress awarded $76,300 to Fulton's heirs, in recompense for the "great benefits" he had conferred on the nation. It was his posthumous consolation prize.

Ingenuity and energy, skill and greed would have transformed America's waterways one way or another, but *Gibbons v. Ogden* gave the process vital assistance. Marshall's vision of a unitary market supervised by Congress remained, enshrined if not quite enacted, as an exciting prospect. (Also an ambiguous one: what Congress could free from state ties, it could also bind with its own.)

As the 1824 term ended, Marshall wrote once again to his wife. "I have not the use of my arm sufficiently to put it into the sleeves of my coat, but I am entirely free from pain." He added that he would return to Richmond and to her by steamboat.

Section IV

CHIEF JUSTICE: THE WANING YEARS

———◆———

Chapter 13

SLAVERS

THE ACCESSION OF SMITH THOMPSON, NOMINATED BY President Monroe in 1823, was pivotal for Marshall and his Court. In the Jefferson administration, the chief justice had withstood serious assaults on the judiciary's independence. From 1811 on, though the assaults continued, the Court had consolidated itself as an institution and as an authority. Every February, the same justices came to Washington, roomed at the same hotel, drank the same wine rain or shine, and followed Marshall's lead regardless of their own party affiliation. Their landmark decisions strengthened contracts, freed commerce, and rebuked the states.

Brockholst Livingston's death had been the harbinger of change. Speculation in Washington about who might replace him began while he still alive and ailing. "This is truly the most heartless place in the country," New York senator Rufus King wrote bitterly.

Some of its most heartless denizens were New Yorkers. The politics of the state was byzantine, and since Livingston had held what was thought to be the New York seat on the Court, it infected the choice of his successor. The obvious candidate was Thompson, former chief justice of the state supreme court, now secretary of the navy. But Thompson thought he might have a shot at the presidency in 1824, as New York's favorite son, to succeed the retiring Monroe. (There were already five candidates in that race: three cabinet secretaries—John Quincy Adams, William Crawford, and John Calhoun, the Speaker of the House, Henry Clay; and General Andrew Jackson, hero of the Battle of New Orleans.) Thompson wrote two letters to his friend—New York's other senator, Martin Van Buren—feeling him out for his support; in a third letter, he offered a favor in return, suggesting that he would back Van Buren for the Court. Van Buren was already backing Crawford for president; since he had missed Thompson's first two letters, he thought Thompson was making an offer with no strings. When the two men figured out where they actually stood, their hopes were dashed and their egos bruised.

When Marshall heard rumors about Van Buren becoming a justice, he wrote Justice Story that he hoped it was "impossible." Van Buren was a smart man but a complete political animal, as he would demonstrate by scrambling into the White House twelve years later. Marshall had been a politician himself and remained a kibitzer on the bench, but he took care to maintain the mask of impartiality. His Federalism appeared in his decisions, not in electioneering. Thompson, however, liked to electioneer. After taking his flier for the White House in the 1824 cycle, he would run for governor of New York in 1828 (against Van Buren, who would beat him soundly).

Thompson overstepped the customs of the Marshall Court in a more serious way, by writing his own opinions. In this, he was now joined by Justice Johnson, who had begun his concurrence in *Gibbons v. Ogden* with this declaration of independence: "In questions of great importance and great delicacy, I feel my duty to the public best discharged by . . . maintain[ing] my opinions in my own way." Johnson felt liberated by his correspondence with Jefferson, in which he had described, and complained of, the Court's pressures to conform. Thompson's presence on the bench further encouraged him. In the twelve years before Thompson was confirmed, all the justices together had issued only eleven dissents. In the twelve years after, there were seven by Thompson, fifteen by Johnson, and twenty-five by other justices, stimulated by the new outspokenness, sometimes against their natural inclination (Story, dissenting in 1830, wrote that he was violating his "usual practice of submitting in silence" to decisions with which he disagreed).

In one respect, Justice Thompson was a good fit with the Marshall Court. Secretary of the navy was a full-time job, but justice of the Supreme Court was part-time; Thompson accordingly sold his house in Washington and located himself in Albany, joining his fellow justices in their boardinghouse when the Court was in session. Their comradeship was unimpaired, though this too would soon change.

B EFORE THE COURT'S 1825 session, Marshall received a visit from his past.

From August 1824 to September 1825, the Franco-American hero Lafayette made a triumphal tour of the United States. Marshall had served alongside him at Valley Forge, when they were both barely in their twenties. The years since had buffeted Lafayette; the radicalism of France's revolution dismayed him, Napoleon and the restored monarchy alike ignored him. America still revered him, and during his visit, every state demanded an opportunity to celebrate him.

In October 1824, Lafayette, after a pilgrimage to Mount Vernon, landed at Yorktown and made progress up the James River to Richmond. There Marshall delivered an address, praising Virginia's great guest and speaking particularly for the Revolutionary War veterans who were present: though time had "thinned our ranks, and enfeebled our bodies"—Marshall was now sixty-nine—it had not diminished their "confidence and love." Lafayette, in reply, saluted Marshall as "the eloquent historian of the Revolution, and of its matchless military chief." So the aging heroes honored each other as the young country honored them.

The young country was also honoring itself: *See what great men won our freedom; what a great place we must be.* But anxiety also lurked in the occasion: *Are we still as great as they were?* The revolutionary past was near enough to be seen and claimed, grand enough to seem overwhelming.

O NE FEATURE OF the American present had been little altered by its great past: slavery. André-Nicolas Levasseur, Lafayette's personal secretary on his American pilgrimage, noted the irony in his published account of their visit: "The soul feels suddenly chilled and the imagination alarmed, at learning that at many points in this vast republic the horrible principle of slavery still reigns, with all its sad and monstrous consequences." Levasseur, like Lafayette himself, tried to put the best face on American conditions: half the existing states were free (thanks to the Missouri Compromise), and Congress had banned the slave trade.

But the trade was a monstrous consequence of slavery that was not so easily abolished.

The Constitution (Article I, Section 9, and Article V) protected the importation of slaves until 1808. Congress then forbade it and in 1820 defined it as piracy, a capital crime.

But the slave trade, though diminished, continued on the sly. American slavers used many dodges. They sailed with false flags or nominal captains from Spain or Portugal (countries that still permitted the trade). They took their cargoes into Spanish or Portuguese colonies or slipped them past American revenue cutters into ports with corrupt customs officials. The wave of revolution that washed over Spanish America in the 1810s created new, sometimes fly-by-night, governments and new opportunities for evasion.

In March 1820, the *Antelope,* a two-masted 112-ton ship, was riding at anchor at Cabinda, a port on the west coast of Africa near the mouth of the Congo River. With a sheltered harbor and a beautiful situation, Cabinda was known as "the paradise of the coast." It was also an old slave depot, where the *mambouk,* the local black ruler, exchanged Africans who had been captured inland with white traders. The *Antelope,* built in Rhode Island in 1802 as an American slaver, had been sold after 1808 to a Spanish firm that used it to bring slaves to Cuba.

This voyage took a sudden turn when the *Arraganta,* a 200-ton vessel carrying seven guns, sailed into Cabinda, opened fire with muskets, and boarded her. The *Arraganta* had sailed from Baltimore as the *Columbia;* once at sea, she raised the colors of the Banda Oriental, the forerunner of modern Uruguay, a revolutionary state at war with Spain and Portugal. On her voyage out, the *Arraganta* had raided a small American brig, the *Exchange,* taking twenty-five slaves (for an American ship to be carrying any slaves was then a crime). In Cabinda, after capturing the *Antelope,* the *Arraganta* attacked three Portuguese ships, burning one, and taking their slaves. The *Arraganta* and the *Antelope* then sailed back across the Atlantic.

Off the coast of Brazil, the *Arraganta* wrecked and was lost. Her first mate, John Smith, took the *Antelope* to Surinam, a Dutch colony, where he offered to sell his cargo, 280 Africans, for $80,000. The Dutch only offered $50,000, so Smith sailed on in search of other buyers. In June, while lurking off the coast of Florida, the *Antelope* was stopped by an American revenue cutter and brought to Savannah on suspicion of being an American slaver.

Smith was charged with piracy but acquitted; his commission from the Banda Oriental converted him from an outlaw to a privateer, licensed by a foreign country to prey on enemy ships. (His attack on the *Exchange* was not mentioned, nor the fact that the Banda Oriental, the country that ostensibly licensed him, was then occupied by Portuguese Brazil.) Three parties now made a claim to the *Antelope* and its cargo: Smith, who claimed them as a prize of war; and the consuls of Spain and Portugal, represented by local lawyers, who each claimed a share of the Africans on behalf of their subjects.

Arguing against them all was the U.S. district attorney for Georgia, Richard Wylly Habersham, a young lawyer from a prominent Georgia family. One of his uncles had served in the Continental Congress; another had been U.S. postmaster general. Habersham would receive little direction or encouragement from his superiors in Washington regarding the captives on the *Antelope,* so the energy with which he pursued their case seems to have been self-generated.

He argued that the Africans should be freed, under an 1819 law, nicknamed the Act in Addition (since it supplemented other laws criminalizing the slave trade). The Act in Addition provided that any Africans brought in illegally be "remove[d] beyond the United States."

The Act in Addition was the child of the American Society for Colonizing the Free People of Color of the United States (known as the American Colonization Society, for short): a benevolent alliance of northern slavery opponents and liberal slave owners. Abolitionists would come to hate it as a distraction and a diversion from the antislavery cause, but its original intent was to encourage manumission by helping free blacks return to Africa. Marshall had attended its first organizational meeting in Washington in 1816, which elected Bushrod Washington its president. Henry Clay, Speaker of the House, was another member. With such support, the society lobbied successfully to get the Act in Addition passed.

Habersham argued that Smith and his crew were Americans, whose privateering violated American neutrality (when the *Columbia/Arraganta* left Baltimore, they had signed papers denying their nationality, but these were obviously bogus). He noted that the *Antelope*'s Spanish papers were not in order—Spain required ships trading slaves south of the equator to have a special license, which the *Antelope* lacked—and that no papers for the Portuguese ships plundered at Cabinda had been presented at all. This raised a "strong suspicion" that their Portuguese ownership was also bogus, "cover[ing] citizens of other countries who cannot lawfully engage in the trade" (i.e., Americans).

The federal district court judge dismissed Smith's claim to the *Antelope*'s cargo but accepted those of Spain and Portugal. Habersham then appealed to circuit court, where the decision was written by Justice Johnson. He backed the district court, with a general statement on the slave trade: "However revolting to humanity may be the reflection, the laws of any country on the slave trade are nothing more . . . than a class of the trade laws of the nation that makes them." Spanish and Portuguese law recognized the slave trade; therefore, the Africans should be divided between the consuls of those countries.

Johnson made one exception, for the slaves taken off the American brig, the *Exchange*. Since the United States had abolished the slave trade, they were held illegally and should be free.

Johnson, however, faced a problem. Which Africans were which? Since they had arrived in Savannah, they had been put to work building a fort for the city or on the plantation of the local U.S. marshal. One had run away; several dozen had died (Savannah had suffered an outbreak of yellow fever). Spanish crew members of the *Antelope* had claimed to identify some of them, but there were no lists.

Johnson decided to sort them out by drawing lots. "The Almighty will direct the hand that acts in the selection." Sixteen were picked for freedom (the original twenty-five, minus a fraction to account for deaths).

In January 1822, Habersham appealed to the Supreme Court.

FOR VARIOUS REASONS, the case was not heard for three years. The American Colonization Society had envisioned a protectorate at Cape Mesurado on the west coast of Africa, to receive those rescued by the Act in Addition, but the site was not fit for settlement until 1824 (hostile tribes menaced it). Washington, DC, meanwhile, was distracted by the upcoming presidential election.

Since none of the candidates won a majority in the Electoral College, the House picked the winner (Adams). Once that contest was resolved, the *Antelope* was scheduled for the Court's 1825 term.

In the long interim, there had been another circuit court decision concerning the slave trade. In 1821, a U.S. Navy ship captured *La Jeune Eugénie,* an empty slaver flying French colors, off the African coast, and brought her into Boston. (The crew claimed they were trading for palm oil, but the ship was fitted with manacles.) Although France prohibited the slave trade, she denied America's right to stop one of her ships, and the French consul sued to retrieve it. Justice Story ruled on the case in 1822.

He decided that the ship was indeed a slaver. More important, he passed judgment on the slave trade, according to the law of nations.

The law of nations was an old and nebulous construct, halfway between the desirable and the real. Blackstone defined it as "a system of rules . . . established by universal consent among the civilized inhabitants of the world, in order to decide [international] disputes."

Story traced it to three sources: "positive law," or the actual laws that nations had passed; "customary observances"—what nations habitually did, law or no law; and "general principles of right and justice"—what nations should do. The slave trade, he argued, failed every test: French law prohibited it; "almost all commercial nations" now denounced it; and "Christian duty," "natural religion," "morality," and "the eternal maxims of social justice" found it "repugnant."

Story nevertheless gave *La Jeune Eugénie* to the French consul on foreign policy grounds. America had just fought a war with Britain, largely out of resentment at British ships stopping American ships on the high seas. Story would not approve a U.S. Navy ship doing the same thing to a French ship. His attack on the slave trade, however, remained on the record.

Defending the Africans of the *Antelope* before the Court in 1825 were William Wirt, the attorney general, and Francis Scott Key, a founder of the American Colonization Society, and author of the "Star-Spangled Banner." One of the spectators noted that Key's features, habitually sad, took on "a noble audacity of tone . . . in moments of special excitement." Key was now excited by the slave trade, which had worsened the practice of slavery. "Slaves are no longer acquired, merely by capture in war. . . . Wars are instigated [by slavers] for the mere purpose of making slaves." That was certainly the economic model of the *mambouk* of Cabinda and his customers.

The keenest point on the other side was made by John Berrien, formerly a Georgia judge, now a U.S. senator, arguing the claim of Spain (another lawyer argued for Portugal). Should the United States, he asked, "assume . . . the character of *censors of the morals of the world* on this subject?" Spain could say, in reply, "For more than thirty years, you were slave *traders;* you are still extensively slave *owners.* If the slave trade be robbery, you *were* robbers, and *are yet* clinging to your plunder." All the principles of right and justice cited by Story could strike uncomfortably close to home.

Six justices heard the case (Todd was ill and missed the entire term). Marshall gave the decision of the Court, with no written dissents or concurrences, though, as he revealed, there had been disagreement among the justices.

It was a shortish opinion, 4,700 words. "The sacred rights of liberty and of property," he began seriously, "[have] come in conflict with each other. . . . This Court," he went on ominously, "must not yield to feelings which would seduce it from the line of duty." Since "feelings" (except for the ever-powerful avarice) would incline to liberty, this did not sound good for Key, Story, or the Africans.

Marshall began with a discussion of "the general question": What was the legal status of the slave trade? After citing some opinions by English admiralty court judges, he unfolded his own.

"That [the slave trade] is contrary to the law of nature will scarcely be denied." The law of nature was a construct more powerful, and more elusive, than the law of nations. It blazed in the first paragraph of the Declaration of Independence, which invoked "the laws of Nature and of Nature's God," and it lived, Jefferson and its votaries believed, in human hearts. Marshall spelled out one of its first principles: "That every man has a natural right to the fruits of his own labour is generally admitted; and that no other person can rightfully deprive him of those fruits, and appropriate them against his will, seems to be the necessary result of this admission."

So Marshall spoke for feelings. Then he turned to duty. Could men, enslaved contrary to the law of nature, be legally traded? "Whatever might be the answer of a moralist to this question, the jurist must search for its legal solution."

Nations could pass laws against the slave trade, as the United States had. But "no [nation] can rightfully impose a rule on another." He illustrated this proposition with a hypothetical: "Russia and Geneva have equal rights." Marshall picked those two countries because of their difference in size: the Russian Empire was huge, while Geneva, the Swiss city-state, was tiny; yet legally, they were equally independent. (There was another difference between them: Russia was an autocracy, while Geneva was a republic. A slave state was no greater than a free state, even if it was larger; but, conversely, freedom had no rights over slavery.)

Marshall drew the point from this discussion. "It follows that a foreign vessel engaged in the African slave trade, captured on the high seas . . . by an American cruiser [should] be restored" to its owners.

Marshall's decision drew a bright line between the law of nature and the law of nations. The law of nature said that all men are created equal; the law of nations said that all nations are created equal. The law of nature belonged in declarations of independence, but the law of nations ruled in courts of law. Story's effort to illegalize the slave trade judicially was rejected; Johnson's deference to the way of the world was upheld.

But this analysis, though it settled "the general question," did not address "the circumstances" in the case of the *Antelope*. Marshall turned now to these.

He dismissed the Portuguese claim brusquely. For five years, no Portuguese person had stepped forward to retrieve his lost slaves. "This total disregard of a valuable property, is so contrary to the common course of human action, as to justify serious suspicion . . . that the real owner belongs to some other nation, and feels the necessity of concealment." Marshall did not spell it out, but his inference was plain: the real owners had been Americans, flying false flags.

The "Portuguese" Africans "ought to be delivered up to the United States, to be disposed of according to the law"—that is, the Act in Addition.

The Spanish claim, however, struck Marshall as different. Richard Habersham had argued, back in the district court, that the

Antelope lacked the Spanish license necessary for slave trading south of the equator. But, Marshall noted, its voyage from Havana, and its ownership by a Spanish firm, were all matters of record.

Was this proof enough of Spanish ownership? Marshall's answer was laconic. "[This] is a question on which much difficulty has been felt. It is unnecessary to state the reasons in support of the affirmative or negative answer to it, because the Court is divided on it." Since the Court could not decide, the decision of the circuit court, in favor of the Spanish claim, prevailed.

What had the justices said to each other at their boardinghouse dinner table? Since they divided evenly, they must have split three to three. Johnson and Story would have followed their opposing circuit court judgments on the slave trade. Thompson was a moderately antislavery Northerner, who had favored freeing all the *Antelope*'s Africans when he was secretary of the navy in Monroe's cabinet. Duvall was a Maryland plantation owner. But in an 1813 decision of the Court, on a freedom petition by an enslaved woman, he had said "the right to freedom is more important than the right of property." (The woman lost; Duvall, in dissent, backed her.) Marshall and Washington must have sided with Spain.

Washington was president of the American Colonization Society, which had pressed for the Act in Addition. He was also an heir of George Washington—a conflicted heir. In his last will and testament, the Father of his Country had, famously, freed all his slaves. He had also left his nephew Bushrod four thousand acres and the Mount Vernon plantation house. But the tidewater soil had been exhausted even in Washington's lifetime; shorn of the investment properties that he had accumulated over years of surveying and speculation, and that he had divided among other heirs, Mount Vernon was a white elephant.

In 1821, Justice Washington, scrambling to stay afloat, sold fifty-four of his own slaves to a planter in Louisiana, which brought him denunciation in the press, and a piece of franglais hate mail. "Je have heard of votre character in Louisiana, where vous rend votre Slaves . . . Vous suppose you are great because named Washington. . . . Wretched being le time is coming when vous have to answer for votre base crimes." Washington answered his critics with an open letter claiming that his ex-slaves had "cheerfully consented" to be sold, complaining (unmindful of the contradiction) that they would have run away if they had not been sold, and asserting his "right, legal [and] moral, to dispose of property."

Washington's opinions and actions could have led him either way in judging the case of the *Antelope*. One of his opinions of longest standing, however, was that John Marshall was generally right. Justice Johnson, in one of his letters to Jefferson, had called the two "one judge." Where Marshall went, Washington would almost certainly have followed.

Marshall had his own mixed motives and influences. He too belonged to the American Colonization Society, having founded its Richmond branch in 1823. After decades of buying, he was also a considerable slave owner, who owned about a dozen house slaves in Richmond, plus over 130 more slaves on plantations in Fauquier and Henrico Counties.

He had begun his *Antelope* decision by distinguishing feelings and moralizing from duty and judging. Counsel for the Spanish claimants had produced a paper trail, and Marshall evidently did not question it.

He did reduce the number of Africans that Spain could claim, since the chief witness to its total, the *Antelope*'s second mate, had relied on memory and hearsay as well as visual identification. "The residue" were to be given to the claimants.

After Marshall's decision, the circuit court sorted the Africans again—not by a lottery this time but by the testimony of Georgians who had seen them responding to commands in Spanish.

One hundred thirty-one were marked for freedom, thirty-nine for slavery (death had reduced their numbers, partly compensated by the births of some children).

Habersham filed yet another appeal on the Africans' behalf (his zeal in their cause was truly remarkable), protesting the shoddiness of the new procedure. The appeal reached the Supreme Court in 1827. Justice Todd had died, replaced by a fellow Kentuckian, Robert Trimble. Key, appearing once again, argued that there was "no credible and competent evidence" to consign "Spanish" Africans to bondage, but Justice Trimble, giving the Court's unanimous decision, found the testimony of the Georgians "sufficient."

Finally, in August 1827, 130 Africans arrived at Cape Mesurado (three had died on the voyage, and two had been born). The agent of the American Colonization Society, who ran the settlement, found them "orderly, peaceable, and industrious." A Georgia congressman bought the Spanish claim, now reduced to thirty-seven Africans, and shipped them to a plantation in Florida.

After Marshall died, Richard Wylly Habersham would be elected to Congress. The American Colonization Society's African settlement would become Liberia.

The secret slave trade continued too. Abraham Lincoln considered the abolition of the trade in 1808 as a sign of the founders' desire to contain slavery, so that it might eventually wither away. Yet he admitted, in his first inaugural, that it had only been "imperfectly suppressed." The first, and last, American slaver to be executed for this capital crime was Nathaniel Gordon, of Portland, Maine, who was apprehended in 1860 not far from Cabinda with a shipload of nine hundred Africans. Gordon was hanged a year and a half later.

It took the Civil War to snuff the slave trade.

NATURAL LAW IS a hard thing to bring into court, and there is a vein of skepticism about it that often appealed to Federalists. They liked to think of themselves as practical men and of their enemies (Jefferson conspicuously) as idle theorists. Alexander Hamilton dropped into the *Federalist* a crack about bills of rights, calling them "aphorisms . . . which would sound much better in a treatise of ethics than in a constitution of government."

Yet there were times when Marshall, even in judicial decisions, smuggled the language of nature and of rights into constitutional law. In *Fletcher v. Peck,* he had defined the contract clause, and other provisions of Article I, Section 10, as a bill of rights. Africans might not be protected by it, but contracts were.

Marshall would reach for natural rights language again, in defense of contracts, and consider it, in defense of another race.

Chapter 14

BANKRUPTS

B Y THE SUMMER OF 1826, THOMAS JEFFERSON KNEW THAT he was dying. Although he was the greatest living Virginian, he was, like many of his planter neighbors, bankrupt. His habits had been too rich and his soil too poor. His last recourse, a special lottery authorized by the State of Virginia for his benefit, had failed to generate enough money to save him.

He never surrendered his dislike of John Marshall. In his last years, he continued to complain to correspondents of Marshall's sins great and small, from his overreach on the Supreme Court to his manhandling of Jefferson in the *Life of Washington:* "Marshall makes history descend from its dignity, and the ermine from its sanctity."

He died on July 4, 1826, the fiftieth anniversary of his Declaration.

Even as Jefferson never surrendered his dislike of Marshall, the chief justice never surrendered his of his cousin. When an edition of Jefferson's letters and papers appeared in 1829, Marshall wrote of it, to an acquaintance, in a spirit of seeming acceptance: "I have become indolent, and age has blunted my feelings." Then he unloaded his feelings. Every good idea that Jefferson had was common to "every patriot"; every idea unique to him was crackpot. Among the latter, Marshall cited Jefferson's beliefs that contracts should last only a generation, that a little rebellion now and then was wholesome, and that judges should be elected. The first two were philosophical trial balloons, released in letters to James Madison and other intimates, never floated publicly; the third was not unique to Jefferson but a commonplace opinion among the Republican Party. Yet Marshall found all three equally crazy and destructive. "From the time I became acquainted with Mr. Jefferson as Secretary of State, I have never believed firmly in his infallibility. . . . I have not changed this mode of thinking." In the determined understatement, one hears the grinding of teeth.

Jefferson was joined in death on July 4 by John Adams, the man who had appointed Marshall to the Supreme Court. He had spent his long retirement—twenty-five years and four months—alternately brooding and enjoying himself, reading tomes and writing peppery letters to numerous recipients, including his nemesis Jefferson. In 1823, some Adams letters abusing various Federalists, chiefly Alexander Hamilton and Timothy Pickering, had been published without his consent. Marshall, ever irenic where fellow Federalists were concerned, deplored the letters but not their author. "I feel great respect for Mr. Adams," he wrote Justice Story, "and shall always feel it whatever he may do."

After these double deaths, one signer of the Declaration still lived, and three of the Constitution; bitterness kept Pickering hale and healthy; aged veterans of the Revolution were still scattered throughout the country, a corps of shadows. But this dramatic exit, on the national birthday, signaled the passing of a generation. The country was middle-aged, its fathers were gone or going. Of that cohort, only John Marshall, who would turn seventy-one in September, remained in active service.

Death had already taken another justice of the Supreme Court, Thomas Todd, who died in February 1826. A eulogy by Story painted a portrait of a shy man; Story called him patient, modest, diffident, and retiring. He also paid him a compliment as impressive as it is rare: "He listened to arguments for the purpose of instruction . . . and not merely for that of confutation or debate." He was replaced in April by Robert Trimble, who had been a judge on both the Kentucky supreme court and federal district court. A local politician described Trimble campaigning for the nomination while Todd still lingered, "running from town to town with ready made recommendations in his pocket" for potential supporters to sign. Despite this eagerness, Todd welcomed Trimble as his successor, and the other justices were happy to have an experienced colleague.

Trimble joined the Court in time for a landmark bankruptcy case. It would be the occasion for Marshall's only dissent on a question of constitutional significance.

M OST DEBTORS IN colonial and early America were undone by land speculation, the hope and trap of the new country. Those who had the least to risk—only their lives and families— carved out subsistence farms on frontier properties they bought, rented, or took by squatting, moving on when they failed, or when some new territory that was (seemingly) more hopeful opened up.

Those who bought large tracts with real money—theirs or borrowed—bet on the hope of resale. After years of careful political and legal attention, the Marshalls had made their slice of the old Fairfax Grant profitable. Less prudent speculators came to grief. Justice James Wilson, who served on the Court in the 1790s, made many other purchases besides his Yazoo holdings and died on the run from creditors. Henry Lee, Marshall's comrade in arms from whom he had borrowed his lapidary tribute to George Washington, plunged again and again, spending time in debtors' prison.

The legal concept of bankruptcy developed to deal, not with real estate high rollers but with merchants, whose ordinary business was subject to mishaps beyond human foresight. Blackstone explained that if "accidental calamities," such as "the loss of a ship in a tempest," caused a merchant to sink under the weight of his debts, "it is his misfortune and not his fault." Bankruptcy law therefore allowed the unfortunate to stay out of jail "upon condition they surrender up their whole estate to be divided among their creditors."

Was this merciful enough for honest men suffering a stroke of bad luck? Was it too merciful (suppose the whole estate of a bankrupt would not cover his debts)? How were honest bankrupts to be distinguished from sharpers trying to shake off their creditors? These were questions with which government at both the federal and state level struggled. The Constitution (Article I, Section 8) gave Congress the power to pass "uniform Laws on the subject of Bankruptcies." Yet it had done so only once, under the Federalists in 1800—a law repealed by the Republicans in 1803. States wanted to keep bankruptcy law in their own hands—and debtors, who felt they could bring political pressure to bear more effectively at the local level, wanted it to remain there.

A significant case in bankruptcy law had come before the Court in 1819. It concerned the debts of Richard Crowninshield, a younger son of a wealthy Salem, Massachusetts, merchant who, before the War of 1812, tried what was for his family a new venture. The disruptions in trade caused by the Embargo and related measures had compelled Americans to manufacture their own cloth. Crowninshield built a woolen factory in Connecticut, which burned down, and another in New York, which went bust. He tried a third time back home, damming a small stream that ran through Salem for power, and this venture prospered.

For his New York venture, he had borrowed $1,543.72 from Josiah Sturgis, a Massachusetts-born merchant then based in Charleston, South Carolina. When that factory failed, Crowninshield declared insolvency under a New York law passed in 1811. In 1816, Sturgis sued in circuit court in Massachusetts to get his money back from his now-recovering debtor, arguing that the New York law infringed on Congress's power to pass uniform bankruptcy laws and violated the obligation of contracts.

Joseph Story, the justice assigned to the Massachusetts circuit, was happy to see the case. He wrote his friend Henry Wheaton, the Court reporter, that he had "meditated much" on the desirability of a national bankruptcy law; a ringing judicial decision might prompt Congress to act. Story wanted a national law, not out of tenderness for debtors but from a desire to nationalize economic laws. He and the district judge who sat with him on the Massachusetts circuit agreed to issue a divided opinion on Sturgis's suit, so that it would have to be decided by the Supreme Court. *Sturges v. Crowninshield* was heard in 1819, the year of *McCulloch* and *Dartmouth* (for some reason—Wheaton's carelessness?—Sturgis's surname was misspelled *Sturges* throughout the record).

Marshall delivered the Court's opinion. There were no concurrences or dissents; it was fairly brief—little more than four thousand words—and it rang with phrases uttered in Marshall's most commanding tone of voice, laying down the law as from Sinai or from the Constitutional Convention: "The words of the Constitution . . . are express, and incapable of being misunderstood. They admit of no variety of construction." But in fact, there had been a variety of understandings among the justices, which Marshall had elided—for a time.

He began by stating the language of Article I, Section 8, giving Congress the power to pass national bankruptcy laws. But Congress, except for the years 1800–03, had failed to do so. Could states fill the gap? Marshall said yes: "until the power . . . be exercised by Congress, the states are not forbidden" from exercising it themselves.

The states, however, were forbidden from "impairing the Obligation of Contracts" (Article I, Section 10). These were the words of the Constitution that prompted Marshall to speak in organ tones. He had already defended contracts from state action in *Fletcher* and had done so once more days before his *Sturges* decision in *Dartmouth*. Now he declared that "contracts should be inviolable." Debts were contracts; debtors must pay.

In a paragraph aimed directly at Richard Crowninshield, Marshall explained that a bankrupt was responsible for the full amount of his debt, even if it exceeded the sum of his property at the moment of going broke: "Industry, talent, and integrity" were assets as real "as property itself." A creditor could therefore call on the "future acquisitions" of his debtor.

So far, so sweeping. But then Marshall introduced a distinction. "The remedy" the law prescribed for fulfilling contracts "may be modified as the wisdom of the nation shall admit." Debtors, as Blackstone had written, did not have to be sent to prison. This punishment, depicted in eighteenth-century prints and ballads as the destination of rakes and wastrels and inflicted in the nineteenth century on Henry Lee, was increasingly seen as inhumane, as well as ineffective (how could a debtor work off what he owed in jail?). It might be wiser, and it was certainly legal, said Marshall, to let him go: "Imprisonment is no part of the contract."

Statutes of limitations, Marshall went on, were another modification of the law's remedies. How long after the fact could an unhappy creditor appear to claim that he had been cheated? Five years (as Josiah Sturgis had done)? Fifty years? Statutes of limitations marked the legal window of an action.

In making these points, Marshall let fall a further distinction: contracts that were "already in existence" before a statute of limitations had been passed could not be brought within it afterward.

This too was aimed at Crowninshield. He had borrowed Sturgis's money in March 1811, but the New York law he invoked to avoid paying it back had not been passed until April. His contract with Josiah Sturgis had been "already in existence." Therefore, the Court ruled that Sturgis could proceed with his suit to recover his money.

Marshall reached for several props to his decision, because his fellow justices had been at loggerheads. Washington, like Story, believed that Article I, Section 8, left the field of bankruptcy law in the hands of Congress, even if Congress had not passed one. But Johnson had ruled, in his circuit, that federal and state governments alike could pass such laws, and Livingston, at that time New York's justice, had upheld, in his circuit, the very law Crowninshield cited. If, as Marshall wrote, there could be no backward-looking remedies, then the justices' disagreements on the validity of state bankruptcy law became moot. So Marshall held his colleagues together.

JOSIAH STURGIS LEFT Charleston to sail and trade along the coast of Oregon. Richard Crowninshield's son, Richard Jr., became famous by robbing and murdering an elderly neighbor in Salem in the middle of the night; Daniel Webster, appearing for the prosecution at young Crowninshield's trial, gave a lurid description of his deed that inspired Edgar Allan Poe's crime classic, "The Tell-Tale Heart."

The legal status of bankruptcy, meanwhile, had become a matter for national concern. The Panic of 1819 hit just as *Sturges* was decided, bringing a wave of business failures. Congress could offer debtors relief—it was not bound by the prohibitions of Article I, Section 10—but Congress failed to act. A case in 1824 brought the issue of state laws before the Court once more.

George Ogden, merchant, was a nephew of Aaron Ogden, the former New Jersey governor who was the defendant in the steamboat case. George was also an old friend of Aaron Burr's, loaning him money for his western schemes (never repaid). In 1806, Ogden endorsed a bill of exchange, or IOU, for $2,100, to John

Jordan, another Burr backer in Kentucky, who then transferred it to a second Kentuckian, John Saunders. When Saunders presented it to Ogden for payment, Ogden pleaded insolvency, citing, in his defense, a New York bankruptcy law—not the 1811 statute invoked by Richard Crowninshield but an earlier one, passed in 1801, five years before his transaction. Saunders took Ogden to court in 1814, arguing, as Josiah Sturgis would, that the New York law was unconstitutional.

The case made its way to the Supreme Court in 1824, but Justice Todd was sick, leaving only six justices, who deadlocked. The case was reargued in 1827, by which time Ogden had died; his executors stood in for him.

Death had also changed the Court since the *Sturges* decision, taking Livingston and Todd, who had been replaced by Thompson and Trimble. Now, for the first time, Marshall lost control of his Court on an issue of constitutional import.

In 1824, when *Ogden v. Saunders* was first argued, Marshall, Story, and Duvall had wanted to strike down the 1801 New York law on the grounds that it interfered with Congress's power to pass bankruptcy laws; Washington, Johnson, and Thompson were for upholding it. (The evolution of Washington's thinking, which had brought him into rare disagreement with Marshall, was complicated; he had originally believed that Congress's power to establish bankruptcy laws preempted the states from doing so. But, after assenting to *Sturges,* he felt committed to the state option.) Marshall hoped that Todd, who always agreed with him on constitutional questions, would ultimately join him in a four-man majority. But Todd had not recovered his health, and Trimble, his replacement, sided with the backers of state laws.

Marshall submitted a dissent, which was joined by Story and Duvall. It was longish, almost eight thousand words. It is possible that he had written it expecting to speak for the Court, although there are some combative touches—"Are gentlemen prepared to say . . . ?" "Will reason sustain this distinction?"—that suggest the ire of an author who finds himself in the unaccustomed position of being outvoted.

Marshall began with a summary of his theory of constitutional interpretation. "The intention of the instrument"—the Constitution—"must prevail . . . This intention must be collected from its words . . . Its words are to be understood in that sense in which they are generally used . . . " By making his method seem simple, he sought to bolster its authority; how could a process so straightforward ever be mistaken?

Marshall's opening flourish paid little heed to the intentions of the framers—it was literalism that he was expounding, not originalism—though he would summon them later.

Ogden's lawyers maintained that New York's 1801 law, in place when his bill of exchange was first drawn, controlled his contract ("The law enters into the contract so completely as to become a constituent part of it," was how Marshall paraphrased their argument). Ogden and his creditors had signed off on the law as surely as they had signed off on Ogden's promise to pay. Therefore, the law could release Ogden from his promise, so long as he met the conditions the law had set forth.

Marshall would have none of it. Laws enforced contracts, but contracts were made by men. Contracts, Marshall declared, "exist anterior to, and independent of society. . . . Individuals do not derive from government their right to contract, but bring that right with them into society." The obligation that a contract creates—in this case, that George Ogden make good on his bill of exchange—"is not conferred . . . by positive law"—the laws that New York State, or other governments, have passed—"but is intrinsic, and is conferred by the act of the parties."

Marshall illustrated his doctrine with a description of a prehistoric contract, set in "the rudest state of nature. . . . One man may have acquired more skins than are necessary for his protection from the cold; another more food than is necessary for his immediate use. They agree each to supply the wants of the other from his surplus." Later, when men formed society, they gave it the right and power of enforcing their agreements about skins and food; society supplied what Marshall had called in *Sturges* the "remedy" for noncompliance. But their agreements—their contracts—came first.

Marshall turned from prehistory to recent history; from men in the state of nature to Americans in 1787. "The august spectacle was [then] exhibited of the assemblage of a whole people by their representatives in Convention, in order to unite thirteen independent sovereignties under one government." It was impossible, he went on, to consider that time—almost forty years ago as he was now writing—"without being sensible of the great importance which was . . . attached" to the sanctity of contracts. He painted a picture of postrevolutionary America as a lawless, deadbeat nation. "The power . . . of interfering with contracts . . . had been used to such an excess by the State legislatures, as to break in upon the ordinary intercourse of society, and destroy all confidence between man and man. The mischief had become so great [as] to sap the morals of the people, and destroy the sanctity of private faith." Natural man had made contracts; Americans, interfering with them, had fallen. The framers of the Constitution (and the ratifying conventions, including John Marshall) had brought redemption through the contract clause.

The contract clause, contra Marshall, had had an almost accidental genesis, inserted into the Constitution at the last minute by Alexander Hamilton. But Marshall's recollection of the framers' anxieties over the wiles and stubbornness of debtors was accurate.

There was near-religious fervor in Marshall's dissent. There was also, in its talk of "the rudest state of nature," an echo of seventeenth- and eighteenth-century political philosophers, of Locke and Rousseau, searching for first principles in hypothetical anthropology—men with buckles on their shoes and powder on their hair, imagining the doings of men in skins, in order to ascertain their own rights. These were tones of voice and modes of thought that Marshall rarely employed. His use of them showed the importance he attached to contracts, and his determination to proclaim it, even (especially) in defeat.

Washington, Johnson, Thompson, and Trimble disagreed with their chief. But without his guiding hand, they produced four separate opinions—a majority of concurrences. Johnson's opinion included a sour note on *Sturges:* "The Court," he told the world, "was, in that case, greatly divided in their views of the [underlying] doctrine." The judgment they had reached "partakes as much of a compromise, as of a legal adjudication." Johnson revealed that the supporters of state bankruptcy laws had accepted Marshall's opinion then only because it forbade laws that operated backward—a prohibition they too endorsed. Lifting the curtain on the internal debates of the Marshall court was as unprecedented as Marshall's failure to carry his point.

T HERE WAS A coda to *Ogden:* an additional argument before the Court, on a question of federalism. George Ogden had been living in New York when he gave his bill of exchange and pleaded a New York law in his defense. But at the time he was sued by John Saunders, of Kentucky, he had moved to New Orleans, where he lived for the rest of his days. Could state bankruptcy laws operate beyond state borders?

On this question a new four-man majority, consisting of Marshall, Story, Duvall, and Johnson, held that they could not. "The power of States over contracts," wrote Johnson, speaking for all of them, "is limited to the controversies of their own citizens." A state could protect bankrupts, but only its own bankrupts, and only if they stayed put. The Court accordingly ruled that Ogden's executors had to pay his debt (which, with interest and damages, had swollen to $4,000). Marshall won the crust but lost the loaf.

The spectacle of shifting four-man majorities, pivoting at the discretion of one justice, chipped the granitic authority that Marshall had sought to confer on the Court.

FOUR YEARS AFTER *Ogden*, Alexis de Tocqueville, the young French aristocrat touring America to study democracy, was dismayed by the number of bankruptcies he found and by the public's indifference to them. It was, he wrote, "one of the greatest stains on the American character." Congress would not pass an effective national bankruptcy law for many years.

Marshall would never again be a dissenter on a constitutional case, but more challenges to him and his Court were coming.

Chapter 15

CHEROKEES

EVEN AS GENERATIONS AGED AND PASSED IN THE NATION, founders giving way to their heirs, so they matured and moved in the Marshall family.

Sometimes the process was attended with friction. Marshall sent his younger sons to Harvard. They had not all flourished there. In 1826, the year before *Ogden,* Marshall's youngest, Edward, fell in love with Harriet Fay, daughter of a Massachusetts judge who was an overseer, or trustee, of the college. Edward must have loved Harriet for herself as much as for her connections; another of her admirers called her "the golden blond." His letters about her were filled with what his father called "the language of a young man who sees nothing but felicity before him."

It was obvious to the chief justice that Harriet's love for Edward must be equally great, since marriage to him would involve leaving the high society of Cambridge for a farm in Fauquier County, Edward's only inheritance as a youngest son. Marshall accordingly wrote a hospitable letter to Judge Fay, assuring him that the entire Marshall clan would give Harriet "the most affectionate and cordial welcome."

He received, in return, a letter informing him that Judge Fay had forbidden the match. Fay's letter and his reasons have not survived; evidently, he wanted what Harriet ultimately got: a marriage to a New Englander. Marshall was doubly embarrassed; he had been deceived, and his son (and, indirectly, himself) had been disrespected by a proud Yankee. Marshall wrote the judge once more, acknowledging that it was for parents "alone to judge" of their daughters' suitors. Men made contracts, but young women could not make their own marriage contracts. Three years later, Edward married an eighteen-year-old Virginian who was a great-great-granddaughter of a Randolph.

Marshall had problems of his own at home. The veil that covers the life of his valetudinarian wife is pierced by an awkward letter Marshall wrote at the end of the decade to a Richmond neighbor, whose barking dog "has scarcely left [Polly] a night of quiet.... Last night she could not sleep two hours. Her situation is deplorable, and if this state of things continues she cannot live." Marshall carefully enumerated and dismissed alternative solutions, besides quieting Fido; he and Polly could retreat to their country house, but "our little place . . . affords her only a confined and hot chamber" (the dog was barking in the middle of July). They could move in with friends, but "my wife cannot travel, and cannot sleep in a house with a family." That a man who loved being everyone's friend could bring himself to write such a letter shows what pain Polly was feeling—and what pain John was feeling from her demands as well as from her suffering.

The good that Polly gave him is reflected in a note to Justice Story. Story had sent Marshall one of his many, many occasional pieces, a speech to the student society Phi Beta Kappa surveying contemporary science and letters. Marshall in reply chided his friend for omitting the great novelist Jane Austen, who had died in 1817, from a list of women writers. "She does not soar on eagle's wings," Marshall wrote—that would describe Sir Walter Scott's hugely popular historical tales—"but she is pleasing, interesting, equable, and yet amusing." Polly, Marshall wrote elsewhere, had "a fine taste for belle lettre reading"; she was also, in private, a wit and a mimic. No doubt it was she who introduced her husband to Austen; he must have thought of Polly as his very own Austen at home.

Marshall's devotion to his wife did not keep him from socializing. One undated story describes him dining with a social club in Philadelphia, which met in a tavern. Members and guests were required to make impromptu rhymes on given words. Marshall was given the word *paradox*. Inspired by some Kentuckians he had just passed drinking in the bar, Marshall said:

> *In the Blue Grass region,*
> *A paradox was born.*
> *The corn was full of kernels,*
> *And the colonels full of corn.*

The pun kernels/colonels may have occurred to him long before, as it might to any verbal person, but to retrieve it on the spot and attach it to the word *paradox*, was quick thinking. Such a genial man might even be able to deal with Harvard overseers and barking dogs.

THE ELECTION OF 1828 was felt to be one of the most momentous in American history. After the collapse of the Federalist Party, everyone for a time was a Republican. But every ambitious Republican soon began fighting with every other. These crosscurrents of self-interest had produced the free-for-all election of 1824, from which John Quincy Adams emerged as president.

Of the losers in that struggle, John Calhoun had contented himself with the vice presidency; William Crawford had retired from politics; Henry Clay, who supported Adams at the last minute, had become his secretary of state; and Andrew Jackson was out for blood. As the candidate who had won a plurality of popular and electoral votes, he felt done out of the White House by the connivance of Adams and Clay. Jackson's 1828 rematch with Adams, a head-to-head contest, was remarkably ugly, even by American standards. Jackson's supporters denounced Adams as corrupt; one Adams campaign song equated Jackson with Satan.

There was an issue, or at least a popular movement, in the clamor. Although Jackson was a wealthy landowner, he was self-made, born a frontiersman, a new man appealing to other new men in the west and in cities alike. The populist rhetoric of Jefferson had found an authentic populist champion. Jackson's followers called themselves Democrats. The word, once a slur among the founders, who equated it with impulsiveness, demagogy, and mob rule—"Our real disease," wrote Alexander Hamilton on the eve of his death, "is DEMOCRACY"—was now a slogan: a winning slogan.

Marshall had made a habit of not voting in recent presidential elections. (Who, given the long withering of his party, could he have voted for, with any prospect of success?) But John Adams had been his friend and patron. John Quincy Adams, for his part, thought Marshall's nomination to the Court "one of the most important services" that his father had ever done for America. It was only natural that Marshall would cast his vote for the family in its hour of need. He was chagrined, however, when a pro-Jackson newspaper in Baltimore quoted him as saying "should Jackson be elected, I shall look upon the government as virtually dissolved."

Marshall wrote a letter to a pro-Adams newspaper in Richmond, protesting that he had said nothing of the kind. (One of his nephews had told an acquaintance that his uncle was supporting Adams, whereupon the acquaintance drew the conclusion that the Baltimore newspaper subsequently reported as Marshall's opinion.) To Story, Marshall complained that he was "a good deal provoked" by the episode. "Intemperate language does not become my age or office and is foreign from my disposition and habits." Marshall was a man of strong views, but he brought them to bear on the bench, not the hustings.

Jackson won in a landslide, carrying fifteen of twenty-four states and 56 percent of the popular vote. John Calhoun, biding his time, was reelected vice president. Justice Story described the scene at the White House after Jackson's inauguration: "[There were] immense crowds of all sorts of people, from the highest and most polished, down to the most vulgar and gross in the nation. . . . The reign of King 'Mob' seemed triumphant."

VIRGINIA, WHICH WENT for Jackson by more than two to one, had a chance to embrace populism at home. The constitution that had governed the state since 1776 pleased nobody. It contained a historic Declaration of Rights, written by George Mason, but the governor was weak, suffrage was restricted to property owners, and the apportionment of the legislature favored the decaying plantation-based counties of the Tidewater. In October 1829, a state constitutional convention met in Richmond to produce a new document.

Thomas Jefferson was dead, but all the other great Virginians of the early republic attended: two ex-presidents, James Madison and James Monroe; the chief justice; John Randolph. These men, assembled together after so many disagreements, must have seemed, if not dead, stepped from the afterlife, visitors from a secular Valhalla. Marshall, ever the host, had them all to his house for dinners and parties.

Marshall chaired the convention's committee on the judiciary. The most controversial point in the report he produced was that judges should serve for life (unless convicted of some crime). This, he believed, was the only security of their independence.

"The Judicial Department," he told the convention, "comes home in its effects to every man's fireside; it passes on his property, his reputation, his life, his all. Is it not, to the last degree important, that [a judge] should be rendered perfectly and completely independent, with nothing to influence or to control him but God and his conscience?"

Marshall was revisiting, a generation later, the issues raised by the Judiciary Act of 1802, when the triumphant Jeffersonians had peeled away layers of the federal judiciary by congressional fiat. Guided by his colleagues on the Court, Marshall had made no move to strike that law down. But he never accepted the principle that legislatures ought to have the power to shorten the tenure of sitting judges, and now he wanted Virginia's new constitution to uphold his own principle. After keen and sometimes florid debate—a dependent judiciary, Marshall declared at one point, was "the greatest scourge an angry Heaven ever inflicted upon an ungrateful and a sinning people"—Marshall prevailed.

There was another scourge that heaven inflicted on sinning (and on innocent) people—slavery. One Virginian, younger than the gathered demigods but still eminent, wanted the convention to address it. Edward Coles was related to Dolley Madison, and he had been James Madison's personal secretary in the White House. In 1819, he had left Virginia with his slaves for the new state of Illinois, where he freed them and set them up as small farmers. In 1822, he ran successfully for governor to block a move to turn Illinois into a slave state. He returned to Virginia for its constitutional convention, hoping that his former home would join his new home in choosing freedom. But Coles was not a delegate, and no one listened to him. Monroe, in one of his speeches to the convention, assured his fellow delegates that emancipation would produce "perfect confusion . . . the thing is impossible." The assembled Virginians left slavery as it was, and though they lessened the property requirement for voting, they left the legislature in the grip of the planter elite.

The convention was a way station on Virginia's by now unstoppable slide into mental and moral insignificance. The state that had once led the world in political thought was hardly capable of keeping its own affairs in order. It could not embrace the Jacksonian ferment, still less be truly bold and humane.

Marshall was no help. The morality of slavery did not concern him in any practical way. It was his greatest deviation from his Federalist idols. George Washington, after a lifetime of slave owning, freed all his slaves in his will in what he knew would be a nationally noted act, and Alexander Hamilton had helped found the New-York Manumission Society that, after decades of lobbying, had ended slavery in his home state in 1827.

Marshall let the institution live and thrive.

D EATH TOOK TWO more justices of the Supreme Court. In August 1828, Robert Trimble, after little more than two years on the Court, died of a bilious fever (one of those nineteenth-century ailments no less deadly for being vague). In November 1829, Bushrod Washington, who had been on the Court since 1798, followed him.

John Quincy Adams made a lame-duck nomination for Trimble's successor, but the Senate, controlled by victorious Democrats, refused to consider it. Both vacancies were therefore filled by Andrew Jackson. He surprised the political world by picking men of relatively moderate views—John McLean, who had been Adams's postmaster general, and Henry Baldwin, a former congressman from Pennsylvania. Daniel Webster hailed their appointments as an "escape" from extremism.

The new justices nevertheless made further changes in the culture of the Court. Justice McLean had been living with his family in Washington, DC, for years and continued to do so. Encouraged by his example, Justice Johnson decided to board on his own when he came to Washington as well. The Court's efficiency suffered: "We cannot carry on our business as fast as usual," Marshall wrote his wife. Even more, so did its camaraderie.

The personalities of the new justices were jarring. McLean was a political animal. He had spent his time at the post office scheming against Clay and sending out feelers to Jackson. (John Quincy Adams, who was the opposite of a political animal, had longed to fire him but couldn't bring himself to do it.) Once McLean got on the Court, he struck out for himself, hoping, like Smith Thompson, to be president one day. He was still hoping a quarter century later; in 1856, Abraham Lincoln would suggest him as the first nominee of the new Republican Party.

The problem with Baldwin was that he was intermittently out of his mind. It is impossible to say, from the twenty-first century, what exactly was wrong with him; money worries apparently contributed. When the fit was on him, he became uncontrollably agitated. "He sits in his room for three or four hours in the dark," one Court observer wrote, then "jumps up and runs down into the judges' consultation room in his stocking feet, and remains in that condition while they are deliberating." In 1833, he missed an entire session. When he was not out of commission, he was prickly and contentious. He particularly disliked Story, who returned the feeling. Marshall, trying to unruffle feathers, wrote Story on the eve of one session that "our brother Baldwin . . . spoke of you in terms not indicating unfriendliness."

Worse for Marshall than these difficult additions was the loss of Washington, his friend since their days at William and Mary, his collaborator in politics, authorship, and judging, his connection—not that he needed an extra one—to the greatest Man on earth. At the opening of the 1830 session, the lawyers of the Supreme Court bar offered a tribute to the late justice. "No man," said Marshall in reply, "knew his worth better or deplores his death more than myself."

T HE MOST CONTROVERSIAL cases of the Court in Jackson's first term involved relations with Indians.

Since the first colonial settlements, white men had been trading with Indians, taking furs and giving guns, tools, liquor, and diseases in exchange. Full-scale battles and piecemeal violence alternated with periods of relative quiet. In the world wars that settled the fate of the continent, Spain, France, Britain, and the United States each recruited Indian allies and fought Indian enemies. One of Marshall's fellow sufferers at Valley Forge was Louis Cook, a pro-American Mohawk, later commissioned as a lieutenant colonel.

White Americans respected Indians more than their black slaves. Indians had been here first; they gave as good as they got; though "savage," they were free. In 1784, Patrick Henry sponsored a bill that encouraged white Virginian men to marry Indians as a measure of frontier peacekeeping. Marshall supported it, calling it "advantageous to this country." (It failed to pass when Henry left the legislature to become governor.) In 1806, Judge George Wythe, Marshall's sometime teacher, ruling on a freedom suit by a slave, made two decisions: the slave was in fact an Indian and thus entitled to freedom; and the Virginia Declaration of Rights granted a presumption of freedom to all men. On appeal, Wythe's second, radical decision was overturned, but his first, pro-Indian one was upheld.

Once Indians had been decisively beaten and displaced, they could be romanticized. James Fenimore Cooper's 1826 best seller, *The Last of the Mohicans,* gave its frontiersman hero an Indian friend, brave, honest, faithful—and doomed (his son is killed in battle, and he will die an old drunk).

Such sentiments, enlightened or tender, had no effect on the land-hungry. Experience showed that white farmers drove off game, which drove away the Indians who lived by hunting and trapping it; if the process was accompanied with murders, massacres, and wars, so be it.

George Washington tried briefly to arrest the process, negotiating, in 1790, a treaty with Alexander McGillivray, the Creek chief who commanded six thousand warriors in western Georgia and beyond. The treaty guaranteed an independent Creek state, protected against the encroachments of settlers and land speculators. Washington, Marshall wrote in his biography, was motivated by "a real respect for the rights of the natives, and a regard for the claims of justice and humanity." But the federal government, with its miniscule army, could not control the tide of white settlement.

The status of Indian land deals came before the Court in two cases early in the new century. In 1812, Marshall, speaking for the whole Court, ruled, in *New Jersey v. Wilson*, that a tax break, granted by the colonial legislature to a tract of land owned by the Delaware Indians, was still valid even though the Delawares had sold the land in 1803 and moved away. The tax break, Marshall wrote, was "a contract, clothed in forms of unusual solemnity. . . . annexed, by the terms which create[d] it, to the land itself."

But Marshall later ruled that Indians could not make their own contracts with private persons. On the eve of the Revolution, Thomas Johnson, a Maryland lawyer and patriot, had bought two tracts of land west of the Appalachians from the Piankeshaw Indians. In 1818, William M'Intosh (or McIntosh) bought the same land from Congress, which was selling off land titles in the Northwest Territory. Johnson's heirs sued the interloper, and the case reached the Court in 1823.

Marshall once again spoke for all the justices. The key phrase of his opinion, which controlled the rest, was marked by frankness amounting to cynicism, boldness amounting to brutality. "Conquest gives a title which the courts of the conqueror cannot deny." Britain had claimed, and defended against European rivals, great tracts of North America, which the United States had then wrested from it. Marshall admitted that the Indians who lived there had legitimate claims to their land. "Indian inhabitants" were "to be protected, indeed, while in peace." But their claims were limited to occupancy; they were "deemed incapable of transferring the ultimate title to others." Indians could live on their land, but only the United States could sell it. McIntosh's title was good, that of Johnson's heirs was not.

Along the way, Marshall praised Indians for their "persevering courage" and observed that "humanity . . . has established, as a general rule, that the conquered shall not be wantonly oppressed." Were these pious sentiments, feelings merely, which would be superseded, as in the *Antelope* decision two years later, by Marshall's duties as a judge?

ANDREW JACKSON AND his enemies made Indian policy a national issue early in his administration. At the end of 1829, Jackson expressed his views to Congress: all Indians east of the Mississippi should move beyond it; those who remained behind would have to abide by the laws of the states where they lived, which would strip them of their identity and consign them to the lowly status reserved for free people of color.

Jackson's policy provoked the Sauk Indians of northwestern Illinois to wage a war of resistance, in which a young Abraham Lincoln served for three months. But Jackson's main targets were the Indians of the old southwest—Choctaws, Chickasaws, Cherokees, Creeks—who occupied millions of acres ripe for cotton cultivation.

The Creeks, having sided with the British in the War of 1812, were by now a minor factor (their destroyer in that war had been General Andrew Jackson).

The Cherokees, however, living in northwestern Georgia, wished to stay where they were. Their mixed-blood leaders had adopted a policy of assimilation. They had given up hunting for agriculture and had abandoned tattooing, nose rings, and (for the most part) polygamy as well. An 1825 census showed that fifteen thousand Cherokees owned thirty-one gristmills, sixty-two smithies, and one thousand black slaves. Three years later, they adopted a constitution, modeled on the United States', for the government of their territory and started a weekly newspaper, the *Cherokee Phoenix*.

The Cherokees had also adopted evangelical Christianity— more so among the upper classes (old customs, such as conjuring, still lingered among the uneducated). The conversion of the Cherokees gave them advocates in the Protestant churches, who sponsored missionaries in the Cherokee homeland.

The State of Georgia was as anxious to dispossess the Cherokees as the Cherokees were to stay and had passed laws in 1828 and 1829 extending the state's power over them. (A gold strike near the Cherokee homeland stoked Georgia's desire.) Jackson articulated the policy of removal; Georgia supplied the goad. In 1830, Daniel Webster and other opponents of Jackson's policy advised the Cherokees to fight it in court, using William Wirt as their lawyer. Wirt, the son of a Swiss tavern keeper in Bladensburg, Maryland, had made his mark both in law and literature. As a young advocate, he had helped George Hay prosecute Aaron Burr; his courtroom denunciation of Burr did not sway Marshall or the jury but became a staple of rhetoric books. His 1817 biography of Patrick Henry was accused, probably unfairly, of improving Henry's "give me liberty, or give me death!" speech.

By turning to Webster and Wirt, the Cherokees put themselves in the whirlwind of national politics. Webster, now a senator from Massachusetts, was a leading critic of Jackson, and Wirt, who had served as U.S. attorney general since 1817, had resigned rather than work for him. Although bullying Cherokees was hugely popular in Georgia, Jackson's enemies thought it might turn voters elsewhere, especially in the north, against him.

Clients hire lawyers for their connections as well as their skills. Wirt now asked Dabney Carr, a Virginia judge who was an old friend of his and a neighbor of Marshall's, to sound out the chief justice as to what arguments Wirt ought to pursue. Should he, for example, bring a suit directly to the Court, on the grounds that the Cherokees were a "foreign nation"? (Article III, Section 2, gave the judiciary power over cases "between a State . . . and foreign States," and the Supreme Court original jurisdiction "in all Cases . . . in which a State shall be a party.")

Marshall answered Carr that his "sense of duty" prevented him from answering Wirt's feeler. But he added that he had followed the debate on Jackson's policy "with deep interest," and wished that the president "had thought differently on the subject. Humanity must bewail the course which is pursued." Although this was not advice, it was certainly encouragement to Wirt to proceed.

WIRT ARGUED THE Cherokees' case in March 1831, claiming them as a "foreign" nation and asking the Court to enjoin Georgia from enforcing its laws. The state, like Virginia in *Cohens,* refused to appear. Marshall gave the opinion of the Court on the eighteenth, four days after Wirt finished.

Cherokee Nation v. Georgia was quite short, less than 2,500 words. Marshall began with an aria of regret: "If courts were permitted to indulge their sympathies, a case better calculated to excite them can scarcely be imagined. A people once numerous, powerful, and truly independent" had sunk "beneath our superior policy, our arts, and our arms." They were, as James Fenimore Cooper might have put it, the last of the Cherokees.

Marshall followed the lament with a question: Could the Court hear their suit?

He answered that it could not, because the Cherokees were not a "foreign nation." He based his judgment on geography—they lived entirely surrounded by the United States—and on the commerce clause, Article I, Section 8, which gave Congress the power to regulate commerce "with foreign Nations . . . and with the Indian Tribes." The verbal distinction, said Marshall, indicated a political and legal one.

Indians, he went on, were "domestic dependent nations . . . completely under the sovereignty and dominion of the United States." Therefore they "cannot maintain an action in the courts of the United States."

Case closed—but not quite. When Marshall read his opinion, there were no dissents; Johnson and Baldwin wrote concurrences, Duvall was absent on family business. Nine days later, however, Thompson produced a dissent, joined by Story. Indian nations, they maintained, were indeed foreign, even if dependent; they ran their own affairs, and the United States made treaties with them. Therefore, the Cherokees could sue in court, and before the Supreme Court, and the State of Georgia was wrong to impose its laws on them.

Thompson and Story had been prompted to issue their opinion by Marshall himself, who also encouraged them to publish it in a pamphlet along with his own. "I should be glad to see the whole case" in print, Marshall wrote the Court reporter. "It is one in which the public takes a deep interest."

Marshall's opinion had ended with a throwaway line, speculating that the rights of the Cherokees "might perhaps be decided by this court in a proper case with proper parties." He was all but inviting further arguments, for the sake of a different decision.

Chapter 16

MISSIONARIES

Two months after Marshall's decision in *Cherokee Nation*, he got a letter from Justice Story—Court business, political gossip. Then this: the Storys had lost a ten-year-old daughter to scarlet fever. Story was trying to work through his grief, but wretchedness overwhelmed him "when alone and left to my reflections. . . . I know not," he added, "if Mrs. Marshall and your self have ever met with like calamities. But I am sure, that you will feel for us in our distress."

Marshall's reply began in the same way as Story's letter: Court business, political gossip. Then he answered that he and Polly indeed knew what the Storys were experiencing. Marshall recalled the double death of newborn son and infant daughter in the summer of 1792. Time had blurred his recollections: he misremembered the order of the two deaths and his daughter's age at the time of hers. He wanted to send Story a poem of consolation he had written Polly and could not find it. But the pain of the almost forty-year-old loss nevertheless came back "fresh to our minds."

Human fragility was never far from the mind of Marshall's favorite poet Alexander Pope, for all his suavity. At the end of "The Rape of the Lock," his mock epic about a purloined lock of hair, he reminded his young lady readers that "those fair suns [their eyes] shall set, as set they must, / And all those tresses shall be laid in dust." John and Polly had not needed poetry to instruct them.

THE SECOND CHEROKEE case to come before Marshall and the Court would pit the State of Georgia not against Indians but against white missionaries serving them. The parties were already on a collision course when *Cherokee Nation* was being heard.

Samuel Worcester was the son of a minister in Peacham, Vermont, who was also a printer; Samuel followed both his father's professions. After graduating from Andover Theological Seminary, an orthodox institution founded to resist the Unitarianism of Harvard, he was sent in 1825 to be a missionary to the Cherokees by the American Board of Commissioners for Foreign Missions, a Congregationalist group headquartered in Boston. The American Board saw the Indians of the old Southwest as homegrown heathens, ripe for Christianity and civilization. Initially, its evangelizing had the blessing of the federal government; during the Madison administration, it contracted with the War Department to set up schools and model farms for its converts.

After two years at a mission in Tennessee, Worcester moved in 1827 to New Echota, the Cherokee capital, halfway between Chattanooga and Atlanta. There he served as postmaster, began a translation of the Bible into Cherokee, and printed the *Cherokee Phoenix;* since the language was written with a unique system of eighty-six characters representing syllables, he had to design his own typeface.

Soon Worcester was caught up in the politics of Indian removal. In December 1830, he called a meeting of fellow missionaries from the American Board, as well as Baptists, Methodists, and Moravians, who declared that the "whole mass of the Cherokee people" opposed the policy. At the same time, the Georgia legislature, meeting at the state capital in Milledgeville, passed a law requiring all white men living in Cherokee territory to have a license from the state and swear an oath of loyalty to it. Anyone who failed to comply after March 1, 1831, would be sentenced to four years of hard labor. The law was intended to force missionaries to toe Georgia's line; Worcester wrote the American Board that taking the oath was "out of the question."

In March, he was arrested. But a Georgia judge freed him on the grounds that, as a contractor with the War Department and a postmaster, he was an agent of the federal government and thus not obligated to take the state's oath. The judge's decision was both principled and opportune: Georgia wanted the power to threaten ministers, not the embarrassment of imprisoning them. But President Jackson had stopped the War Department contract the year before, and his postmaster general, after receiving a complaint from the governor of Georgia, promptly fired Worcester. His protective status as a federal agent thus vanished.

In the face of Georgia's show of force, Worcester's missionary colleagues now broke ranks. Was their resistance expressive of true "Christian meekness" or merely a move in a "political contest"? Worcester thought it was both. Christian voters, he wrote, should choose leaders who would "save our country from the guilt of covenant-breaking." He was willing to suffer for his faith, for his Cherokee parishioners, and for the cause of defeating Andrew Jackson's reelection.

In July 1831, he was arrested again, along with another steadfast American Board missionary, Elizur Butler. They were marched, in chains, eighty miles to prison and tried and convicted in September. Worcester and Butler were not Indians claiming to be a foreign state, but American citizens. Here, perhaps, were the "proper parties" Marshall had written of in *Cherokee Nation*.

I N SEPTEMBER 1831, Marshall touched the politics already swirling around Jackson's reelection. On his way from Richmond to Philadelphia, he stopped in Baltimore to observe the first American presidential nominating convention.

George Washington had been elected and reelected without nominations of any kind. His life was his nomination; he was drawn to the presidency as if by gravity. His would-be successors, Federalist and Republican, had been tapped as candidates by caucuses of each party's senators and congressmen.

The first party to adopt the new system—a convention of delegates from many states—was the first American third party: the Antimasons. Antimasonry sprang up in response to the case of William Morgan, a renegade Mason in upstate New York who was abducted, and presumably killed, after promising to reveal the order's secrets. When the local authorities investigating Morgan's disappearance turned out to be Masons themselves, a panic ensued.

Antimasonry was equal parts paranoia and an earnest concern that the young republic harbored a fraternal order with ranks, oaths, and secret rituals, willing to set itself above the law. It was also a way for certain shrewd politicians to be more populist than the populists, for the most prominent Mason in America happened to be Andrew Jackson.

The Antimasons invited Marshall to be their guest out of respect for his eminence—after thirty years on the Court, the chief justice was an icon, like the Liberty Bell—and he accepted their invitation out of courtesy. (He had joined the Masons himself during the Revolution—the order was popular among officers—and continued to join in public ceremonies, like welcoming Lafayette, a fellow Mason, to Richmond, though he had not been active for years.) He must also, however, have wanted to judge how respectable the new party was. He had just turned seventy-six. "You know how much importance," he wrote Justice Story, "I attach to the character of the person who is to succeed me." If the next president were politically congenial, Marshall could retire after the inauguration, confident that the chief justiceship would pass to a like-minded judge, very likely to Story himself.

The Antimasons had appealed in vain to Henry Clay to be their candidate (he would run as the nominee of a coalition of anti-Jacksonians called the National Republicans, in a desperate effort to recall the unitary politics of the Monroe years). The Antimasons ended up giving their nomination to the Cherokees' lawyer, William Wirt.

MARSHALL'S REASON FOR traveling, via Baltimore, to Philadelphia was medical. He had been an active man all his life, fond of his quoits and his daily miles-long walks; for years, he had been an active old man. "In his youth," wrote a marveling congressman from Massachusetts, Marshall "gamed, bet and drank. In my youth I was a demure lad, indulg[ing] in no dissipation." Yet the young Puritan had to drive himself up Capitol Hill in a gig, "while the old chief justice walks."

But since the spring of 1831, Marshall had been suffering from abdominal pains that had finally become too painful to ignore. In Philadelphia, he consulted Philip Physick, America's preeminent surgeon, who diagnosed bladder stones. The condition was treated with a lithotomy, an incision in the anal region, followed by a removal of the stones with forceps. It was performed in October without anesthesia and took an unusually long time because Marshall was found to have so many stones. Before and after this ordeal, he wrote upbeat letters to Polly, confessing that he was gorging on pears against medical advice, fretting about his doctor's health rather than his own. By November, he was well enough to return to Richmond; he gave Physick a wine cooler as a present.

He returned to the greatest pain of his life. After years of seclusion, enforced by physical and emotional sensitivity, Polly fell ill indeed. In mid-December, Marshall wrote his brother James that his fears for her "are stronger than my hopes." On December 24, she gave her husband the locket containing the snip of hair that the bold girl had sent after her lover fifty years earlier. She died on Christmas.

Poetry had been a medium of their romance, and Marshall turned to a poem to express his grief—a Revolutionary-era relic, lines written by the British general and playwright John Burgoyne in memory of his own wife; Marshall inserted Polly's given name into the text. Burgoyne's poem is a slight thing—unless it is about you, when it becomes a melodized sob.

> My Mary's worth, my Mary's charms
> Can never more return.
> What now shall fill these widowed arms?
> Ah, me! My Mary's urn!
> Ah, me! My Mary's urn!

Marshall recited the lines to Story when the Court next met. "I saw at once that he had been shedding tears," Story wrote home. "[He] rarely goes through a night without weeping over his departed wife."

WILLIAM WIRT, THE Cherokees' lawyer, took on the case of Samuel Worcester and Elizur Butler. He argued it before the Court in February 1832. Once again, the State of Georgia refused to appear.

Marshall gave his decision in *Worcester v. Georgia* on March 3, joined by Story, Thompson, and Duvall. (McLean concurred;

Baldwin dissented, though he neglected to give a copy of his opinion to the Court reporter; Johnson was out sick.)

Marshall invoked the language of duty, as he had in Burr's treason trial twenty-five years earlier. Then, defying a president bent on hanging a man, he had said, "This court dares not shrink from its duty." Now, about to defy a state and a president determined to bully two missionaries and an Indian tribe, he said, "This duty, however unpleasant, cannot be avoided." As he usually did when he wished to cover all the bases, he wrote at length—over eleven thousand words.

The hinge of his decision, as in *Johnson v. McIntosh,* was conquerors' rights: "Power, war, conquest give rights which, after possession, are conceded by the world, and which can never be controverted by those on whom they descend."

In Marshall's earlier Indian decisions, their status as history's losers had deprived them of the right of making unapproved land sales or of suing in court as independent nations. Now, however, that same status conferred responsibility for their fate on history's winners—the federal government, not any state. "According to the settled principles of our constitution," wrote Marshall, the regulation of "the relations established between the United States and the Cherokee Nation . . . are committed exclusively to the government of the union." Article I, Section 10, forbade states from making treaties; Article II, Section 2, reserved that power to the president, with the advice and consent of the Senate.

How had the government of the Union decided to treat the Cherokees? Marshall made a long survey of America's Indian treaties and concluded that they "explicitly recognize[d] the national character of the Cherokees and their right of self government." The Cherokees were free to manage their own affairs, and "the faith of the United States" backed the arrangement.

Georgia's law requiring missionaries to obtain a license and swear an oath violated federal policy and trespassed on federal prerogative. It was "repugnant to the Constitution, treaties and laws of the United States and ought therefore to be reversed and annulled." Worcester and Butler had suffered "disgraceful punishment, if punishment could disgrace when inflicted on innocence." They should be freed.

Marshall alluded in passing to a different standard of judgment, which would perhaps have yielded an even more sweeping decision—the standard of natural rights. "It is difficult," he admitted, "to comprehend the proposition . . . that the discovery" of one-quarter of the globe by the inhabitants of another "should give the discoverer rights . . . which annulled the preexisting rights of its ancient possessors." The Cherokees and other Indians were here first; who could dispossess them?

Similarly, in his decision in the *Antelope,* he had noted that "every man has a natural right to the fruits of his own labour." Slavery was unjust; how could the slave trade be justified?

In both cases, he alluded to natural rights in passing—and then passed on. Courts expound rights conferred by law. Conquest, recent or remote, underlies all law; the purchase of chattel in the course of legal trade conforms to it. In *Worcester,* however, red men were found to have more rights than black men in the *Antelope* because the laws of the United States had treated red men better.

"Well," said President Jackson after the Court had ruled, "John Marshall has made his decision, now let him enforce it." This remark, published thirty years after the fact by a journalist on the hearsay of a congressman, may never actually have been said. What Jackson did write, in a letter to one of his confidants, was that Marshall's decision "fell stillborn." Thomas Jefferson had told his attorney general privately that he wished *Marbury* might be "denounced as not law." Now Georgia behaved as if

Marshall's verdict against it was not law, keeping Worcester and Butler at labor, and the president did nothing to rebuke it.

ELECTION POLITICS BOILED on. Jackson tangled with the Supreme Court on another campaign issue. The second Bank of the United States, after its rocky start, had become an honest and effective institution. But Jackson, a foe of banks quite in the style of Thomas Jefferson, had expressed hostility to it at intervals throughout his term. Partisans then and since cast him as a tribune of the people, waging war against a moneyed elite. Critics cast him as an economic ignoramus, manipulated by advisors seeking power for local banks in the ruin of their national rival. Marshall inclined to the latter view; he wrote Story that New York—represented in Jackson's inner circle by his 1832 running mate, Martin Van Buren—"has sagacity enough to see her interest in putting down the present bank. Her mercantile position gives her . . . a commanding control over the currency and the exchanges of the country, if there be no Bank of the United States."

Congress, at the urging of Henry Clay, called for a fifteen-year extension of the Bank's charter (due to expire in 1836). In July 1832, Jackson vetoed the bill.

His veto message was a broad condemnation of the Bank as an uncontrollable monopoly. But in the course of it, he assailed Marshall's opinion in *McCulloch* for limiting the power of states to tax. And in a bold paragraph, he seemed to set himself up as a coequal judge of the constitutionality of laws. "The Congress, the Executive, and the Court must each for itself be guided by its own opinion of the Constitution. . . . The opinion of the judges has no more authority over Congress than the opinion of Congress has over the judges, and on that point the President is independent of both."

Jackson's attorney general at the time, Roger Taney, would later argue that Jackson in this passage was speaking of himself as a partner of the legislature—as one who signed or vetoed bills. In that capacity, he had the right, and the duty, to judge whether the bills presented to him were constitutional or not. He was not proposing to defy bills that had been passed by Congress, signed into law, and upheld by the Court. But Jackson's aura of willfulness was such that there was no telling what he might mean or do.

The voters did not seem to care. In their eyes, Jackson's positions on Indian removal and the second Bank were merits, not black marks. Of the twenty-four states voting in 1832, Wirt and the Antimasons carried only Vermont. Clay and the National Republicans won the old bastions of Federalism—Maryland, Delaware, and three New England states—plus Clay's home state of Kentucky. South Carolina voted for a favorite son (John C. Calhoun, displaced on Jackson's ticket by Van Buren, was engaged in a mortal feud with his former ally). Jackson took the sixteen remaining states, and almost 55 percent of the popular vote; Virginia went for him by a three-to-one margin.

Marshall had seen the landslide coming. "I yield slowly and reluctantly to the conviction that our constitution cannot last," he wrote Story in September. His hopes for retirement were dashed. He had outlasted two terms of Jefferson's enmity, but then he had been in the prime of life, not its end.

SOON AFTER JACKSON'S reelection, however, a new issue reordered American politics. Calhoun's feud with Jackson was personal—the two quarreled over trivialities, such as the character of the secretary of war's wife (Calhoun thought she was a loose woman; Jackson maintained she was a wronged one). But their enmity was also political and ideological. During the campaign of 1828, Jackson's supporters, hoping to win the manufacturing states of Pennsylvania and New York, had backed a steeply pro-tectionist tariff, which bit hard on cotton-growing slave states. In office, Jackson supported a reduction of the tariff, but it was not enough to satisfy South Carolina. Calhoun now argued that protective tariffs favoring particular regions of the country were unconstitutional. At his direction, on November 26 his state passed an ordinance declaring the tariff "null, void and no law," adding that it was not to be collected within the state's borders after February 1, 1833.

Georgia was defying the Supreme Court in the Cherokee cases. Now South Carolina was defying Congress and the president. Jackson wished to judge the constitutionality of laws, but he refused to extend that privilege to states, particularly Calhoun's state. On December 10, he issued a proclamation blasting the nul-lification ordinance as "contradicted expressly by the letter of the Constitution" and "inconsistent with every principle on which it was founded."

Marshall, in a letter to Story, wryly noted the effect on Jack-son's most populist admirers in Virginia, who reached for the worst epithets they could bestow: "They said Andrew Jackson had become a Federalist . . . a convert to the opinions of Wash-ington." Marshall knew who to blame. "We are now gathering the bitter fruits of the tree . . . planted by Mr. Jefferson."

In their Georgia prison, Samuel Worcester and Elizur Butler found their status as anti-administration martyrs transformed by the nullification crisis. On the very day that South Carolina passed its nullification ordinance, the missionaries asked Wirt to take the next step in their case: informing the Court at the opening of its 1833 term that Georgia had refused to release them and asking the justices to notify the president. The Constitution (Article II, Section 3) required the president to "take Care that the Laws be faithfully executed." Jackson could either refuse and put himself in the same position as South Carolina; or he could do his job, which would drive Georgia (and possibly Alabama and Mississippi, which had their own Indian populations) into the ranks of the resistance along with South Carolina. If Jackson were forced to act, one course—defying the Court—would be embarrassing, the other—upholding it—might bring on a civil war.

The weight of the political world now fell on the imprisoned missionaries. They were assured by supporters and foes alike that it was up to them to save Andrew Jackson and the Union. The Cherokees, facing a hostile state and a reelected unfriendly president, were doomed. Would Worcester and Butler risk the peace of the nation to pursue their personal lost cause?

On January 8, 1833, they asked Wirt to abandon their appeal. On January 14, the governor of Georgia pardoned the missionaries and set them free; it was no longer necessary to punish the friends of Georgia's defeated enemies. On January 16, Jackson, his southern flank secure, asked Congress for a bill allowing him to collect the tariff in South Carolina by force, if necessary.

At the end of January, Story wrote his wife, describing a dinner at the White House, during which he and Jackson had drunk glasses of wine together. He and Marshall had, willy-nilly, become the president's "warmest supporters. . . . Who would have dreamed of such an occurrence?"

Jackson's will (and a reduced tariff, brokered by Henry Clay) broke South Carolina's will. The state withdrew its ordinance of nullification, and the Union was saved. Marshall enjoyed a moment of truce with the president, though he had lost his battle with him. *Worcester v. Georgia* remained in the Court's reports, a signpost to nothing. The last shreds of Washington's Indian policy were swept away.

At the end of the decade, the Cherokees were marched to Indian Territory, the future Oklahoma. Samuel Worcester and Elizur Butler accompanied them.

Chapter 17

BILL OF RIGHTS

.

T HE MARSHALL COURT'S LAST MAJOR CASE WAS DECIDED
in the 1833 term; it concerned silt and the Bill of Rights.

Baltimore was America's postindependence boom-
town, vaulting from nowhere to becoming the country's third-
largest city by 1800. It profited by its position in the northern
reaches of Chesapeake Bay as an outlet for the produce of central Pennsylvania; it profited as an outfitter of privateers during
the War of 1812 and the South American revolutions. The city's
prosperity explained why the Cohens moved there, why the British tried to sack it, and why the *Arraganta* sailed from it. It also
explained the hopes of John Barron, an Irish immigrant lumber
merchant, and John Craig, a grocer, who, after investing successfully in privateers, bought a wharf in 1815 at Fell's Point, just
east of the inner harbor, capable of serving the largest ships. The
price was steep, $25,000; Barron and Craig put $10,000 down
and owed the rest.

Soon, they were in trouble. In 1817, the city embarked on a
program of improvements to control the drainage of Fell's Point,
paving and grading the streets down which streams once flowed
and diverting their channels. A new runoff emptied into the outer
harbor just north of Barron's and Craig's wharf; the sediment it

dropped formed a sandbar that blocked access, rendering their property, in the words of another wharf owner, "wholly forsaken." Barron and Craig fell behind on their payments and went into hock to Luke Tiernan, a more successful entrepreneur. In 1822, they sued the city of Baltimore for $20,000 in damages. When the case finally went to trial six years later—lawyers on both sides had filed numerous requests for extensions—a jury ordered the city to pay $4,500, the amount the wharf had depreciated in value. Craig had died shortly before the judgment, Barron followed him shortly after; Tiernan would pocket the award.

Baltimore appealed the decision, and the two sides went at it again in Maryland's appeals court in December 1830. This time, the city won; the higher court threw out the award and ordered Barron (actually Tiernan) to pay Baltimore's legal bills. Unlike the original wharf owners, Tiernan was a wealthy man who did not need the money he had been awarded, but he would welcome it if he could get it. In January 1831, his lawyers appealed to the Supreme Court.

The case was heard in February 1833. Baldwin missed the entire term, because the fit was on him. Appearing for Barron/Tiernan was Charles Mayer, a Baltimore lawyer and state senator. Representing the city was Roger Taney, a scarecrow of a man whose face, according to one contemporary, was "without one good feature." But Taney was one of the best lawyers in Maryland, indeed the country, a fitting successor to Luther Martin and William Pinkney. Once the state's attorney general, he was now the attorney general of the United States. (Attorneys general, like senators such as Webster, maintained sideline careers as Washington lawyers.)

Mayer argued that depriving his clients of the value of their wharf, without compensation, was a tort, or an injury, under both the laws of Maryland and the Fifth Amendment to the

Constitution, which declared that "private property [shall not] be taken for public use, without just compensation."

Marshall told Mayer to focus on the latter point, since the Court would have no power to judge a suit between two Marylanders—a person and a city—unless some constitutional question were involved. Mayer spoke for two days.

Taney had represented Baltimore in the state appeals court, where he had argued, among other things, that the city had taken no property, only altered the water that flowed alongside it. What he might have told the Court will never be known, because after Mayer finished making his case, Marshall, in an unusual intervention, told Taney to say nothing at all. Marshall's opinion, speaking for all the justices present, was ready five days later. He and his colleagues must have made up their minds in advance.

Marshall began by saying that the case raised a question "of great importance, but not of much difficulty." Unlike his invocations of "delicacy" in other landmark cases, this was not a politeness about to be exploded but the simple truth. Marshall's opinion was curt, less than 1,800 words long.

In his *Life of Washington,* Marshall had described the passage of the Fifth Amendment and its nine fellows. By the end of 1791, Congress had passed and the states had ratified ten amendments. The Ninth and Tenth were general statements about the division of rights and powers among the federal and state governments and the people. The First through the Eighth, by contrast, listed specific prohibitions—no establishment of religion or warrantless searches—and guarantees—freedom of the press, the right to keep and bear arms. The inclusion of this compendium, according to Marshall, had been a matter of political and emotional housekeeping. The "friends" of the government "were anxious to annex to the constitution those explanations and barriers against . . . possible encroachments . . . on the liberties of the people which had been loudly demanded, however unfounded . . . might be the fears by which those demands were suggested." The Constitution as it left Philadelphia in 1787 was fine, but nervous folk feared imaginary dangers; to please them, Congress drew up the Bill of Rights.

In Marshall's view, the real bill of rights in the Constitution was not these amendments but the restrictions imposed on Congress and the states in Article I, Section 9 and Section 10. There habeas corpus was protected from Congress and contracts protected from states; bills of attainder and ex post facto laws were forbidden to both. As long ago as *Fletcher,* he had called Section 10 "a bill of rights for the people of each state." Now in *Barron v. Baltimore,* he called Section 9 "a bill of rights . . . imposed on the power of the general [that is, federal] government."

Marshall, as he had in *Gibbons,* sought guidance in words: "words . . . which directly express" the constitution's intent. Were there words that might show how the Fifth Amendment was to be applied? Marshall found them in the contrast between the two bills of rights in Article I, Section 9, which declared baldly, "No bill of attainder or ex post facto law shall be passed." "No language," Marshall added, could be more sweeping. Yet in Section 10, it had been felt necessary to say, "No state shall pass any bill of attainder or ex post facto law."

Why the seeming repetition? Because, Marshall argued, it was no repetition at all. The Constitution was a road map for the new government it created, the federal government of the United States. Unless the states were specifically referenced, all the Constitution's powers and restrictions referred to that government alone. Therefore, "the fifth amendment must be understood as restraining the power of the general [federal] government, not as applicable to the states."

There was a counterargument to Marshall's textualism, lodged within the text of the first eight amendments themselves. The

First Amendment begins, "Congress shall make no law respecting," and goes on to enumerate freedom of religion, speech, the press, assembly, and petition. The Seventh Amendment imposes a restriction on federal courts. But other amendments say nothing about the federal government or any of its branches. The Second and Fourth refer to "the right of the people," the Sixth to "the accused"; the Third, Fifth, and Eighth are blanket prohibitions.

If two of the first eight amendments restrict only the federal government, should not the others, the Fifth included, be understood to apply, by contrast, to both the federal government and the states?

Marshall foreclosed this interpretation with a second argument, drawn not from the Constitution's words but from its history, reprising his account of the first ten amendments in the *Life of Washington*. "It is universally understood, it is a part of the history of the day, that the great revolution which established the constitution of the United States, was not effected without immense opposition." Too many Americans had feared that "those powers which the patriot statesmen, who then watched over the interests of our country, deemed essential . . . might be exercised in a manner dangerous to liberty." This was a coda to Marshall's by-now-familiar creation story of the Constitution. To better run their affairs, the people had created a federal government. But some people were afraid of what they had done. To quiet those fears, the first ten amendments were written and ratified. "These amendments demanded security against the apprehended encroachments of the general [federal] government—not against those of the local [state] governments."

There is no question that Marshall the historian was correct. He had lived through the history and remembered the arguments on all sides.

His enemy Jefferson would have agreed with his account. Jefferson had urged that a bill of rights be added to the Constitution and had raised the alarm when Congress seemed to violate the First Amendment with the Sedition Act. Yet he was happy, as president, to see seditious (Federalist) journalists prosecuted at the state level. "A few prosecutions," he had written a friendly state governor while he was in the White House, "would have a wholesome effect in restoring the integrity of the presses. Not a general prosecution, for that would look like persecution: but a selected one." Marshall was of course unfamiliar with this letter (Jefferson had labeled it "entirely confidential"), but he was quite familiar with Jefferson's principles and practice.

"This court," Marshall concluded his opinion, "has no jurisdiction of the cause; and it is dismissed." The Fifth Amendment's prohibition on taking property without just compensation restricted only the federal government. The Bill of Rights would not be applied to the states until the twentieth century, and then only because the Court decided that the Fourteenth Amendment (ratified in 1868), which was meant to guarantee "due process of law" to freed slaves, secured the rights listed in the first eight amendments against the states.

TIERNAN LOST HIS case but kept his status; a local newspaper called his death, a few years later, "a public deprivation." Barron's impoverished heirs sank from sight; Craig's (evidently helped by Tiernan) fared better financially but all died young.

Why had Marshall decided so quickly and written so tersely? Ruling on the Fifth Amendment took him away from those parts of the Constitution with which he was most comfortable. Confirming the power of the states, and so broadly, was equally unusual for him. And when *Barron v. Baltimore* was litigated, the most prominent defender of the Constitution was not the Court but Andrew Jackson.

Altogether, Marshall was in unfamiliar territory. He had been so for much of his career as chief justice, especially in his earliest days, when there were precedents to establish and enemies to be fought. But now Marshall was old.

JUST THEN, MARSHALL's life was sweetened by a tribute from his most devoted and most intelligent friend. Joseph Story had completed a three-volume set of *Commentaries on the Constitution*. Story wished to be the American Blackstone, explaining and expounding America's fundamental law. In January 1833, he had written Marshall to say that he wanted to dedicate the work to him.

"Your expositions of constitutional law," Story wrote, "enjoy a rare and extraordinary authority. . . . They are destined to enlighten, instruct, and convince future generations; and can scarcely perish but with the memory of the constitution itself. . . . They remind us of some mighty river of our own country, which, gathering in its course the contributions of many tributary streams, pours at last its own current into the ocean, deep, clear, and irresistible."

So Story praised the thinker and the exponent. In his next paragraph, he praised the man. "I dwell with even more pleasure upon the entirety of a life adorned by consistent principles, and filled up in the discharge of virtuous duty; where there is nothing to regret, and nothing to conceal; no friendships broken; no confidence betrayed; no timid surrenders to popular clamour; no eager reaches for popular favour." This was high praise. But Story finished with the highest praise of all: "Who does not listen with conscious pride to the truth, that the disciple, the friend, the biographer of Washington, still lives, the uncompromising advocate of his principles?"

Story knew what Marshall most wished to do with his life and told him that he had done it.

Marshall read the *Commentaries* when it came out and replied to Story in July with praise of his own. It was a "great work," which should be read by "every statesman, and every would-be statesman" in the country. (Or perhaps not all statesmen: Southerners, he noted, were too far gone in "frenzy" to benefit from it.)

Then he replied with a laugh. He thanked Story for "the very flattering terms" in which he had written of him. Yet he could not "suppress the fear that you will be supposed . . . to have consulted a partial [biased] friendship. . . . Others may not contemplate this partiality with as much gratification as its object."

A VEXATIOUS CASE landed at the Court in 1834. Henry Wheaton had stepped down as reporter seven years earlier to take a diplomatic job, being succeeded by Richard Peters Jr., a Philadelphia lawyer. Peters, like Wheaton and Cranch before him, affixed explanatory summaries to his reports of the justices' opinions and the lawyers' arguments. His summaries, unfortunately, were haphazardly done, often missing the main points. But he was an imaginative publicist, producing a set of condensed reports of all the Court's past decisions (Story, always eager to educate the public, liked the idea). Wheaton did not like it, however, claiming Peters's condensations recycled material he had prepared without paying him for it. In 1831, Wheaton sued, the case reaching the Court three years later.

Johnson was out sick for the entire term. Story, who had been friends with both the dueling reporters, fled Washington in a fit of awkwardness before the opinions were read. A law student of his who stayed behind described what happened next in a letter to the runaway justice. McLean delivered the opinion of the Court,

Thompson and Baldwin dissenting; after Thompson and Baldwin read their opinions, McLean answered them publicly. Marshall tried to cut short their cross talk, but Thompson was in a "broil" and Baldwin in a "passion," while Duvall, who had been deaf for years, sat "in utter unconsciousness of the strife around him." Marshall ordered Peters to make no mention of the squabble in his notes. The case, bucked back to circuit court, was not decided until 1850, by which time both Wheaton and Peters were dead. The decision was Solomonic: the opinions of the Court were public property, and hence not copyrightable, but reporters' summaries were; Peters's estate paid Wheaton's $400.

The mighty river pouring into the ocean was chopped by embarrassing crosscurrents.

M ORE JUSTICES FELL by the wayside, opening new vacancies. William Johnson died in August 1834, age sixty-two, after an operation (without anesthesia) to remove a cancer of the jaw. Gabriel Duvall retired, age eighty-three, in January 1835, to live nine more years at his Maryland estate.

Johnson had been Jefferson's first man on the Court and an often prickly presence (though not a patch on Baldwin). He had utterly failed, however, to steer the Court in Jefferson's direction. On the occasions when he wrote concurrences, he was sometimes more bluntly nationalistic than Marshall himself. Duvall, Madison's first pick, had quietly seconded Marshall in almost everything.

To replace Johnson, President Jackson tapped James Wayne, an anti-nullification congressman from Georgia, whose nomination pleased everyone. To replace Duvall, he turned to Roger Taney, who had become a lightning rod. Jackson had intended to exalt his second term by destroying the second Bank of the

United States, removing from it all the deposits of the federal government. Though long hinted, the move seemed so radical that two of his own treasury secretaries had refused to do his bidding; he kicked one upstairs to become secretary of state and fired the second, whereupon Attorney General Taney had agreed, in the fall of 1833, to move to Treasury to do the deed.

Both Marshall and Duvall respected Taney's legal acumen, but the Bank's supporters in the Senate were angry enough and numerous enough to block Taney's elevation to the Court; Duvall would not be replaced for another year.

Marshall presided over the Court's 1835 session, his last. On his way back to Richmond, the stagecoach he was riding in overturned, causing an injury to his spine. He recovered, but not with his former vigor. In April, he sent a chipper, stoical letter to Richard Peters. "My old worn out frame"—he was seventy-nine and a half—"cannot I believe be repaired. Could I find the mill which would grind old men, and restore youth," he might revive. "But as that is impossible, I must be content with patching myself up and dragging on as well as I can." In June, he went to Philadelphia to be patched up by its doctors—without success.

Marshall had made his will three years earlier. George Washington had freed all his slaves in his will—an act noted, with praise, in Mason Weems's biography, though not in Marshall's much longer one. Marshall offered freedom to Robin, his long-time personal servant, and one hundred dollars if he moved to Liberia, fifty dollars if he moved out of state, nothing if he stayed where he was. Robin, who was over seventy years old by 1835, chose to remain enslaved to Marshall's daughter. In this, Marshall had not followed where Washington led.

He was spared one pain. At the end of the month, his eldest son, Thomas, traveling to be at his father's bedside, was killed in a freak accident in Baltimore. (He had ducked out of a storm into a building whose chimney collapsed on him.) No one told the dying man.

The last thing Marshall ever wrote, on the Fourth of July, was his own epitaph.

JOHN MARSHALL
SON OF THOMAS AND MARY MARSHALL
WAS BORN THE 24TH OF SEPTEMBER 1755
INTERMARRIED WITH MARY WILLIS AMBLER
THE 3RD OF JANUARY 1783
DEPARTED THIS LIFE
THE — DAY OF — 18

Himself, his parents, his wife; birth, marriage, death. It was as simple as he was.

He died on July 6. Around his neck, he was wearing the locket containing Polly's hair.

MARSHALL'S DEATH WAS treated as the passing of a remarkable man and of an era; of his important peers, only James Madison and Aaron Burr survived him. Mourning dress was worn, speeches were given, bells rung. A persistent though untrue story held that the Liberty Bell cracked while tolling for him.

Andrew Jackson released a statement that was both acute and gracious—far more gracious than anything Jefferson would have said or than anything Marshall said about Jefferson. The president identified the main chapters of Marshall's life—service in the Revolution, in the ratification struggle, and on the bench—omitting only the intense politicking of the 1790s. He acknowledged Marshall's "learning, talents and patriotism," and "the good he has done his country in one of its most exalted and responsible offices." He admitted in an aside that he "dissent[ed] from some of [Marshall's] expositions of our constitutional law," but concluded by praising "the energy and clearness" of "his strong mind."

The most heartfelt tribute came from Richmond. Since Marshall was irreplaceable, the Quoits Club resolved that it should always have one fewer member.

LEGACY

Marshall, Jefferson, Lincoln

WHAT DID JOHN MARSHALL ACCOMPLISH AS CHIEF JUSTICE? He gave the office what its first occupant, John Jay, had complained it lacked: dignity. Some of that dignity was imparted by mere staying power. Marshall served alongside six presidents, swearing in five of them in nine inaugurals.

Marshall's manner radiated dignity. Jefferson called him lax and lounging; friends spoke of him as simple. But once he mounted the bench, he was sober, focused, direct. His thoughts seemed well arranged and logical; his rhetoric typically had a quality that we, standing after and away from it, associate with the century in which he grew up—balanced, sometimes ringing, minus the flourishes and reaching for effect of romantic orators (Clay, Webster, Lincoln).

He instilled his dignity into his Court. Whatever backstage maneuvers he and his brother justices engaged in, the high number of unanimous decisions they issued gave them solidity and mass. Justices during his tenure still ran hither and yon on circuit duty (and several of Marshall's most consequential decisions—in *Stuart v. Laird* and in the trial of Aaron Burr—were delivered in Richmond); when the justices met together in Washington, it was in ground-floor quarters in the Capitol, at worst squalid, at best modest. But when they decided, the nation listened. As much as possible, Marshall made them not six or seven men but one body. This was why McLean's public spat with Thompson and Baldwin in *Peters v. Wheaton,* or Johnson's indiscreet discussions of how a judicial sausage had been made in *Ogden v. Saunders,* were so wounding to Marshall's project.

Justice Story called Marshall the advocate of George Washington's principles, a description he repeated in a eulogy, in which he hailed Marshall as "a Federalist of the good old school of which Washington was the acknowledged head." What principles had he upheld? To what school had he belonged?

In Marshall's view, America's earliest days of independence were a chaos of slipshod legislating and power grabs by interest groups, chiefly debtors. To cure the evil, he spoke for the validity of contracts, even contracts made by crooked politicians (*Fletcher v. Peck*) or George III (*Dartmouth v. Woodward*). In his only dissent on a constitutional question (*Ogden v. Saunders*) he wrote of contracts in almost sacred terms.

Twenty-five years after the fact, he inserted himself into one of the defining arguments of the Washington administration, declaring (in *McCulloch v. Maryland*) that the power to charter a Bank of the United States was constitutional (even if not explicitly enumerated) and, by implication, wise. Hamilton proposed a Bank, Washington approved it; the Republican Party resisted it, accepted it, killed it, then revived it. Marshall anchored it in the Constitution.

When states claimed the power to ignore this and other decisions and go their own legal way—breaking into bank vaults (*Osborn v. Bank of the United States*) or refusing to hear appeals from their wayward actions—fining lottery promoters (*Cohens v. Virginia*), overturning a land deal made by Marshall's brother (*Martin v. Hunter's Lessee*)—he, or Justice Story, called them to account. States had many powers reserved to them, but where a power was given to the federal government, Marshall and his Court defended it zealously.

Some of his principles were a shade less definite. He considered with sympathy the proposition that the United States was meant to be a single economic unit—*E Pluribus Unum,* as Daniel Webster romantically called it—though when he struck down a state-approved transportation monopoly, he did it on a smaller point (*Gibbons v. Ogden*). In the early 1790s, the Washington administration had considered establishing free Indian nations within America's borders. Marshall would not go so far; he defined Indian tribes as "domestic dependent nations" (*Cherokee Nation v. Georgia*) and denied them standing to sue in federal courts as foreign countries. But he recognized the sovereignty of these nations as defined by treaties with the federal government and defended it (*Worcester v. Georgia*) against state incursions and presidential hostility.

He rebuked the crooked dealings of some slave traders (*Antelope*), though he left the resolution of the problem of slavery to private charity and to the states, which is to say, in limbo.

These (with the partial exception of his views on slavery) were substantially the policies of Washington and his most trusted aide, Alexander Hamilton. Marshall served with both in the Revolution; they went on to politics and administration; he went on to the judiciary, where he defended their handiwork, using their arguments, sometimes (as in *Cohens v. Virginia*) their very words.

Marshall's greatest accomplishment, though congruent with Washington's and Hamilton's way of thinking, was something elaborated by Marshall himself: defending the Constitution as the people's supreme act. The Philadelphia Convention of 1787 had been a secret conclave, with no one besides the delegates admitted and no words of theirs escaping until the very end. But the ratification struggle of 1787–8 had been a yearlong, wide-open process, played out in newspapers, pamphlets (of which the *Federalist* was only one of many), and state ratifying conventions. The people had made a new government, giving it new powers, and binding it with new prohibitions. It was, as Marshall wrote in *McCulloch,* a government of the people, emanating from them, its powers granted by them, to be exercised on them and for their benefit. Marshall devoted his decades as chief justice to explicating and upholding the people's government against the attacks of men he deemed demagogues in Congress, in the states (including his own Virginia), and in the White House (including his own cousin).

In defending the Constitution, he used two weapons. Sometimes he relied, in almost Hebraic fashion, on its words (literalism). They had issued, as from a cloud, and should be read and pondered in splendid isolation. "The intention of the instrument must prevail," as he wrote in his dissent in *Ogden v. Saunders.* "This intention must be collected from its words." Sometimes he relied, additionally or instead, on the historical context of its creation: the particular ills the framers and the American people had faced, the desires and the fears reflected in the remedies they had chosen. "The great revolution which established the constitution of the United States," as he put it in *Barron v. Baltimore,* "is universally understood . . . is a part of the history of the day."

Marshall's key to that history was his own history: observing the ratification struggle as it unfolded nationwide, participating in the Richmond ratifying convention, following as always George Washington's imperative lead.

Washington died, Hamilton died, the Federalist Party died. But for thirty-four years, Marshall held his ground on the Supreme Court, showing the steady firmness and vigorous performance of duty that had riveted him when he witnessed it at White Marsh outside Philadelphia when he was twenty-two years old.

Marshall himself, at the end of his life, saw his accomplishments differently. He feared he had failed and that the Union might fail. After Thomas Jefferson's retirement, the Court for a time no longer had to defend itself, and Marshall and his colleagues had reaped a harvest of decisions. But in the mid-1820s, things began to come unstuck. Andrew Jackson was a much more resolute advocate of his own ideas than Jefferson had been; he neither schemed nor theorized—he acted. He destroyed the second Bank of the United States and articulated a principle of executive power that equally destroyed Marshall's reasoning in *McCulloch*. He let Marshall's last Cherokee decision fall stillborn. He quashed nullification but was otherwise friendly to the prerogatives of states not dominated by John Calhoun.

In October 1834, nine months before his death, Marshall wrote a sober letter to Thomas Grimké, a South Carolina lawyer who was a supporter of the Union (and thus a lonely man). Is our Constitution, wrote Marshall, "a LEAGUE" or "A GOVERNMENT" (his capital letters)? "This is the true and substantial dividing line between parties in the United States. One of more vital importance cannot be drawn. As the one opinion or the other prevails, will the union, as I firmly believe, be preserved or dissolved." Dissolution and preservation would come some thirty years later.

JACKSON MADE HIS most important contribution to the Supreme Court when he tapped Roger Taney to be Marshall's successor. The Senate of the Twenty-Third Congress, which last met in March 1835, had included enough enemies of Jackson and friends of the Bank to block Taney's nomination to succeed Gabriel Duvall. But in the Senate of the Twenty-Fourth Congress, the balance shifted slightly but decisively. Taney was confirmed in March 1836 (Philip Barbour, a Jackson Democrat from Virginia, replaced Duvall). "Judge Story thinks the Supreme Court is *gone*, and I think so too," wrote Daniel Webster.

Would Taney's ascendancy mark a new era or a gradual evolution? Several cases raising constitutional questions that had come before the Court in the early 1830s had been held from judgment by Marshall because illness and madness had thinned the bench, and he had not wanted them settled by fewer than four justices—a majority of the full Court, not merely of the justices present. (Marshall's head-counting for jiggering majorities was itself a sign of his loss of control of the Court.)

These cases were finally heard and decided in 1837, and Story, dissenting, declared that he spoke for his dead chief. I "know . . . full well," Story keened, that Marshall would have found the Court's decisions "unconstitutional. . . . I am sensible that I have not done that justice to his opinion which his own great mind and exalted talents would have done." Then he quoted Virgil, favorite poet of educated lawyers, describing Aeneas's visit to his dead father in the underworld: *His saltem accmulem donis et fungar inani munere* (These offerings at least let me leave, and discharge this unavailing duty).

One of the Taney Court's 1837 decisions, *Briscoe v. Bank of Commerce of Kentucky,* was a clear rebuke to Marshall. States unhappy with the Bank of the United States had sought other ways to thwart it besides taxing its branches or breaking into its vaults; one popular recourse was to issue paper—loan certificates, banknotes—that could pass as legal tender, thus evading its tight credit policies. In 1830, the Marshall Court had struck down one such scheme, hatched by Missouri, as a violation of Article I, Section 10 ("No State shall . . . emit Bills of Credit"). After Jackson and Taney killed the Bank, the Taney Court approved another easy-money scheme sponsored by Kentucky (this was the case that prompted Story's lament).

A second apparently anti-Marshall decision, *Proprietors of the Charles River Bridge v. Proprietors of the Warren Bridge et al.,* concerned two bridges over the Charles River in Massachusetts, connecting Boston and Cambridge. The owners of the older, a toll bridge, claimed a monopoly on cross-river traffic, conferred by charters that Massachusetts had granted them in 1650 and 1785. Since walking or riding between Boston and Cambridge was not interstate commerce, they did not fall afoul of *Gibbons*. They argued, in the spirit of *Dartmouth*, that their charters gave them a property right.

The Taney Court rejected their argument in language that echoed Jefferson's thoughts on the *Dartmouth* case: "The object and end of all government is to promote the happiness and prosperity of the community. . . . New channels of communication are daily found necessary both for travel and trade, and are essential to the comfort, convenience and prosperity of the people. . . . While the rights of private property are sacredly guarded, we cannot forget that the community also have rights." When the times change, change the law.

Yet the break with the Marshall Court in the bridge case was less than it seemed. The language of the old charters was unclear. The 1650 charter, for a ferry, had been exclusive, forbidding other ferries to compete with it; the 1785 charter, for a bridge, had said nothing about other bridges. The *Dartmouth* precedent was of doubtful relevance. Neither Dartmouth College's charter from the king nor Marshall's decision had conferred a monopoly; the trustees of the college were not insisting on educating all the students in New Hampshire, only on educating their own as they wished. The owners of the old bridge over the Charles River claimed a lonely eminence and were rebuked for it.

Story died in 1845, still at his post on the Court, unreconciled to the new order. But Taney's intellect and gentle manner won over other critics. In 1857, his twenty-first year on the Court, he passed the age that Marshall was when he died and seemed able and determined to keep going for years more.

The year 1857 also saw Taney's most memorable gift to the Court and to the nation.

Dred Scott v. Sandford was an appeal of Dred Scott, a slave, for freedom on the grounds that, although he had once been and was now being held in Missouri, a slave state, he had in the interim been held for years in Illinois and the Wisconsin Territory, both free.

The Court decided on March 6, with a majority opinion endorsed by six justices, one concurrence, and two dissents (Congress had raised the number of justices to nine). Taney wrote the majority opinion, and everything about it excited controversy.

The new president, James Buchanan, had been observed chatting with Taney on March 4, the day of his inauguration, inquiring, it was assumed, what the decision would be (Buchanan approved the verdict; Taney's conversation with him suggested collusion).

One portion of the opinion, holding that Scott's status depended on the laws of Missouri, seemed to give slave states extraterritorial powers: once a slave, always a slave, wherever you might later go.

Taney's opinion included a long analysis of the history of slavery in America, meant to show that blacks had always been considered a race of inferior beings, outside the pale of citizenship even if freed. Their inferior status, Taney wrote, was assumed when the Declaration of Independence and the Constitution were written; hence Scott was unable to sue in court.

Taney's most dramatic argument was made in passing: he overturned the Missouri Compromise. One of Dred Scott's claims to freedom was that he had been held in a portion of the Wisconsin Territory that had once belonged to the northern reaches of the Louisiana Territory—the great tract between the Mississippi and Missouri Rivers that the Compromise had reserved for freedom. The Missouri Compromise, Taney now declared, was unconstitutional, since Congress had no power to deprive citizens of their property. The Fifth Amendment, as Marshall had explained in *Barron v. Baltimore*, applied only to the federal government—which meant, according to Taney, that it applied to territories. Slave owners could take their chattels into any territory where the stars and stripes waved. This judgment of Taney's was the first time, since *Marbury*, that the Court had struck down a law passed by Congress, though the effect of this rebuke was far more sweeping: in *Marbury*, the Marshall Court had deprived itself of the power of issuing a mandamus; in *Dred Scott*, the Taney Court rewrote the character of a vast swath of frontier—and, since slavery was all but impossible to uproot wherever it was once planted, determined its fate and the future balance of slave and free states in Congress.

Dred Scott provoked the most furious reactions to a Court decision in history. The most interesting were uttered by future president Abraham Lincoln.

Lincoln was a self-educated, small-town lawyer and politician, a follower of Henry Clay, and an enemy of Andrew Jackson. But he criticized *Dred Scott* with Jacksonian fervor.

He attacked specific elements of the decision, particularly Taney's lecture on the history of blacks in America. Taney's survey was not unlike Marshall's review of the history of Indian relations in *Johnson v. McIntosh;* both chief justices looked to the past to guide them in deciding the status of nonwhite races in the present. But Lincoln, echoing one of the two dissenting opinions to Taney's decision, by Justice Benjamin Curtis, argued that Taney had gotten his facts wrong. Free blacks, so far from being considered by all the framers to be forever unsuited to citizenship, could vote in several states in 1787–8, the years that the Constitution was ratified. Lincoln quoted Curtis: in those states, free blacks "had the power to act, and, doubtless, did act, by their suffrages, upon the question of its adoption." The Constitution did not exclude them; they had helped create the Constitution.

But Lincoln made a wider assault on the Court itself. Lincoln admitted that its decisions on constitutional questions "should control . . . the general policy of the country." But he distinguished between decisions that were "settled" and decisions that were "erroneous." A settled decision was one that had received the "unanimous concurrence of the judges"; that showed no "apparent partisan bias"; that accorded "with [governmental practice] throughout our history"; and that was not "based on assumed historical facts which are not really true."

Lincoln was proposing a probationary review of Supreme Court decisions. Since *Dred Scott* did not satisfy him and his allies, they would consider it stillborn. (His criteria, if rigorously applied, would have overset several of Marshall's most significant decisions. Although Marshall strove for unanimity, he did not always achieve it, even in his heyday—consider the snarl of opinions in *Dartmouth*. Marshall could be acquitted of partisanship after 1816 on the grounds that his party had ceased to exist, but that his thought had a bias throughout his career his warmest admirers admitted.)

Over the next four years, Lincoln, campaigning for the Senate, then the presidency, attacked *Dred Scott* and the Court again and again, culminating in his first inaugural address in March 1861, with Chief Justice Taney sitting behind him on the podium (looking, according to one observer, like a "galvanized corpse"). Lincoln conceded that poor Dred Scott had to remain in slavery: the Court's "decisions must be binding in any case upon the parties to a suit, as to the object of that suit." He also allowed that its decisions were "entitled to very high respect and consideration, in all parallel cases." But respect had its limits. "If the policy of the government, upon vital questions, affecting the whole people, is to be irrevocably fixed by decisions of the Supreme Court, the instant they are made . . . the people will have ceased to be their own rulers, having, to that extent, practically resigned their government into the hands of that eminent tribunal."

Andrew Jackson had said nothing more combative and nothing as dismissive.

In 1862, ignoring Taney's opinion, Congress passed and Lincoln signed a ban on slavery in all territories. In 1865, the Thirteenth Amendment, ending slavery throughout the United States, was ratified. (Slavery among the Cherokees and other Indian tribes removed to Oklahoma ended a year later.) Roger Taney had died in 1864, after twenty-eight years as chief justice.

The prestige of the Court was damaged by its decision in *Dred Scott*. "Judicial baseness," said one contemporary, "reached its lowest point on that occasion." But, thanks to Marshall, it could not be permanently dissipated. He had laid down a marker, an upper boundary of influence and respect, which it could reach once again.

M ARSHALL'S YEARS ON the bench were a long series of disputes: debating, for the most part genteelly, with fellow justices; presiding over the arguments of lawyers and litigants; answering or ignoring critics in the press and in Congress.

His most significant antagonist throughout his long career was Thomas Jefferson. Jefferson does not appear well in a biography of Marshall. The third president schemes, whines, and behaves unethically. Time and again, his cousin eludes him. In every one of their showdowns, Marshall seems to be right and Jefferson wrong: the cases against both Justice Chase and Aaron Burr were political and flimsy; the State of New Hampshire should not have simply taken over a college, even one run by Federalist clergymen; the State of Virginia should not have presumed to pick and choose which cases originating in its courts might be appealed to the Supreme Court.

Yet Jefferson had a point against the subject of this book that is still unresolved. Should the Supreme Court be the sole arbiter of constitutional questions?

Jefferson expressed his thoughts on the Court most clearly in his correspondence with Marshall's colleague, Justice William Johnson. Jefferson quibbled with the Marshall Court's reasoning, "hanging inference on inference, from heaven to earth, like Jacob's ladder," or showing "the slipperiness of the eels of the law." Jefferson shared the exasperation that all laymen feel before legal adepts (although Jefferson himself had legal training, from no less than Marshall's own teacher, George Wythe): "Laws are made for men of ordinary understanding and should therefore be construed by the ordinary rules of common sense. Their meaning is not to be sought for in metaphysical subtleties, which may make any thing mean every thing or nothing."

His most serious point, however, was that relying on the Court to settle constitutional questions was undemocratic. He expressed his creed, and the creed of his followers, this way: "We believed . . . that man was a rational animal, endowed by nature with rights, and with an innate sense of justice, and that he could be restrained from wrong, and protected in right, by [a government of] moderate powers, confided to persons of his own choice, and held to their duties by dependence on his own will." Jefferson's first four assertions, about rationality, rights, the innate sense of justice, and governments of moderate powers, reflected the philosophical and political convictions of his lifetime. The last two assertions were directly relevant to the Court: the people should choose their governors, who should be guided by and answerable to the people's will. The people choose the Court, since the justices are chosen by elected officeholders. But once justices are on the Court, they are answerable only to themselves.

Marshall in his own way was a populist, as his creation story of the Constitution, iterated in years of decisions, showed. He first outlined it in the first decision to excite Jefferson's wrath, *Marbury v. Madison:* "That the people have an original right to establish, for their future government, such principles as, in their opinion, shall most conduce to their own happiness, is the basis on which the whole American fabric has been erected." The "American fabric" was the Constitution, an act of "original and supreme will."

The defender of this act of popular will was the Court—when cases that raised constitutional questions came before it. "It is emphatically the province and duty of the judicial department to say what the law is. . . . If then the courts are to regard the constitution; and the constitution is superior to any ordinary act of the legislature—the constitution, and not such ordinary act, must govern the case to which they both apply."

Marshall's devotion to the Constitution was sincere. He had followed Washington, as he had during the Revolution, in the great act of framing of 1787–8. His political biases—in favor of contracts and a national bank; sympathetic to, if not definitely in favor of, the idea of a national market—were not his alone but in the air when the Constitution was new. He saw the fabric being erected; he was there when the original will moved.

But as time passes, can Marshall's devotion to the Constitution survive? If it does not, what becomes of the Court's role as its guardian?

Marshall was virtually the last jurist, and certainly the last justice of the Supreme Court, to have a living relationship to the Constitution. How can those who follow him recapture his intimacy with a document ratified over a dozen decades before they were born?

Words preserve intentions, and the Constitution's words survive. So does the history of its making. But in explaining words and history, men necessarily use their own words, which can generate new intentions. (Marshall himself hinted at this process in *Dartmouth*.) Atop the Constitution, there rises a coral reef of constitutional law, explicating, embellishing, and burying the document that supports it.

This is what happens when judges and justices have the best will in the world. But what if they rely not on the Constitution but on their own wills? One eminent federal judge, recently retired, admitted that he paid "very little attention to legal rules, statutes, [or] constitutional provisions" in deciding cases. "A case is just a dispute. The first thing you do is ask yourself—forget about the law—what is a sensible resolution of this dispute?" He was an outlier, but the temptation to wing it always exists.

Jefferson had no easy alternative to offer to Marshall's view of the federal judiciary as the Constitution's guardian. Some of his followers, in the first flush of victory at the dawn of the nineteenth century, dreamed of government by congressional fiat. "You hold dangerous opinions," said one, explaining the Republican Party's desire to impeach Federalists on the Court, which would at that moment have meant all its justices. "We want your offices, for the purpose of giving them to men who will fill them better." Jefferson, as it proved, was not willing, or not determined, to go so far as that. In his late-life correspondence with Justice Johnson, he toyed instead with the idea of recurring constitutional conventions as a possible check on the Court. "The ultimate arbiter" of constitutional questions "is the people of the union, assembled by their deputies in convention, at the call of Congress, or of two thirds of the states. Let them decide."

Multiple (ongoing?) constitutional conventions would be a difficult remedy: "Too tardy, too troublesome, and too expensive," wrote James Madison when Jefferson ran the idea by him. Jackson and Lincoln, for all their blunt criticisms of the Court, proposed no checks at all.

In the twentieth century, Franklin Roosevelt, irked at a Court that struck down New Deal legislation, pushed for a bill that would have allowed him to appoint new justices (up to six) for every justice age seventy years six months or older. (There were, as it happened, six such justices at the time.) If Roosevelt's plan had been in operation during the Marshall Court, Cushing in 1803, Duvall in 1823, and Marshall himself in 1826 would have been offset by newcomers. Roger Taney would have been paired in 1847. The Court's prestige and Roosevelt's mismanagement of his bill ensured its defeat in Congress; his own vice president held his nose and gestured thumbs-down in the Senate when the plan was announced.

Court decisions can always be overruled by amendments. The Eleventh Amendment, which protects a state from being sued by citizens of other states, was a swift response to *Chisholm v. Georgia;* the Thirteenth, which ended slavery, and the Fourteenth, which established birthright citizenship, were responses to *Dred Scott* (and, more importantly, to the Civil War). But the ratification process is designedly difficult. The Twenty-Seventh Amendment, regulating congressional pay raises, was approved by Congress in 1789 but not ratified by the states until 1992—the record for long gestation. The majority of proposed amendments—including all of Senator Richard Johnson's measures for curbing the Court in the early 1820s—die on the vine.

The fabric of the Constitution is not simply democratic. Besides the judiciary, the Senate and the Electoral College are obvious anomalies—bodies in which democracy is alloyed with the principal of state equality. The existence of different branches of government is a complication and therefore an anomaly. Representation itself is a step away from pure democracy (H. Ross Perot, independent presidential candidate in the 1990s, proposed referendums conducted by home computer terminals).

Yet there are degrees of deviation from democracy. As the distance between us and the act of "original and supreme will" lengthens, and the Court fills the space with its own will, to that extent the people cease, as Lincoln said, to be their own rulers, resigning their government into the hands of that eminent tribunal.

M ARSHALL, JEFFERSON, AND Lincoln were not only populists. They also believed in rights, grounded in nature. Jefferson and Lincoln were most eloquent on the subject, but Marshall, when he wrote about contracts, in *Fletcher* or his dissent in *Ogden* ("Individuals do not derive from government their right to contract, but bring that right with them into society"), could almost match their pitch.

Believing in rights sometimes involved them, as practical men, in contradictions. Jefferson the politician could deny the popularity of illiberal measures he opposed, such as the Alien and Sedition Acts when first passed, and the illiberality of popular measures he supported, such as New Hampshire's attempted takeover of Dartmouth College. Marshall, heeding the laws that enslaved blacks and regulated Indians, could only allude to natural rights ("every man has a right to the fruits of his own labour") from a distance.

Every theory generates its own difficulties. The conviction, or the hope, that there is such a thing as natural rights offers a perspective for viewing the politics of the Court as something other than a struggle of will—the will of the people, whether in 1787–8 or now, versus the wills of the nine men and women who happen to be justices. It may be that the American fabric is right—not only because the people of Marshall's and Jefferson's lifetime said so but because those people had right ideas about man and society. These ideas found expression in the war for independence, in revolutionary declarations of principle, and in the Constitution. The most momentous changes to the Constitution, the Thirteenth and Fourteenth Amendments, were not, as Chief Justice Taney might have thought, repudiations of it and of the founders' ideas but, as Lincoln would have argued, refinements of them.

If the American fabric is right, then lawyers and judges, mindful of the inroads of time and the wayward power of language, must do their best to read the Constitution as Marshall did, as it was written and as it was meant. They may hope to avoid his mistakes. No doubt they will make their own. Rather than looking, à la Jefferson or Franklin Roosevelt, for Rube Goldberg remedies for bad decisions, we may expect that right understanding and steady firmness will produce good ones.

Constitutions, wrote Marshall, are "framed for ages to come." But men live only for their own age. Young Marshall played a small but worthy role in two great works, the Revolution and the Constitution (through the struggle to ratify it). In his maturity, he feared that the second work, the legacy of himself and his great companions, was under attack. So this simple, lax, deeply serious man did his best to defend it.

Eight years after Marshall died, Joseph Story told one of his law school classes that men such as the late chief justice "are found only when our need is the greatest." This is almost exactly right. Such men are found when our need for them is the greatest. Marshall addressed the perplexities and the challenges that he needed to face. When we have other needs, we must look for other men to address them.

ACKNOWLEDGMENTS

I WOULD LIKE TO THANK SUSAN DUNN, MATTHEW FRANCK, Annette Gordon-Reed, the Honorable Thomas P. Griesa (RIP), Jibran Khan, Eugene Meyer, Nicole Seary, Michael Uhlmann, and Kevin Walsh for their help, guidance, and encouragement.

Jason G. Coleman of the University of Virginia Press was most helpful in my using the Papers of John Marshall Digital Edition.

Akhil Amar suggested I write this book, as he did my last. I am grateful for his insight and his friendship.

I must thank my editor and publisher, Lara Heimert, and my agent, Michael Carlisle. My wife, Jeanne Safer, heard every word and improved many.

NOTES

THE PAPERS OF JOHN MARSHALL ARE AVAILABLE ONLINE, behind a paywall, at a site maintained by the University of Virginia (see below). The decisions of the Supreme Court, known collectively as United States Reports, are also available online. Each volume prepared in Marshall's lifetime and for several decades thereafter is identified by the surname of the reporter who compiled it, preceded by the year of the reporter's tenure; a citation to a particular page is followed by the proper number (e.g., 3 *Wheaton* 120).

The volumes by Goebel (*Antecedents and Beginnings to 1801*) and by Haskins and Johnson, cited below, belong to the Oliver Wendell Holmes Devise History of the Supreme Court of the United States, a series commissioned by Congress. White's volume, also cited below, is an abridgement of his contributions to the series.

Letters are cited either by their location in books or (when found online) by the correspondents and the date. Prominent correspondents are identified by obvious initials (*JM* is John Marshall, *JMad* is James Madison, *JMon* is James Monroe).

Quotations from famous poems are footnoted by line, from Blackstone's *Commentaries on the Laws of England* by book and chapter. The Constitution is cited in the text by article and section; the King James Bible, by chapter and verse.

ABBREVIATIONS OF MOST-CITED WORKS

H Hamilton, Alexander. *Writings.* New York: Library of America, 2001.

J Jefferson, Thomas. *The Life and Selected Writings of Thomas Jefferson.* Edited by Adrienne Koch and William Peden. New York: Modern Library, 1944.

M Marshall, John. *Writings.* New York: Library of America, 2010.

MLife Marshall, John. *The Life of George Washington.* New York: Wm. H. Wise, 1925.

PJM Hobson, Charles, ed. *The Papers of John Marshall.* Charlottesville: University of Virginia Press, 2014. Digital edition.

INTRODUCTION

1   **"dignity"** Jay, IV: 285.

1   **"weakest"** H, 421, *Federalist Papers* 78.

1   **"Man on earth"** M, 8, JM to JMon, January 3, 1784.

3   **"to encounter"** MLife, II: 349–353.

3   **"of his countrymen"** Quoted everywhere, see Beveridge, II: 443–445.

5   **"of commerce"** H, 206, *Federalist Papers* 11.

5   **"in government"** H, 432, *Federalist Papers* 80.

6   **"a stronghold"** TJ to John Dickinson, December 19, 1801.

7   **"acknowledged head"** Dillon, III: 367.

7   **"of individuals"** Blackstone, *Commentaries,* book 1, part 1, section 2.

7   **"ponds"** Smith, 500.

CHAPTER 1: SOLDIER

12   **"rarely to be seen"** M, 640–641, memorandum by Jared Sparks, January 1, 1826.

13   **"the heart"** M, 635, JM to Thomas W. White, November 29, 1824.

14   **"to the bar"** M, 389, JM to Joseph Delaplaine, March 22, 1818.

14   **"every man knows"** Kronenberger, 638.

14   "intelligent companion" M, 677, JM to Joseph Story, July 1827.

15   "give me death!" Widmer, 20–21.

15   "my age" M, 692, JM to Joseph Story, July 1827.

15   "scalping knife" Slaughter, 107.

18   "of anecdote" Howe, 266.

18   "extreme" MLife, II: 356.

18   his injury at Germantown See Smith, 548.

19   "prevailed" MLife, II: 143.

19   "in season" Ibid., III: 156.

19   "system itself" Ibid., III: 161.

19   "he marched" Ibid., III: 218.

19   "its support" Ibid., III: 234–235.

19   "without food" Ibid., III: 280.

20   "despond" Ibid., II: 229.

20   "steady mind" Ibid., II: 415.

20   "through a glass" Ibid., III: 7.

20   "excite enthusiasm" Ibid., III: 22.

20   "independence" Ibid., II: 235.

20   "can succeed" Ibid., II: 427. Washington's original, however, used different wording. See GW to Continental Congress Camp Committee, January 29, 1778.

21   "my country" M, 680, JM to Joseph Story, July 1827.

21   "one's country" Ellis, *Sphinx,* 61.

22   "poor distracted brain" *Atlantic Monthly,* 573.

22   "his eyes" Ibid., 547.

22   "an idea of" Ibid.

23   one of Wythe's students Smith, 79.

24   "slender Chains" Alexander Pope, "The Rape of the Lock," canto II, ll. 23–24.

24   One of Marshall's modern biographers Smith, 85–86.

25   "gratitude" M, 8, JM to JMon, January 3, 1784.

CHAPTER 2: LAWYER

27   "what it was" Goebel, *Hamilton,* 8.

27   "mother country" Blackstone, *Commentaries,* book 1, part 1, section 4.

28   "judges of law" M, 12, JM to Charles Simms, June 16, 1784.

28   rest of her days Paxton, 25–26.

29   "full of resources" Burke, I: 241–242.

29   Marshall agreed Howe, 266.

30   "unknown to any body" PJM, I: 153–157, *Hite v. Fairfax,* argument in the Court of Appeals, May 5, 1786.

31   "she was bred" M, 829, eulogy for Mary Marshall, December 25, 1832.

33   "talking ribaldry" Schoepf, 64.

33   "with contracts" M, 12, JM to Charles Simms, June 16, 1784.

33   "another revolution" M, 17, JM to James Wilkinson, January 5, 1787.

34   "ready to fall" Washington, 643.

34   "a rat" Grigsby, 32.

34   "ample discussion" Beveridge, I: 247.

37   they liked him Barbarossa, 160.

37   "To get out" Brookhiser, *Madison,* 74.

37   "our decision" Maier, 299.

38   "insecure and unprotected" M, 24–29, speech on adopting the Constitution, June 10, 1788.

38   "rest my safety" M, 35, speech on the Militia, June 16, 1788.

39   "a protection" M, 38–39, speech on the Judiciary, June 20, 1788.

39   "in the Federal Court?" Ibid., 45.

39   "on our side?" Brookhiser, *Madison,* 73.

40   "for this government" Maier, 318.

CHAPTER 3: LOCAL POLITICIAN

42   "writ of ejectment" Munford, 333–335.

43   "peep with?" Brookhiser, *Gentleman Revolutionary,* 189.

44   "guilt to her" PJM, II: 168–178, *Commonwealth v. Randolph,* notes of evidence, c. April 29, 1793.

45   "an orator indeed!" Kukla, 373.

46   "is discharged" PJM, V: 306, *Ware, Administrator of Jones v. Hylton,* argument in the circuit court, May 29–May 30, 1793.

47   huge risks See editorial note, "Fairfax Lands," PJM, II: 140–149.

47   "which bestowed it" M, 48, JM to GW, October 14, 1789.

47   "political life" M, 682, to Joseph Story, July 1827.

48   "sergeant-at-arms" Ames, I: 564.

48   "striking resemblance" Brookhiser, *Alexander Hamilton,* 103.

49   "censured" M, 682, JM to Joseph Story, July 1827.

49   "citizens to support" Brookhiser, *Gentleman Revolutionary,* 109.

50   "political heresies" Brookhiser, *Madison,* 96–98.

50   "the Republic," "the whole earth" J, 518, TJ to GW, September 9, 1792; J, 522, TJ to William Short, January 3, 1793.

51   "perpetual fetes" Brookhiser, *Madison,* 114.

52   "high indignity" M, 51–54, resolutions and address in support of the neutrality proclamation, August 17, 1793.

53   apprentices, schoolboys Beveridge, II: 151–154.

53   "to the treaty" M, 78, JM to AH, April 25, 1796.

53   he had won M, 683, JM to Joseph Story, July 1827.

54   "his opinion" Ibid., 684–685.

54   "with flattery" TJ to JMad, June 29, 1792.

54   "people of Richmond" TJ to JMad, November 26, 1795.

54   "as I please" Brookhiser, *Madison,* 1312.

55   "these gentlemen" M, 685, JM to Joseph Story, July 1827.

55   "spirit of party" Washington, 969, farewell address.

CHAPTER 4: DIPLOMAT, CONGRESSMAN, SECRETARY OF STATE

59   "whore England" TJ to Philip Mazzei, April 24, 1796. Mazzei printed the letter in Italian, which was then reprinted in French, and later in English. The version that appeared in the New York *Minerva,* May 2, 1797, is the one quoted here.

60   "good-tempered" M, 81, JM to Mary Marshall, July 3, 1797.

60   "learned" Beveridge, II: 218.

61   "polite and easy" PJM, III: 160, *Paris Journal,* October 8, 1797.

61   "confidential friend" Ibid., 164.

61   "for the pocket" Ibid., 165.

62   "not a sixpence" Ibid., 171.

62   "power and violence" Ibid.

62   "in America" Ibid., 180.

62   "an answer" M, 112, JM to Timothy Pickering, October 22, 1797.

62 "surprised" M, 122, JM to Timothy Pickering, November 8, 1797.

63 "by Marshall" J, 547.

63 "own esteem" Beveridge, II: 378–379.

64 "the truth" Hardy, 482–483.

64 poem of condolence Marshall described it in a letter to Joseph Story, June 26, 1831, and added that the poem was lost.

64 "concerning you" M, 92, JM to Mary Marshall, September 9, 1797.

64 "amiable lady" M, 137–138, JM to Mary Marshall, November 27, 1797.

65 "yourself and me" M, 147, JM to Mary Marshall, August 18, 1798.

66 the trip to Mount Vernon See Beveridge, II: 376–389.

66 "this objection" M, 688, JM to Joseph Story, July 1827.

66 "this representation" M, 850, JM to James K. Paulding, April 4, 1835.

67 lavishly on barbecues Beveridge, II: 409.

67 "into service" Munford, 208–209.

68 "of his countrymen" Beveridge, II: 443–445.

69 "by the judiciary" M, 167–168, speech on the case of Thomas Nash, March 7, 1800.

69 "sole representative" Ibid., 177.

70 "unanswerable" Henry Adams, *Gallatin,* 232. Ekirch doubts the story but notes that Jefferson wrote that Marshall had distinguished himself "greatly" (Ekirch, 164).

70 "jealousies" H, 971, letter concerning John Adams, October 24, 1800.

72 Some Federalists toyed An anonymous article floating this idea appeared in a Federalist newspaper in the new capital in January 1801. Republicans accused Marshall of writing it, a charge the newspaper denounced as "a lie." Beveridge credited the Republican charge (see Beveridge, II: 541–543).

73 "aid Mr. Jefferson" M, 213–214, JM to AH, January 1, 1801.

74 "weight and dignity" Jay, IV: 285.

74 "'nominate you'" M, 691, JM to Joseph Story, July 1827.

CHAPTER 5:
THE CASE OF THE MISSING COMMISSION

77 Washington was less a city See Haskins and Johnson, 77; Wood, 289–290.

77   "very inconvenient" Haskins and Johnson, 82.

78   "knot of lawyers" Maclay, 97.

78   strike down, laws See Justice Chase's caution about doing so, 3*Dallas* 175.

79   judicial procedure Goebel, *Antecedents,* 541.

79   invalid veterans Warren, I: 70–72.

79   international law McDonald, *Presidency,* 227.

79   "a fool" Warren, I: 131.

80   Hamilton had to advise Goebel, *Antecedents,* 665–666.

80   "next day" McRee, II: 347.

80   fell into the Susquehanna Goebel, *Antecedents,* 569.

80   "intolerable" King, I: 506.

80   "to the people" John Adams, IX: 144.

80   "bunches of oakum" Warren, I: 48.

81   "manner of dwarfs" Haskins and Johnson, 101.

81   "not to quote" Ibid., 100.

82   "through the storm?" Brookhiser, *Gentleman Revolutionary,* 168.

83   "Mr. Jefferson" M, 219, JM to Charles C. Pinckney, March 4, 1801.

83   "contemplation of Congress" J, 330.

83   "the last session" TJ to Benjamin Rush, December 20, 1801.

83   "to make it" Beveridge, III: 71.

83   "irresponsible?" Ibid., 85–86.

84   "wrong-doer?" Haskins and Johnson, 72–75.

84   "my brothers" M, 222, JM to William Cushing, April 19, 1802.

85   "insufficient" 1*Cranch* 302.

86   "resolute manner" Sloan and McKean, 52.

87   Marshall supposedly said Parton, 586.

87   James Marshall later declared 1*Cranch* 146.

87   "of the deed" TJ to William Johnson, June 12, 1823.

88   "office and duty" Blackstone, *Commentaries,* book 3, chapter 7, section 1.

89   "power . . . invading" Sloan and McKean, 99.

89   "distance of time" 1*Cranch* 142.

90   "two capacities" 1*Cranch* 149.

90   "irrevocable" 1*Cranch* 151.

90   "to no man" 1*Cranch* 153.

91   partly disagreed See *M'Ferran v. Taylor and Massie,* 3*Cranch* 282.

91   "unremitting pace" Wirt, 108–111.

91   "real difficulty" M, 229, *Marbury v. Madison*, February 24, 1803.

91   "appointment is made" Ibid., 236.

92   "vested legal right" Ibid., 237.

92   "for a remedy" Ibid., 240.

92   "all other cases" Ibid., 246.

93   "deemed fundamental" Ibid., 248–249.

93   "by that instrument" Ibid., 252.

93   "disregard the former" H, 424, *Federalist Papers* 78.

94   "declare it void" M, 38–39, speech on the judiciary, June 20, 1788.

94   "CONSTITUTION VIOLATED" Sloan and McKean, 166.

94   "not law" TJ to George Hay, June 2, 1807.

95   "to be disturbed" 1*Cranch* 309.

CHAPTER 6: IMPEACHMENT

98   "my hatchet" Weems, 24.

99   "of genius" MLife, IV: 323.

99   "inflexible integrity" Ibid., 325.

99   "subject of government" Ibid., 328.

99   "the United States" MLife, V: 271.

99   "unpublished documents" J, 117.

99   "three cheers" J, 131.

100   "shall be of opinion" Haskins and Johnson, 212.

101   "in your corners" Conrad, 491.

101   "posse comitatus" Ibid., 502.

102   "all possible governments" Haskins and Johnson, 218.

102   "not interfere" Ibid., 219.

102   "the legislature" M, 262, JM to Samuel Chase, January 23, 1804.

103   "fill them better" John Quincy Adams, I: 116.

103   "intemperance" Haskins and Johnson, 238–239.

104   "the devil" Brookhiser, *Gentleman Revolutionary*, 181.

105   "really guilty" Gales and Seaton, 224.

105   "young gentlemen," "damned" Ibid., 482.

105   "the word 'very'" Ibid., 489.

105   "state the facts" Ibid., 266.

105   "too much cunning" Beveridge, III: 196.

CHAPTER 7: TREASON

107 "political principles" Haskins and Johnson, 390.

108 "to the current" White, 189.

108 "directed to deliver" 3*Cranch* 282, *M'Ferran v. Taylor and Massie.*

109 "of that description" PJM, XII: 67, JM to Joseph Story, May 23, 1831.

109 "highest judicial authorities" TJ to Congress, January 22, 1807, message on Aaron Burr.

110 moved to Kentucky Wilkinson wrote Marshall from Kentucky, evidently at the end of 1786, requesting a passport from the governor of Virginia to travel to Spanish New Orleans; Marshall told him that the governor (Edmund Randolph) could not issue such a document. See M, 16, JM to James Wilkinson, May 1787.

110 "Things written," he would say, "remain" Brookhiser, *Hamilton,* 166.

110 "*chère diable*" Lomask, 27.

112 "widespread conspiracy" Linklater, 253.

112 "deserve the boon" Malone, 264, and Burr, II: 973–986.

113 "distinct offenses" 4*Cranch* 126, *Ex parte Bollman* (Bollmann's name was shorn of one *n* throughout.)

113 "high misdemeanor" Ibid., 131.

113 "a tribunal" Ibid., 136.

114 "not proved?" Lomask, 231.

114 "necessary testimony" Haskins and Johnson, 266.

115 seven thousand men Henry Adams, *Jefferson,* 820.

115 when did Burr Beveridge, III: 341. Kline thinks the author of the cipher letter was former New Jersey senator Jonathan Dayton, another friend of Burr's. See Burr, 985–986.

115 "scene of the action" 4*Cranch* 126.

116 "expression of contempt" Lomask, 252.

116 "a villain" Beveridge, III: 464.

117 "impartial trial" M, 269–276, circuit court opinion in *United States v. Burr* regarding a motion for a subpoena.

117 Marshall apologized Beveridge, IV: 447–449.

117 a force of Marines This bold attack was the inspiration for the line, "to the shores of Tripoli," in the Marine Corps hymn.

119 "virulent" Madison, *Debates,* 468.

120 "to embrace" M, 328–329, circuit court opinion in *United States v. Burr* on the law of treason, August 31, 1807.

121 "the future" TJ to George Hay, September 4, 1807.

121 "governed by laws" M, 339, JM to Richard Peters, November 23, 1807.

122 "the United States" Lomask, 309.

CHAPTER 8: CORRUPTION AND CONTRACTS

123 "oppressed minority" M, 340, JM to Charles C. Pinckney, October 9, 1808.

124 "any one of us" PJM, VII: 219, Gouverneur Morris to JM, December 2, 1809.

124 "the malignant" Ibid., 221, JM to Gouverneur Morris, December 12, 1809.

125 "not greedy" Magrath, 6.

126 "keep out the din" Ames, 835.

126 "good temper" Magrath, 9.

126 "their lives" Magrath, 123–126. These words are from a reminiscence Jackson wrote in later years, but they recall his arguments at the time.

126 "burned the papers" Magrath, 13.

127 first appeared in the final draft See McDonald, *Novus*, 270–275.

127 "pronounce it so" Hamilton's opinion in Magrath, 149–150.

128 "a Yazoo man" Henry Adams, *Randolph*, 171.

129 "much delicacy" M, 342, *Fletcher v. Peck*, March 16, 1810.

130 "incompatibility" Ibid., 342–343.

130 "control their conduct" Ibid., 344.

130 "absolute power" Ibid., 348.

130 "without compensation" Ibid., 349.

131 "each state" Ibid., 349–350.

131 "the Constitution" Ibid., 352.

132 "feigned case" 6*Cranch* 147.

132 "all the points" Warren, I: 395. John Quincy Adams, who had been cocounsel with Harper for Peck in 1809, recorded the remark in his diary.

133 "my scruples" 6*Cranch* 148.

CHAPTER 9: A SMALL COLLEGE

137 "superior talents" M, 340, JM to Charles C. Pinckney, October 19, 1808.

138 "to unite" M, 355–356, JM to Robert Smith, July 27, 1812.

138 "John Marshall" Beveridge, IV: 31.

138 "these feelings" M, 357, JM to Robert Smith, July 27, 1812.

139 The case with the most winning name 8*Cranch* 398.

139 "canal mania" Brookhiser, *Founding Father,* 49.

140 "more powerful" M, 362–787, report of the Virginia River Commission, December 26, 1812.

140 "every part" H, 206–207, *Federalist* 11.

141 "cordiality" PJM, XII: 432, JM to Gabriel Duvall, January 16, 1835.

141 "a victim" TJ to Albert Gallatin, September 27, 1810.

142 "'I can't tell'" Hayes, I: 115.

142 "strange questions" White, 365.

142 "positively in love" Beveridge, IV: 81.

143 "raining somewhere" Ibid., 88.

143 "dissolute conduct" PJM, VIII: 84, Harvard faculty records, March 20, 1815.

143 "intelligent companion" M, 677, JM to Joseph Story, July 1827.

144 "concurred in every word" White, 173. White presents Marshall as deeply interested in the case, but see also the editorial note in PJM, VIII: 119, which is more skeptical and more charitable.

144 "to have been argued" White, 397. The words are Wheaton's, from his notes to a case.

144 This room was furnished PJM, VII: 257, Benjamin H. Latrobe to JM, June 5, 1810.

144 for their benefit Smith, 419.

146 "infidel," "murderer" Peabody, 329.

147 "to mankind" Ibid., 438.

147 "are attached" Ibid., 439.

147 "nation itself" TJ to William Plumer, July 21, 1816.

148 "of a few" Beveridge, IV: 234–236.

148 "any other man" White, 268.

148 Webster concluded White, 616–617.

149 "able argument" Smith, 437.

149 "delicacy" M, 391, *Dartmouth College v. Woodward,* February 2, 1819.

150 "integrity" Ibid.

150 "confer rights" Ibid., 394.

150 "eleemosynary institution" Ibid.

150 "public property . . . ?" Ibid., 397.

151 "powers would be" Ibid., 398–399.

151 "of the donors" Ibid., 401.

151 "operation likewise" Ibid., 404.

151 "totally changed" Ibid., 408–410.

151 "repugnant to the Constitution" Ibid., 411.

152 "unfortunate" Peabody, 460.

152 "our Constitution" M, 352, *Fletcher v. Peck.*

152 "not the living" TJ to William Plumer, January 21, 1816.

153 "the society" TJ to JMad, September 6, 1789.

153 Scholars debate See Newmyer, 246–253.

CHAPTER 10: BANKERS AND EMBEZZLERS

156 "the importance" MLife, IV: 393.

156 "ever formed" Chernow, 647.

157 "expressly granted" Brookhiser, *Madison,* 192.

158 "amicable arrangement" Richard Ellis, 72.

158 worth a trip White, 246.

159 "the classics" White, 352–353.

159 "a large part" White, 239; *Aeneid,* II: 6.

159 "act" M, 414, *McCulloch v. Maryland,* March 6, 1819.

160 "submitted" Ibid.

160 "have assembled?" Ibid.

160 "for their benefit" Ibid., 415.

160 "to the people" Widmer, 233.

160 "from the earth" Lincoln, *1859–1865,* 536, the Gettysburg Address.

161 "sphere of action" M, 415.

161 "are expounding" M, 416.

161 *"conducive to"* H, 618, opinion on the constitutionality of a national bank, February 23, 1791.

161 "powers of government" M, 421.

162 "national authority" H, 621.

162 "are constitutional" M, 426.

162 "great principle" M, 429.

162 "separated from it" Ibid.

162 "its own sphere" Ibid.

162 "power to destroy" Ibid., 432; for Webster, see 4*Wheaton* 327.

163 "the judicial department" M, 432.

163 "of the states" M, 433.

163 "unconstitutional" M, 436.

163 "crowbar law" Richard Ellis, 151.

164 "ruffian-like manner" Ibid., 153.

164 in 1824 *Osborn* was argued in 1823, then reargued the following year.

164 "national purposes" 9*Wheaton* 360, *Osborn v. Bank of the United States*.

164 "therefore void" Ibid., 368.

165 "controverted and exposed" Smith, 447.

165 "every tittle of them" TJ to Spencer Roane, September 6, 1819.

165 "vindictive hate" M, 468, "A Friend of the Constitution" #I, June 30, 1819.

166 "to be effected" M, 480, "A Friend of the Constitution" #III, July 2, 1819.

166 embargo trade, fight wars M, 469, 471, "A Friend of the Constitution" #I.

166 "masterly" M, 486, "A Friend of the Constitution" #III.

166 "much *extended*" Richard Ellis, 128.

166 "the whole nation" M, 511, "A Friend of the Constitution" #VIII, July 14, 1819.

166 "by themselves" M, 481, "A Friend of the Constitution" #III.

166 "or ever can" M, 500, "A Friend of the Constitution" #VI, July 6, 1819.

166 "legislative power" M, 518, "A Friend of the Constitution" #IX, July 15, 1819.

167 were acquitted See Hammond, 260–262, 268–272.

CHAPTER 11: JEWISH LOTTERY RUNNERS

167 "a superior" Virginian, 27.

169 **"rapacity"** PJM, VIII: 111, editorial note on Marshall and the Fairfax litigation.

169 **"instructions"** Haskins and Johnson, 362.

170 **"those of the nation"** 1*Wheaton* 324–325, *Martin v. Hunter's Lessee.*

170 **The Cohens came** Barroway, 357–376.

171 **"dangerous expedient"** H, 592.

171 **Marshall had voted** Beveridge, II: 56.

171 **"important improvement"** 6*Wheaton* 285.

172 **"in our legislature"** M, 526, JM to Bushrod Washington, February 8, 1821.

172 **"examine and correct"** White, 505.

172 **"a mere league"** 6*Wheaton* 353–354.

172 **"shall endure"** 6*Wheaton* 344.

173 **"present Constitution"** M, 531, *Cohens v. Virginia,* March 3, 1821.

173 **"subdivision of them"** Ibid., 536–537.

173 **also be appellate** Newmyer, 370, summarizes Marshall's reasoning thus: "Heads, the Court wins; tails, Virginia loses."

173 **"be decided"** M, 533, *Cohens v. Virginia,* March 3, 1821.

173 **"celebrated statesman"** Ibid., 556.

173 **"ONE WHOLE"** H, 450, *Federalist* 82.

174 **"can proceed"** H, 43, *Federalist* 80, quoted in M, 554, *Cohens v. Virginia,* March 3, 1821.

174 **"it is competent"** M, 553.

174 **"its bands"** Washington, 966–968, farewell address, September 19, 1796, quoted in MLife, V: 286–289.

174 **"not sustained"** M, 564, *Cohens v. Virginia,* March 3, 1821.

176 **"going with him"** Beveridge, IV: 358–359.

176 **"engulfing"** TJ to Spencer Roane, March 9, 1821.

176 **"of character"** M, 565, JM to Joseph Story, June 15, 1821.

176 **"of the mountains"** M, 569, JM to Joseph Story, September 18, 1821.

176 **"independent judiciary"** M, 567, JM to Joseph Story, July 13, 1821.

177 **"by Judge Marshall"** TJ to William Johnson, June 12, 1823.

177 **"like other people"** Martineau, I: 257.

177 **"through all time"** Beveridge, IV: 372.

178 **none of Johnson's amendments** His, and similar ones, were tabled or squelched in committee. See Beveridge, IV: 379–380.

178 **"of the mind"** TJ to Spencer Roane, March 9, 1821.

178 **no Virginian on the horizon** Henry Clay and William Crawford had been born in Virginia but were identified with the states they had grown up in (Kentucky and Georgia).

178 **"between the states"** PJM, IX: 181, JM to Charles Miner, July 15, 1821.

179 **"in the night"** J, 698.

CHAPTER 12: STEAMBOATS AND COMMERCE

183 **"here I disembark"** Morris, II: 533–534.

184 **"highest consideration"** Chernow, 721.

184 **"*contradictory* and *repugnant*"** H, 302, *Federalist* 32.

184 **"triumphant success"** Baxter, 24.

185 **"caught no buddy"** Ibid., 36.

187 **"encroachment and confusion?"** 9*Wheaton* 14.

187 **"[those of] Congress"** 9*Wheaton* 88.

187 **"while recollection remains"** M, 605–606, JM to Mary Marshall, February 23, 1824.

187 **"feeble voice"** White, 573.

187 **"to [them] implicitly"** M, 608, *Gibbons v. Ogden,* March 2, 1824.

188 **"they have said"** Ibid., 609.

188 **"fornication laws"** White, 576.

188 **"the subject exists"** M, 614, *Gibbons v. Ogden,* March 2, 1824.

188 **"mother's milk"** White, 287.

188 **"every part"** H, 206–207, *Federalist* 11.

188 **"growth and comfort"** Washington, 965–966, farewell address, September 19, 1796.

189 **"other states"** M, 613, *Gibbons v. Ogden,* March 2, 1824.

189 **"been refuted"** Ibid., 623.

189 **"do that thing"** Ibid., 625.

189 **"reversed and annulled"** Ibid., 632.

190 **"entire approbation"** 9*Wheaton* 222.

190 **"a wall in sport"** M, 601, JM to Joseph Story, September 26, 1823.

190 **The planter class would fear** Baxter, 58–60.

190 **New York would not welcome** Ibid., 63.

191 **"destroys the health"** 2*Peters* 249.

191 **"of a highway"** Ibid., 246.

191 **"circumstances of the case"** Ibid., 252. Marshall's opinion is vague as well as short; the Taney Court would understand him to have said that the most important "circumstances" were not Delaware's concern for public health, but Congress's failure to have passed any laws about navigating Blackbird Creek and similar streams. See also Baxter, 90–91, and White, 584.

191 **"minute interests," "desirable cares"** H, 232–233, *Federalist* 17.

191 **"free from pain"** PJM, X: 87, JM to Mary Marshall, February 23, 1824.

192 **steamboats** Warren, II: 75.

192 **"great benefits"** Baxter, 72.

CHAPTER 13: SLAVERS

195 **"in the country"** White, 331–332.

196 **"impossible"** M, 599, JM to Joseph Story, July 2, 1823.

196 **"my own way"** 9*Wheaton* 222.

197 **"submitting in silence"** 3*Peters* 145.

198 **"military chief"** PJM, X: 123, speech, October 27, 1824.

198 **"monstrous consequences"** Levasseur, I: 203.

199 **"of the coast"** Bryant, 50.

200 **"beyond the United States"** Noonan, 19.

201 **"in the trade"** Ibid., 56.

201 **"that makes them"** Ibid., 63.

201 **"in the selection"** Ibid., 65.

202 **"[international] disputes"** Blackstone, *Commentaries,* book IV, chapter 5.

203 **"repugnant"** White, 693.

203 **"special excitement"** Foote, 13.

203 **"making slaves"** 10*Wheaton* 79.

203 **"your plunder"** Ibid., 86.

204 **"line of duty"** Ibid., 114.

204 **"general question"** Ibid., 123.

204 **"this admission"** Ibid., 120.

204 **"legal solution"** Ibid., 121.

204 **"equal rights"** Ibid., 122.

205 **"be restored"** Ibid., 123.

205 "necessity of concealment" Ibid., 130.

206 "divided on it" Ibid., 126.

206 "right of property" 7*Cranch* 299, *Mima Queen and child, petitioners for freedom, v. Hepburn.*

207 "votre base crimes" White, 353–354.

207 "of property" "Letter," 70–72.

207 "one judge" William Johnson to TJ, December 10, 1822.

207 considerable slave owner See Finkelman, 36–48.

207 "The residue" 10*Wheaton* 132.

208 "competent evidence" 12*Wheaton* 552.

208 "sufficient" Ibid., 554.

208 "peaceable, and industrious" Noonan, 137.

208 "imperfectly suppressed" Lincoln, *1859–1865,* 221, first inaugural address.

209 "constitution of government" H, 470, *Federalist* 84.

209 as a bill of rights M, 350, *Fletcher v. Peck.*

CHAPTER 14: BANKRUPTS

211 "its sanctity" TJ to Martin Van Buren, June 29, 1824.

212 "mode of thinking" M, 727–728, JM to Henry Lee, October 25, 1830.

212 "he may do" M, 602, JM to Joseph Story, December 9, 1823.

213 "confutation or debate" Story, I: 498.

213 "in his pocket" White, 303.

214 "among their creditors" Blackstone, *Commentaries,* book II, chapter 31, section 1.

215 "meditated much" Story, I: 271.

215 "no variety of construction" 4*Wheaton* 198, *Sturges v. Crowninshield.*

215 "not forbidden" Ibid., 196.

216 "inviolable" Ibid., 206.

216 "future acquisitions" Ibid., 198.

216 "shall admit" Ibid., 200.

216 "the contract" Ibid., 201.

216 "in existence" Ibid., 207.

219 "this distinction?" M, 647, *Ogden v. Saunders,* February 19, 1827.

219 "generally used" Ibid.

219 "part of it" Ibid., 652. For the lawyers, see 12*Wheaton* 231.

219 "of the parties" M, 659–660, *Ogden v. Saunders,* February 19, 1827.

220 "his surplus" Ibid., 659.

220 "private faith" Ibid., 668.

221 "legal adjudication" 12*Wheaton* 272–273.

221 "their own citizens" 12*Wheaton* 366.

222 The spectacle See Warren, II: 151.

222 "American character" Tocqueville, 245.

CHAPTER 15: CHEROKEES

223 "golden blond" Smith, 495.

223 "before him" M, 644, JM to Samuel Fay, October 15, 1826.

223 "cordial welcome" M, 643, JM to Samuel Fay, September 15, 1826.

224 "alone to judge" M, 644, JM to Samuel Fay, October 15, 1826.

224 "with a family" M, 708, JM to James Rawlings, July 25, 1829.

224 "yet amusing" M, 646, JM to Joseph Story, November 26, 1826.

225 "belle lettre reading" M, 828, Eulogy for Mary Marshall, December 25, 1832.

225 "full of corn" Beveridge, IV: 83.

226 "DEMOCRACY" H, 1022, AH to Theodore Sedgwick, July 10, 1804.

226 "important services" John Quincy Adams, II: 360.

226 "virtually dissolved" Beveridge, IV: 463.

226 "disposition and habits" PJM, XI: 94, JM to Joseph Story, May 1, 1828.

227 "seemed triumphant" Story, I: 563.

228 "his conscience?" M, 714, speech in the Virginia constitutional convention on the judiciary, December 11, 1829.

228 "a sinning people" Ibid., 718.

228 "is impossible" Guasco, 148–149.

229 "escape" Warren, II: 172.

230 "as usual" M, 719, JM to Mary Marshall, January 31, 1830.

230 "are deliberating" White, 302.

230 "indicating unfriendliness" M, 845, JM to Joseph Story, October 21, 1831.

231 "than myself" 3*Peters* xii.

231 "to this country" M, 13, JM to JMon, December 2, 1784.

232 **"justice and humanity"** MLife, IV: 292. See also Joseph Ellis, *Creation*, 127–164.

232 **"land itself"** 7 *Cranch* 167, *State of New Jersey v. Wilson.*

232 **a Maryland lawyer** Johnson served as a justice of the Supreme Court for less than half a year, 1792–3.

233 **"cannot deny"** M, 586, *Johnson v. McIntosh*, February 28, 1823.

233 **"to others"** Ibid., 588.

233 **"persevering courage"** Ibid., 584.

233 **"wantonly oppressed"** Ibid., 586.

234 **An 1825 census showed** McLoughlin, 125.

235 **"which is pursued"** PJM, XI: 380–381, Dabney Carr to JM, June 25, 1830; JM to Dabney Carr, June 26, 1830.

236 **"our arms"** M, 731, *Cherokee Nation v. Georgia*, March 18, 1831.

236 **"dominion of the United States"** Ibid., 733.

236 **"courts of the United States"** Ibid., 735.

236 **"a deep interest"** M, 738, JM to Richard Peters, May 19, 1831.

236 **"proper parties"** M, 736, *Cherokee Nation v. Georgia.*

CHAPTER 16: MISSIONARIES

237 **"in our distress"** PJM, XII: 68, Joseph Story to JM, May 29, 1831.

237 **"to our minds"** M, 741, JM to Joseph Story, June 26, 1831.

238 **"laid in dust"** Alexander Pope, "The Rape of the Lock," canto V, l. 147–148.

238 **"of the Cherokee people"** McLoughlin, 256.

239 **"of the question"** Ibid., 258.

239 **"political contest"** Ibid., 260.

239 **"covenant-breaking"** Ibid., 262.

241 **"succeed me"** M, 739, JM to Joseph Story, June 26, 1831.

241 **"chief justice walks"** Smith, 510.

242 **"my hopes"** PJM, XII: 135, JM to James M. Marshall, December 19, 1831.

242 **lines written** General Burgoyne's song was written for the libretto of a comic opera, *The Lord of the Manor*; see Burgoyne, I: 159. For Marshall's version, see Smith, 515.

242 **"his departed wife"** Story, II: 87.

243 **"its duty"** M, 337, *United States v. Burr.*

243 "cannot be avoided" M, 758–759, *Worcester v. Georgia,* March 3, 1832.

243 "they descend" Ibid., 760.

243 "of the union" Ibid., 778.

243 "faith of the United States" Ibid., 773.

244 "annulled" Ibid., 779.

244 "inflicted on innocence" Ibid.

244 "its ancient possessors" Ibid., 760.

244 "his own labour" 10*Wheaton* 120.

244 never actually have been said See Warren, II: 219.

244 "fell stillborn" White, 737.

244 "not law" TJ to George Hay, June 2, 1807.

245 Partisans, Critics For classic dueling interpretations of Jackson, see Arthur Schlesinger Jr., *The Age of Jackson,* and Bray Hammond, *Banks and Politics in America from the Revolution to the Civil War.*

245 "Bank of the United States" M, 821–822, JM to Joseph Story.

245 "independent of both" Jackson's veto message, July 10, 1832.

246 Roger Taney, would later argue See Warren, II: 222–224. Taney was making this argument when he was chief justice, so he had an interest in minimizing Jackson's criticisms of the Court.

246 "cannot last" M, 824, JM to Joseph Story, September 22, 1832.

247 "null, void and no law" South Carolina ordinance of nullification, November 24, 1832.

247 "on which it was founded" Proclamation regarding nullification, December 10, 1832.

247 "by Mr. Jefferson" M, 825–826, JM to Joseph Story, December 25, 1832.

248 "such an occurrence?" Story, II: 119.

CHAPTER 17: BILL OF RIGHTS

250 "wholly forsaken" Mercer, 103.

250 "one good feature" White, 581.

251 Marshall told Mayer 7*Peters* 245–246; PJM, XII: 260, headnote, *Barron v. Baltimore,* February 16, 1833.

251 water that flowed alongside it Mercer, 129.

251 say nothing at all 7*Peters* 246–247.

251 **"much difficulty"** M, 830, *Barron v. Baltimore,* February 16, 1833.

252 **"were suggested"** MLife, IV: 318.

252 **"each state"** M, 351, *Fletcher v. Peck,* March 16, 1810.

252 **in *Gibbons*** M, 610, *Gibbons v. Ogden,* March 2, 1824.

252 **"directly express"** M, 832, *Barron v. Baltimore.*

252 **"No language"** Ibid., 831.

252 **"to the states"** Ibid., 830.

252 **within the text** This argument was made at the time by William Rawle, a Philadelphia jurist, in a commentary on the Constitution: "The first amendment expressly refers to the powers of Congress alone, but some of those which follow are to be more generally construed . . . as applying to the state legislatures as well as that of the Union." See White, 590.

253 **"local [state] governments"** M, 833, *Barron v. Baltimore.*

254 **"a selected one"** TJ to Thomas McKean, February 19, 1803.

254 **"is dismissed"** M, 833, *Barron v. Baltimore.*

254 **"public deprivation"** Mercer, 258.

255 **"his principles?"** PJM, XII: 257, Joseph Story to JM, January 1833.

256 **"its object"** M, 839–840, JM to Joseph Story, July 31, 1833.

257 **"around him"** White, 422.

258 **"as I can"** M, 851, JM to Richard Peters, April 30, 1835.

259 **his own epitaph** M, 852.

260 **"his strong mind"** Warren, II: 272–273.

LEGACY

262 **"acknowledged head"** Dillon, II: 367.

264 **for their benefit** See M, 415, *McCulloch v. Maryland,* March 6, 1819.

264 **"its words"** M, 647, *Ogden v. Saunders,* February 19, 1827.

264 **"of the day"** M, 833, *Barron v. Baltimore,* February 16, 1833.

265 **"or dissolved"** M, 845, JM to Thomas S. Grimké, October 6, 1834.

265 **"think so too"** Warren, II: 284.

266 **a majority of the full Court** 8*Peters* 122.

266 **unavailing duty** 11*Peters* 350, *Briscoe v. Bank of Commerce of Kentucky; Aeneid,* VI: 885–886.

266 **the Taney Court approved** 11*Peters* 350, *Briscoe v. Bank of Commerce of Kentucky*.

267 **"have rights"** 11*Peters* 422, *Proprietors of the Charles River Bridge v. Proprietors of the Warren Bridge et al*.

267 **Taney's intellect and gentle manner** Warren, II: 289–290.

268 **suggested collusion** Buchanan's correspondence shows that he colluded with other justices, if not Taney. See Buchanan, X: 106–108.

269 **applied to territories** Taney's argument concerning the Fifth Amendment is at 19*Howard* 450, *Dred Scott v. Sandford*.

269 **"its adoption"** Lincoln's speech is in Lincoln, *1832–1858*, 395, speech on the Dred Scott decision, June 26, 1857. For Curtis's opinion, see 19*Howard* 576, *Dred Scott v. Sandford*. Curtis was wrong about New York State, which, while it allowed free blacks who met the property qualification to vote in ordinary elections, allowed free white males age twenty-one and over to vote for delegates to the ratifying convention (Maier, 327).

270 **"not really true"** Lincoln, *1832–1858*, 392–393.

270 **"galvanized corpse"** Brookhiser, *Founders' Son*, 191.

270 **remain in slavery** After the Court ruled, Scott was freed by his owners and worked as a hotel porter until he died in 1858.

271 **"eminent tribunal"** Lincoln, *1859–1865*, 221, first inaugural address, March 4, 1861.

271 **"that occasion"** Senator Charles Sumner, quoted in Finkelman, 173.

272 **"his own will"** TJ to William Johnson, June 12, 1823.

273 **"supreme will"** M, 248–249, *Marbury v. Madison*, February 24, 1803.

273 **"both apply"** Ibid., 250.

274 **"this dispute?"** Liptak.

274 **"fill them better"** John Quincy Adams, I: 116.

274 **"Let them decide"** TJ to William Johnson, June 12, 1823.

274 **"too expensive"** Madison, *Writings*, 800.

276 **"into society"** M, 660, opinion in *Ogden v. Saunders*, February 19, 1827.

276 **"his own labour"** 10*Wheaton* 120.

277 **"ages to come"** M, 536, *Cohens v. Virginia*, March 3, 1821.

277 **"the greatest"** Hayes, I: 114.

BIBLIOGRAPHY

Adams, Henry. *History of the United States During the Administrations of Thomas Jefferson*. New York: Library of America, 1986.

Adams, Henry. *John Randolph*. Armonk, NY: M. E. Sharpe, 1996.

Adams, Henry. *The Life of Albert Gallatin*. Philadelphia: J. B. Lippincott, 1880.

Adams, John. *Works of John Adams*. Edited by Charles Francis Adams. Boston: Little, Brown, 1854.

Adams, John Quincy. *The Diaries of John Quincy Adams*. Edited by David Waldstreicher. New York: Library of America, 2017.

Ames, Fisher. *The Works of Fisher Ames*. Edited by W. B. Allen. Indianapolis: Liberty Classics, 1983.

Atlantic Monthly. "An Old Virginia Correspondence." October 1899.

Barbarossa [John Scott]. *The Lost Principle*. Richmond, VA: James Woodhouse, 1860.

Barroway, Aaron. "The Cohens of Maryland." *Maryland Historical Magazine*, December 1923.

Baxter, Maurice G. *The Steam Boat Monopoly Gibbons v. Ogden 1824*. New York: Alfred A. Knopf, 1972.

Beveridge, Albert J. *The Life of John Marshall*. Boston: Houghton Mifflin, 1916–19.

Brookhiser, Richard. *Alexander Hamilton, American*. New York: Free Press, 1999.

Brookhiser, Richard. *Founders' Son: A Life of Abraham Lincoln*. New York: Basic Books, 2014.

Brookhiser, Richard. *Founding Father: Rediscovering George Washington.* New York: Free Press, 1996.

Brookhiser, Richard. *Gentleman Revolutionary: Gouverneur Morris, the Rake Who Wrote the Constitution.* New York: Free Press, 2003.

Brookhiser, Richard. *James Madison.* New York: Basic Books, 2011.

Bryant, Jonathan M. *Dark Places of the Earth.* New York: Liveright, 2014.

Buchanan, James. *The Works of James Buchanan.* Edited by John Bassett Moore. Philadelphia: J. B. Lippincott, 1910.

Burgoyne, John J. *The Dramatic and Poetical Works.* London: C. Whittingham, 1808.

Burke, Edmund. *Selected Works.* Indianapolis: Liberty Fund, 1999.

Burr, Aaron. *Political Correspondence and Public Papers of Aaron Burr.* Edited by Mary-Jo Kline. Princeton, NJ: Princeton University Press, 1983.

Chernow, Ron. *Alexander Hamilton.* New York: Penguin Press, 2005.

Conrad, Robert T., ed. *Sanderson's Biographies of the Signers of the Declaration of Independence.* Philadelphia: Thomas Cowperthwait, 1846.

Dillon, John F. *John Marshall: Life, Character and Judicial Services.* Chicago: Callaghan, 1903.

Ekirch, A. Roger. *American Sanctuary.* New York: Pantheon Books, 2017.

Ellis, Joseph J. *American Creation.* New York: Alfred A. Knopf, 2007.

Ellis, Joseph J. *American Sphinx.* New York: Alfred A. Knopf, 1997.

Ellis, Richard E. *Aggressive Nationalism.* New York: Oxford University Press, 2007.

Finkelman, Paul. *Supreme Injustice.* Cambridge, MA: Harvard University Press, 2018.

Foote, H. S. *Casket of Memories.* Washington, DC: Chronicle, 1874.

Gales, Joseph, and William Winston Seaton. *Debates and Proceedings in the Congress of the United States: Eighth Congress—Second Session.* Washington, DC: Gales and Seaton, 1852.

Goebel, Julius, Jr. *Antecedents and Beginnings to 1801.* New York: Macmillan, 1971.

Goebel, Julius, Jr. *The Law Practice of Alexander Hamilton.* New York: Columbia University Press, 1964.

Grigsby, Hugh Blair. *The History of the Virginia Federal Convention of 1788.* Richmond: Virginia Historical Society, 1890.

Guasco, Suzanne Cooper. *Confronting Slavery.* DeKalb: Northern Illinois University Press, 2013.

Hammond, Bray. *Banks and Politics in America from the Revolution to the Civil War.* Princeton, NJ: Princeton University Press, 1957.

Hardy, Sallie E. Marshall. *The Green Bag.* Boston: Boston Book Company, 1896.

Haskins, George Lee, and Herbert A. Johnson. *Foundations of Power: John Marshall, 1801–15.* New York: Macmillan, 1981.

Hayes, Rutherford B. *Diary and Letters of Rutherford B. Hayes.* Edited by Charles R. Williams. Columbus: Ohio State Archeological and Historical Society, 1922.

Howe, Henry. *Historical Collections of Virginia . . .* Charleston, SC: W. M. R. Babcock, 1852.

Jay, John. *The Correspondence and Public Papers of John Jay.* Edited by Henry P. Johnston. New York: G. P. Putnam's Sons, 1893.

King, Charles R. *Life and Correspondence of Rufus King.* New York: G. P. Putnam's Sons, 1894.

Kronenberger, Louis. *The Portable Johnson & Boswell.* New York: Viking Press, 1947.

Kukla, Jon. *Patrick Henry.* New York: Simon & Schuster, 2017.

"Letter from Justice Washington." *Niles Register,* September 29, 1821.

Levasseur, A. *Lafayette in America.* Translated by John D. Goodman. Philadelphia: Carey and Lea, 1829.

Lincoln, Abraham. *Speeches and Writings 1832–1858.* New York: Library of America, 1989.

Lincoln, Abraham. *Speeches and Writings 1859–1865.* New York: Library of America, 1989.

Linklater, Andro. *An Artist in Treason.* New York: Walker, 2009.

Liptak, Adam. "An Exit Interview with Richard Posner, Judicial Provocateur." *New York Times,* September 11, 2017.

Lomask, Milton. *Aaron Burr: The Conspiracy and Years of Exile 1805–1836.* New York: Farrar, Straus and Giroux, 1982.

Maclay, William. *The Diary of William Maclay.* Edited by Kenneth R. Bowling and Helen E. Veit. Baltimore: Johns Hopkins University Press, 1988.

Madison, James. *Debates in the Federal Convention of 1787.* Edited by James McClellan and M. E. Bradford. Richmond, VA: James River Press, 1989.

Madison, James. *Writings.* New York: Library of America, 1999.

Magrath, C. Peter. *Yazoo*. New York: W. W. Norton, 1966.

Maier, Pauline. *Ratification*. New York: Simon & Schuster, 2010.

Malone, Dumas. *Jefferson the President: Second Term 1805–1809*. Boston: Little, Brown, 1974.

Martineau, Harriet. *Retrospect of Western Travel*. London: Saunders & Oatley, 1838.

McDonald, Forrest. *The American Presidency*. Lawrence: University of Kansas Press, 1994.

McDonald, Forrest. *Novus Ordo Seclorum*. Lawrence: University of Kansas Press, 1985.

McLoughlin, William G. *Cherokees and Missionaries*. Norman: University of Oklahoma Press, 1984.

McRee, Griffith J. *Life and Correspondence of James Iredell*. New York: Appleton, 1863.

Mercer, William Davenport. *Diminishing the Bill of Rights*. Norman: University of Oklahoma Press, 2017.

Morris, Gouverneur. *Diary and Letters of Gouverneur Morris*. Edited by Anne Cary Morris. New York: Da Capo, 1970.

Munford, George Wythe. *The Two Parsons*. Richmond, VA: J. D. K. Sleight, 1884.

Newmyer, R. Kent. *John Marshall and the Heroic Age of the Supreme Court*. Baton Rouge: Louisiana State Press, 2001.

Noonan, John T., Jr. *The Antelope*. Berkeley: University of California Press, 1977.

Parton, James. *Life of Thomas Jefferson*. Boston: Houghton, Mifflin, 1883.

Paxton, W. M. *The Marshall Family*. Cincinnati, OH: Robert Clarke, 1885.

Peabody, A. P., ed. *Life of William Plumer*. Boston: Phillips, Sampson, 1857.

Schoepf, Johann David. *Travels in the Confederation*. Translated by Alfred J. Morrison. Philadelphia: William J. Campbell, 1911.

Slaughter, Philip. *A History of St. Mark's Parish* . . . Baltimore: Innes, 1877.

Sloan, Cliff, and David McKean. *The Great Decision*. New York: Public Affairs, 2009.

Smith, Jean Edward. *John Marshall, Definer of a Nation*. New York: Henry Holt, 1996.

Story, William W. *Life and Letters of Joseph Story*. London: John Chapman, 1851.

Tocqueville, Alexis de. *Journey to America*. Edited by J. P. Mayer. Translated by George Lawrence. New Haven, CT: Yale University Press, 1959.

Virginian. *Letters on the Richmond Party*. Washington: n.p., 1823.

Warren, Charles. *The Supreme Court in United States History*. New York: Cosimo Classics, 2011.

Washington, George. *Writings*. New York: Library of America, 1997.

Weems, Mason Locke. *A History of the Life and Death, Virtues and Exploits of General George Washington*. Cleveland: World Publishing, 1965.

White, G. Edward. *The Marshall Court and Cultural Change: 1815–35*. New York: Oxford University Press, 1991.

Widmer, Ted, ed. *American Speeches: Political Oratory from the Revolution to the Civil War*. New York: Library of America, 2006.

Wirt, William. *Letters of the British Spy*. London: Sharpe and Hailes, 1812.

Wood, Gordon S. *Empire of Liberty: A History of the Early Republic*. New York: Oxford University Press, 2009.

INDEX

RICHARD BROOKHISER is a senior fellow of the National Review Institute, a senior editor of *National Review,* and a columnist for *American History* magazine. His thirteen books include *Founders' Son: A Life of Abraham Lincoln; Alexander Hamilton, American;* and *Founding Father: Rediscovering George Washington.* He lives in New York City.

Photo credit: Lara Heimert